# THE MACCABEES

*endpapers* A woodcut by
Julius Schnorr von Carols-
feld of Judah the Maccabee
defeating the Seleucid
enemy and purifying the
Temple

*frontispiece* The opening page
of the Book of Maccabees
from an 11th-century Latin
Bible

INCIPIT LIBER
MUS MACHABEOR

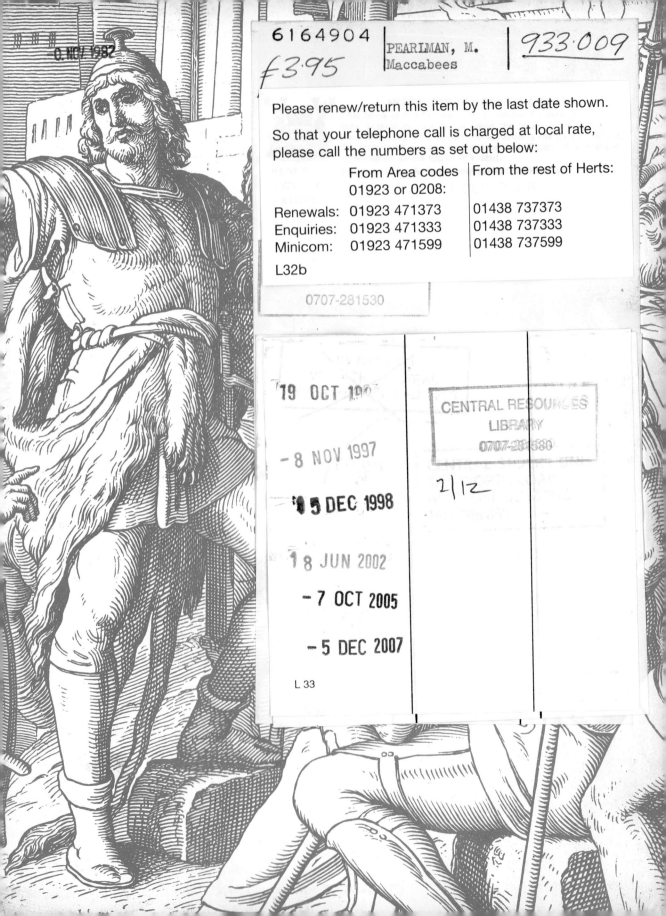

# THE
# MACCABEES

## MOSHE PEARLMAN

Weidenfeld and Nicolson

Weidenfeld and Nicolson
11 St John's Hill
London SW 11

Weidenfeld and Nicolson Jerusalem
19 Herzog Street
Jerusalem

Copyright © 1973 by Moshe Pearlman

Designed by Alex Berlyne for Weidenfeld and Nicolson Jerusalem
Picture research and selection by Irène Lewitt

ISBN 297 76582 5

Composed and bound by Keter Press, Jerusalem;
printed by Japhet Press, Tel Aviv, Israel, 1973

# Contents

# Acknowledgements

The quotations from the First and Second Books of Maccabees are from the translation in the New English Bible (second edition, copyright 1970, by permission of Oxford and Cambridge University Presses) and from Sidney Tedesche's translation of the First Book of Maccabees (copyright 1950 by Harper & Row, Publishers, Inc.) and the Second Book of Maccabees (copyright 1954 by Harper & Row, Publishers, Inc.) in the Dropsie College Apocryphal Literature series. The extracts from the Fourth Book of Maccabees are taken from Moses Hadas' translation (copyright 1953 by Harper & Row, Publishers, Inc.), also in the Dropsie College edition. I am grateful to the publishers for their kind permission to quote from these sources.

I also thank Harvard University Press, Cambridge, Mass., publishers of the Loeb Classical Library series, for permission to quote from their editions of Appian (tr. by Horace White, 1912–13, 1968); Diodorus Siculus (tr. by C. H. Oldfather, C. L. Sherman, C. B. Welles, R. M. Greer, and F. R. Walton, 1933–57, 1970); Livy (tr. by B. O. Foster, F. G. Moore, Evan T. Sage and A. C. Schlesinger, 1919–51, 1967); Polybius (tr. by W. R. Paton, 1922–27, 1968); and Strabo (tr. by Horace L. Jones, 1917–32, 1969).

The quotations from Justin are taken from John Selby Watson's 1902 translation of 'Justin's History of the World, extracted from Trogus Pompeius', which appears (pp. 2–304) in his *Justin, Cornelius Nepos and Eutropius* (George Bell and Sons, Publishers).

The extracts from Josephus are largely from the 1794 translation by Charles Clarke; but I have also used the translations of H. St. J. Thackeray, Ralph Marcus and L. H. Feldman (1926–65) in the Loeb Classical Library edition.

I am grateful to Mr Yeshayahu Gafni of the Hebrew University, Jerusalem, who read the manuscript and made valuable suggestions; to Mrs Irène Lewitt, who was responsible for the illustrations; to Carta, Jerusalem, who drew the maps; to the book's designer, Mr Alex Berlyne; and to Miss Ina Friedman of Weidenfeld and Nicolson Jerusalem, ingenious and ever helpful, who saw this book through the press.

Jerusalem
July 1973

Moshe Pearlman

# Photography Credits

The author and publishers wish to express their gratitude to the Encyclopaedia Judaica, Jerusalem, and the Jerusalem Publishing House for permitting generous access to their archives and to Dr Arnold Spaer, Jerusalem, for his kind aid and for permission to photograph his coins. We further wish to thank the following individuals and institutions for their gracious cooperation, aid and permission to reproduce the illustrations appearing in this work:

Denise Bourbonnais, front cover, 101; Musée de Cluny, front cover, 101; David Harris, back cover, 8, 17, 18 (bottom), 36, 49 (left), 51, 72, 73, 86, 99, 107, 140, 153, 212, 221, 239; Israel Museum, Jerusalem, back cover, 36, 49 (left), 59, 71, 85, 86, 110, 139, 153, 162, 168, 176, 231, 253, 258; Snark International, frontispiece; Biblioteca Laurenziana, Florence, frontispiece; A. Spaer Collection, Jerusalem, 8, 18, (bottom), 221; Ronald Sheridan, 11, 37, 45, 63, 90–1, 118–19, 125, 187, 194–5, 226; Torlonia Museum, Rome, 15; Hirmer Photoarchive, 16, 18 (top), 26, 31, 32, 44, 48, 60, 78, 96, 97, 104–5, 112 (left, top right), 130–1, 184, 190, 228–9, 242; Archaeological Museum, Istanbul, 16, 228–9; Maurice Chuzeville, 19, 64; Louvre, Paris, 19, 25, 56, 64, 78, 97, 127, 170, 186, 190; Hillel Burger, 20; Israel Department of Antiquities, 20, 40, 150–1, 156–7, 172, 225, 232, 251; Landesmuseum, Trier, 24; Giraudon, 25, 56, 81, 127, 170; National Museum, Rome, 26; Scala, 28–9, 47, 135; The Vatican, 28–9, 54, 233, 235, 255; National Museum, Athens, 31, 37, 63, 93; British Museum, London, 32, 65, 112 (left), 145, 199; Bibliothèque Nationale, Paris, 33, 38, 41; Alinari, 42, 54, 182, 186, 202, 220, 255; National Museum, Naples, 42, 47, 220; Glyphothek, Munich, 44, 112 (top right); Agyptisches Museum, Berlin, 46; Staatliche Antiken Sammlung, Munich, 48, 60; Nir Bareket, 59, 71, 110, 139, 162, 168, 176, 231, 249, 251, 253; Staatliche Universitätsbibliothek, Hamburg, 61; Universitäts und Staatsbibliothek, Cologne, 62; Michael Holford, 65, 199; Bibliothek of the Rijksuniversiteit, Leyden, 68, 132; Winchester Cathedral Library, 70, 207; Israel Defence Forces Archives, 79; Archaeological Museum, Châtillon-sur-Seine, 81; Staatliche Museum, Berlin, 82 (left), 124; John Donat, 82 (right); Arje Volk, 85, 116, 173; Jerusalem Publishing House, 85, 116, 173; Israel Ministry of Defence Publishing House, 94, 117; Museum of Delphi, 96, 130–1; Villa Giulia, Rome, 104–5; Werner Braun, 108, 210, 243; Greco-Roman Museum, Alexandria, 109; Haganah Archives, 112 (bottom right); Keren Hayesod, Jerusalem, 129; Archaeological Museum, Florence, 135, 185 (top); Holyland Hotel, Jerusalem, 140, 212; Eliyahu Cohen, 148; Metropolitan Museum of Art, N.Y., 158 (left), 164; Cincinnati Art Museum, 158 (right); Oronoz, 167; Duke of Alba Collection, 167; 'The Hermitage', Leningrad, 171; Museum of the Therme, Rome, 182; National Museum, Chieti, 185 (bottom); Ann Muchrow, 192; Bibliothèque de l'Arsénal, Paris, 204, 217; Rhode Island School of Design, 218; Burrell Collection, Glasgow Art Gallery, 224; Anderson, 233, 235; Alex Straijmayster, 237; Ze'ev Radovan, 244; Baruch Rosenzweig, 247; Hebrew University Collection, 249; Editions Arthaud/Franceschi, 122, 254; Cabinet des Médailles, Bibliothèque Nationale, Paris, 254; Ze'ev Meshel, 256.

# Prologue: The Sacrifice

*It was the end of the season of rain in Judea and Samaria, but there was no sound and no movement in the olive groves, vineyards and cornfields of the Jewish village of Modi'in, 17 miles north-west of Jerusalem. They were as silent as on the holy Sabbath; yet this was not the Sabbath day. There was silence near the entrance to the village. The threshing floor was still; so was the huge stone olive press – both favoured playgrounds for the children when not in use. The houses were empty. In the kitchens, the ashes were cold beneath the mud stoves. The alleyways were deserted.*

*Everyone was in the market-place, but there was no produce on display and no one spoke. Indeed, the market-place wore an unusual look. It had been cleared some hours earlier, and all the villagers were now ranged in the form of the Hebrew letter* het, *on three sides of a square. They were dressed, as they had been commanded, in their Sabbath clothes, their long, sombre-coloured galabiyas reaching down to their sandalled feet. Their faces, framed by dark head-cloths, were sullen. The sun was high, and the scent of pine hung heavy in the air.*

*In the centre of the fourth side of the square rose a pagan altar to the Greek god Zeus. It had been erected that morning. Tethered to the left of it, and soon to be sacrificed, was a pig. On the other side of the altar, lounging on a grounded litter, was the officer Apelles, representative of the imperial Seleucid court, showing little trace of his lean, hard life as a seasoned campaigner. His heavy jowls and sagging dewlap, his flabby body now straining at his tunic, bespoke the easy living of an occupation commander. His forehead and fleshy cheeks glistened with sweat. The only martial sign he bore was the sword at his side, sheathed in a handsome scabbard. Swaggering in the middle of the square was a small detachment of Seleucid troops, his armed escort.*

*The ceremony was about to begin. Apelles surveyed the crowd. He well knew that this was to be no simple ritual and that more was at stake than the life of a pig. His eyes roved contemptuously over the villagers, finally*

Obverse of a silver tetra-drachm of Emperor Seleu-cus IV showing Zeus hold-ing an eagle, typical of hellenistic-period coins

9

coming to rest on the patriarchal figure at the head of the front row nearest to him. This was Mattathias, the Jewish priest and head of the leading family in the village, whom he had met that morning and to whom he had given certain instructions. Mattathias, the only one in white robes, stood erect, for all his heavy years and for all the pain and anger in his heart, as he glanced first at the pig, animal of abomination to the Jews, and then at the officer. He, too, knew that this was to be no ordinary ceremony. This was to be a fateful test of wills – and much else – between his people, the peasants of Modi'in, and the might of the emperor Antiochus IV Epiphanes, represented by Apelles. He could not know the outcome; but he well knew what he would do when he was bidden – as he had been told by Apelles that he would be bidden – to take part in the sacrifice, eat of the pig and thus formally acknowledge the submission of his community to the edict of Antiochus. So did the five grave-looking young men who stood at his side, his sons.

The officer rose. The troops jerked to attention. The villagers stopped shuffling. All eyes turned to the royal emissary as he began to speak. He was there, he told them, to carry out the command of His Imperial Majesty, the all-wise and all-powerful, and initiate the villagers into the noble worship of the god Zeus. This would be marked by the public sacrifice of the animal, and they, the populace, would mark their acceptance of the new faith by tasting of the flesh of the offering. Thus had the king ordered, said Apelles; and the king's will, he added, tapping his sword hilt, would be done.

He paused, and there was a deep hush, pregnant with horror and fear. The villagers looked at the ground, each afraid of meeting the eyes of his neighbour. All except Mattathias and his sons. They kept staring at the officer, their expressions unchanged.

Despite his appearance, Apelles was a soldier, more at home on the battlefield than on an apostasy mission in a village square, and accustomed to unquestioning compliance with his commands. But he had been briefed before setting out and advised that prompt compliance was not to be expected on this particular operation. The Jews might be reluctant to 'cooperate'. If they proved troublesome, he would know what to do. But he was to try diplomacy first, for if all went well and peaceably at Modi'in, other villages in the area would be more complaisant. The briefing officer who supplied Apelles with intelligence on the village mentioned the name of Mattathias and suggested that it might be politic to offer him inducements. If he were won over, the entire village would follow his example.

Apelles was aware of the mood in the market-place as he ended his introductory words, satisfied that they had had the desired effect. The people seemed cowed. Now, recalling his briefing, he turned to Mattathias and encountered the unwavering stare of the priest. Apelles was no fool.

Today's village on the site of ancient Modi'in, birthplace of the Maccabee revolt

*Whatever he saw in the eyes of the old Jew, it was not submissiveness, and he knew at once that the advice of the briefing officer was not likely to be effective. But he would try it anyway. If it did not work, it would be a pleasure to apply the alternative.*

*He addressed himself to Mattathias, and the words are recorded in the Apocryphal First Book of Maccabees:*

*You [he said] are a leader here, a man of mark and influence in this village, and firmly supported by your sons and your brothers. Be the first to come forward and carry out the order of the king. All the other people have done so, as have the leading men in Judea and the people left in Jerusalem. Do this, and you and your sons will be counted among the Friends of the King; you will all receive high honours, rich rewards of silver and gold, and many further benefits (2: 17, 18).*

*Apelles had tried to soften his martial tone to suit his wheedling plea. He now called upon Mattathias to take up position at the altar.*

*The proud figure in white did not move. His head held high, his long beard jutting forward, he opened his mouth to make reply. None could know that the few words which followed were to change the course of history.*

# 1 The Ultimatum

While Apelles was expressing the king's will in Modi'in, the monarch himself, Antiochus IV Epiphanes, was in Antioch, the spacious capital (which he had enlarged) of the Seleucid empire, situated in the north-west corner of Syria overlooking the Mediterranean. It is unlikely that at this time (166 BC) Antiochus had ever heard of Mattathias or of his remote village on the Judean border, though he would hear about both before long. From the reports of ancient historians, he was more urgently preoccupied with the military and diplomatic moves of Rome, the newly risen power in the region and the gravest threat to his own empire; with Egypt, which he still hoped to annex; and with Persia, where he sought to tighten his control.

Not that Antiochus was uninterested in or unfamiliar with Judea, his southernmost province. He knew it well – as a troublesome area; but it was hardly a menace, and he could leave it to his local officials, to whom he had issued directives to keep it in check. He knew Judea at first hand, just as he knew – and had left his grim mark on – its capital, Jerusalem. But not Modi'in. Yet had he but known, he had passed within only a few miles of it some twenty months earlier, returning from a mission he would have wished desperately to forget. It was a mission in which he had suffered the most galling humiliation of his life. Later, much later, perhaps only on his deathbed – if a certain ancient record is to be believed – would he be struck by the sudden revelation of a direct link between that catastrophic journey and the events at Modi'in.

The scene of his discomfiture had been the outskirts of Alexandria, and the humiliation was all the more bitter because victory had been almost within his grasp. In the year 170 he had invaded and gained possession of almost the whole of northern Egypt (though he had failed to take Alexandria), established a protectorate there (after

The cornucopia held by a goddess in this hellenistic silver medallion represents the wealth of Alexandria, site of Antiochus' humiliation by the Roman legate

13

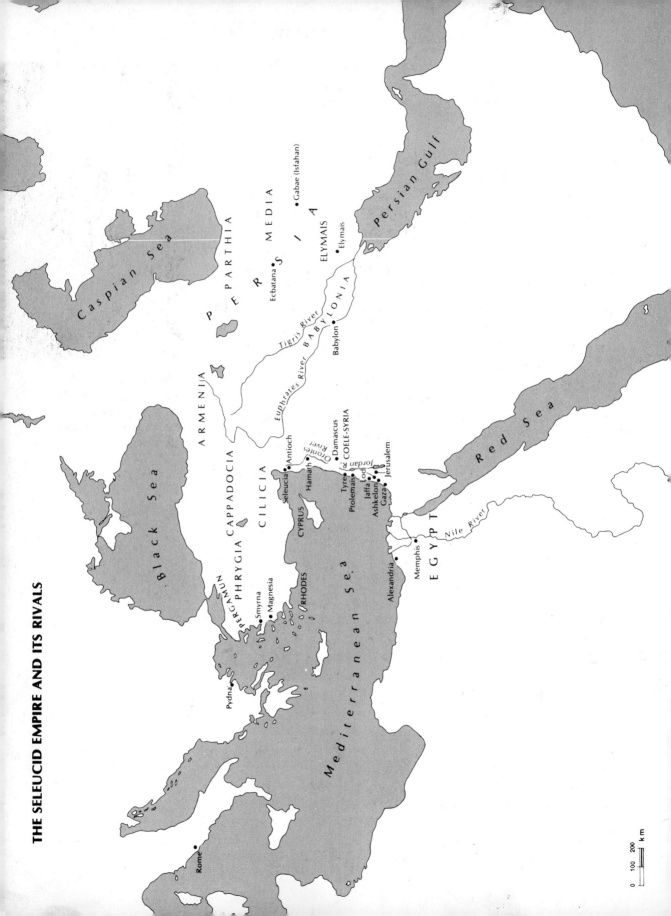

**THE SELEUCID EMPIRE AND ITS RIVALS**

Caspian Sea

PARTHIA

P E R S I A

MEDIA

ELYMAIS

• Gabae (Isfahan)

• Ecbatana

Tigris River

Euphrates River

BABYLONIA

• Babylon

• Elymais

Persian Gulf

ARMENIA

CAPPADOCIA

PHRYGIA

CILICIA

CYPRUS

PERGAMUN

• Smyrna

• Magnesia

RHODES

Black Sea

• Pydna

Antioch

Seleucia

• Hamath

Orontes River

Damascus

COELE-SYRIA

Jordan River

Tyre

Ptolemais

Jaffa

Lod

Ashkelon

Gaza

Jerusalem

Red Sea

Mediterranean Sea

• Alexandria

Memphis •

E G Y P T

Nile River

• Rome

k m

0  100  200

having himself crowned at Memphis) and retired to Antioch; but his control had not long survived his withdrawal. He accordingly returned in 168, penetrated deeply into the country and was about to put Alexandria under siege.

Rome at the time was heavily engaged in her Macedonian campaign, and Antiochus calculated that she would therefore do nothing to stop his Egyptian venture. But the intelligence he received was faulty, and he was unaware that the Roman Senate, upon learning of his march southwards, had assigned an embassy of three, headed by a distinguished no-nonsense officer named Caius Popilius Laenas, to wait upon him with a harsh message. As Polybius, the contemporary Greek historian of Rome, puts it: 'The Senate, when they heard that Antiochus had become master of Egypt and very nearly of Alexandria itself, thinking that the aggrandisement of this king concerned them in a measure, dispatched Caius Popilius as their legate to bring the war to an end, and to observe what the exact position of affairs was.'

A Roman patrician, possibly a member of the very Senate which issued the ultimatum to the Seleucid monarch

It is suggested by another early historian that Popilius was advised to linger over his journey and await news of Rome's fortunes before seeing the Seleucid emperor. In the third week of June 168, the envoys (who are believed to have been waiting in Delos) received a report of the decisive Roman victory over Macedonia's King Perseus at Pydna. They promptly took ship for Egypt and by the end of the month reached the encampment of Antiochus some 4 miles from Alexandria.

Livy, the most famous of Roman historians, writing in the first century BC, describes their meeting: 'On their approach he [Antiochus] saluted them, and held out his right hand to Popilius; but Popilius put into his hand a written tablet, containing the decree of the Senate, and desired him first to peruse that.' Failure to grasp the monarch's hand in friendship was a fearsome snub, but Antiochus thought it wise to ignore it (he too had heard by now of the victory at Pydna) and began reading the Senate's message. It was a crisp order to put an end to his Egyptian campaign and retire. The shocked emperor said he would 'call his friends together' and 'consult on what was to be done'.

But he was in for a more grievous shock. The swaggering Popilius was carrying a stick (Polybius provides the detail that the stick was 'cut from a vine'), and he now added 'a spontaneous ultimatum of his own, acting, says Polybius with touching understatement, 'in a manner which was thought to be offensive and exceedingly arrogant'. Using the stick to draw a circle round Antiochus' feet, Popilius told him 'he must remain inside this circle until he gave his decision about the contents of the letter':

(The third-century AD Roman historian Justin says Popilus told him 'to decide on the spot and not go out of that ring until he had given an answer whether he would have peace or war with Rome'.)

Polybius continues: 'The king was astonished at this authoritative proceeding, but, after a few moments' hesitation, said he would do all that the Romans demanded.' It was only then that 'Popilius and his suite all grasped him by the hand and greeted him warmly . . . So, as a fixed number of days were allowed to him, he led his army back into Syria, deeply hurt and complaining indeed, but yielding to circumstances for the present.'

Antiochus made the slow journey northwards back to Antioch through Palestine, following the route by which he had come to Egypt. He moved southwards from the area of Alexandria to Memphis, then cut north-east across northern Sinai to reach the Mediterranean coast at a point just west of today's El Arish. From there he continued along the ancient 'Way of the Sea', the coastal road, through Gaza and on towards Jaffa (Joppa), expecting to move on to Ptolemais (Acre) and to proceed home through Tyre. He had just got beyond Judea – only a few miles away from the then quiet and obscure village of Modi'in – when he received news of certain events which had just occurred in Jerusalem. He was still under the impact of the Alexandria meeting, still irate at the frustration of his imperial design and mortified by the manner in which it had been effected. It was in this dark mood that he responded to the news from Jerusalem, taking action against the Jews of Judea and touching off a series of events which led up to the ceremony at Modi'in.

The palms of El Arish on the ancient 'Way of the Sea', which was traversed by the frustrated Antiochus when forced by Rome to abandon his Egyptian campaign

*opposite* Relief of Alexander the Great on a 4th–3rd-century BC marble sarcophagus found in Sidon which bears beautifully carved battle scenes from his campaigns

Judea had been part of the Syrian-based Seleucid empire for twenty-five years when Antiochus IV reached the throne in 175 BC. Before that it had fallen within the Ptolemaic empire. Seleucus and Ptolemy, the founders of their imperial dynasties, were two of the outstanding generals of the redoubtable Alexander the Great. By his decisive victory over the Persians in 332 BC, this youthful wonder-king of Macedonia gained the territorial possessions of the Persian empire, which included Judea.

Alexander died nine years later, and his dream of a huge, united, long-lasting Greek empire died with him. By then the lands he had conquered stretched from Egypt and Asia Minor in the west to India in the east. These were now divided among his leading Macedonian chiefs – and savage fighting promptly broke out between these former comrades in arms. Ptolemy was assigned the satrapy of Egypt, but he soon established himself as monarch and set up his capital in Alexandria. Seleucus had been given the satrapy

*above* Emperor Seleucus I
on a silver tetradrachm
*below* Emperor Ptolemy I
on a silver diobol minted
in Alexandria

of Babylonia, and he, too, made himself king, with his capital at Seleucia. A little while later, he extended his control to Syria, establishing a new capital at Antioch.

Between Syria in the north and Egypt in the south lay Palestine, and for obvious strategic reasons it was coveted by both Ptolemy and Seleucus. Though Ptolemy had promised it to Seleucus in return for key military aid against another of Alexander's generals, he incorporated Palestine into his own empire, and for the next one hundred years (except for a few brief interruptions), Jerusalem and Judea came under the authority of his dynasty, the 'Greeks of Egypt'. In 198 BC Antiochus III, father of Antiochus IV, succeeded in wresting Palestine from the Ptolemies, and Judea now came under the 'Greeks of Syria', the Seleucids.

Apart from an oppressive annual tribute, the Jews of Judea had enjoyed, on the whole, benevolent rule under the Ptolemies. According to the first-century AD historian Josephus, they were left in peace and allowed to manage their own affairs, practising their religion and maintaining their Temple in Jerusalem without molestation or interference. While formally subservient, they were in fact autonomous. When Antiochus III became the new suzerain, he continued this favourable treatment. Josephus quotes documents showing that Antiochus III even made grants for the repair of the Temple, remitted taxes – particularly of priests, scribes and others associated with Jewish religious life – and issued a charter endorsing the rights of the Jews to live in accordance with their own laws and customs. (There is scholarly controversy over the authenticity of these documents, but it is generally agreed that they reflect the trend during the reign of Antiochus III.) This policy towards the Jews was pursued by his son and successor, Seleucus IV. It changed with the accession of Antiochus IV, brother to Seleucus (in whose murder he is thought to have been implicated).

This change was partly a by-product of Antiochus' immediate ambition to bring Egypt within the sphere of Seleucid control, an aim prompted both by the urge to emulate Alexander's accomplishments and by fear of Rome. Antiochus knew Rome, having lived there as a hostage for more than a decade. In 190 BC, his father's armies had been ignominiously vanquished by the Romans at the battle of Magnesia, in Asia Minor, and under the harsh treaty of Apamea contracted two years later, Antiochus III had to renounce Seleucid claims over extensive areas, surrender his fleet and war elephants and pay a heavy indemnity over several years. To guarantee payment, he had to hand over to the Romans twenty selected hostages. His son was one of them. The young prince was well treated by his Roman hosts, and he learned much of their long-range

Marble bust of Antiochus III (an ancient copy of a hellenistic work) which was discovered in Italy and acquired by Napoleon

policies and the art of their diplomacy. He was impressed by their spectacular power and was convinced that it was matched by their appetite. (Not for nothing had he submitted, long after his years as hostage, to Popilius' ultimatum in Alexandria.) An eventual Roman-Seleucid military confrontation was inescapable, and now that he was emperor he wanted to be prepared. If Antiochus was unable to build up a matching strength, he was anxious at least to stiffen his southern flank by the incorporation of Egypt. Palestine was already his; and if Egypt could also be brought under his control, he would be better able to prevent a Roman landing on the eastern edge of the Mediterranean.

Judea was thus of interest to him not because it posed a military threat – he feared no revolt from this hilly enclave at that time – but because it was that part of his territory which lay closest to Egypt, closest to possible hostile landing sites and close to the coastal highway, the main line of communications between Egypt and Syria. It could become an area of danger if it were to be exploited by the Ptolemies – and he had heard that they were making overtures to the Judeans. He therefore sought to ensure that his hold upon it remained undisturbed and undisputed. He estimated that his

A terracotta statuette of the goddess Aphrodite from the hellenistic period found in a cave on Israel's Carmel Range and used in pagan worship which Antiochus IV sought to impose on the Jews

best course was to appoint men he could trust to positions of local responsibility. In so doing, he was to touch the Jews at their most sensitive spot – their religion. It is ironic that had he followed the policy of his predecessors, leaving the Jews to run their own affairs and choose their own leaders, Judea might never have given him any trouble – and the trouble which did arise was to contribute to the ultimate collapse of his empire. By his interference, Antiochus created the very explosive situation he had sought to avert.

His active intervention in Judean communal life was greatly facilitated by the intrigues and jockeying for power of members (and their highly placed supporters) of a Jewish patrician family known as the Tobiads, or 'Sons of Tobias'. It was their aim, unprecedented in Jewish life, to topple the reigning High Priest and secure that office for one of themselves.

Since the fifth century BC, when Judea was under benign Persian rule and was receiving waves of Jewish returnees from Babylonia, the high priesthood, a hereditary office, provided both the spiritual and temporal leadership of the Jews of Judea. The Jews were, for the most part, a hard-working, God-fearing, farming community scattered in hillside villages. They scrupulously followed the injunctions of the Torah and the time-honoured customs of their people, brought the fruits of their terraced fields as offerings to the Temple in Jerusalem at festival time and revered their High Priest. They remained largely unaffected by the winds of hellenism which had begun to sweep the Middle East with the arrival of Alexander the Great and his successors. The tone had been set by their High Priests, the most notable of whom in the third century BC was Simon the Just, considered to have been the ideal combination of sage, teacher and community leader. His descendants in the sacerdotal office took him as their model (as did the rabbis in the generations immediately following the destruction of the Temple in AD 70).

But there were those in Jerusalem, mostly among the wealthy upper class, who were attracted by the commercial opportunities opened to the region by the Greeks, and who were responsive to the new fashions, new ideas and the more worldly outlook introduced by the hellenistic dynasties. This tendency, says historian Cecil Roth, was similar to that of 'the more backward colonies of the European powers in the 19th and 20th centuries. The native population avidly adopted all the superficial characteristics of its conquerors, their language, their costume, their architecture, their diversions, their social and domestic habits – under the impression that this constituted the essential part of a civilisation greater, because materially more powerful, than their own.' The aping of

Original notation on a papyrus by Zeno of Egypt, commercial agent of Ptolemy II, who visited the estates of 'Tobias the Jew' in Transjordan in 259 BC

imperial customs – a trend which had been developing since the days of Alexander the Great – was now widespread among the subject peoples within the Ptolemaic and Seleucid empires. In Judea alone it had made little headway; but even Judea had not been totally immune, and leading the small but influential group of would-be assimilationists were members of the House of Tobiad.

One of them was a certain Joseph, whose unusual family background gave him an association both with the hellenists and the traditionalists. His father, a Tobiad, had married the daughter of the previous High Priest and sister of the reigning High Priest, Honya II (better known as Onias II, the Greek form of the Hebrew Honya), a man of piety who held office towards the end of the third century BC. Joseph's character reflected the influence of both families: he was a traditional Jew with moderate hellenistic tastes – and a keen interest in finance.

This interest stemmed, no doubt, from his paternal ancestors, who were Jewish potentates with land holdings on the eastern side of the Jordan River, opposite Jericho. One of the early ones may well have been the fifth-century BC 'Tobiah the Ammonite' mentioned in the Book of Nehemiah (4:3) and so called possibly because of his possessions in the land of Ammon. One much closer to the time of Joseph was 'Tobias the Jew', who appears in the Zeno papyri as having maintained commercial relations with the royal office of supplies in Alexandria and was sufficiently important to have been visited in 259 BC at his estates in Transjordan by Zeno. (Zeno was a high official under the Egyptian monarch Ptolemy II in what today would be called the Ministry of Commerce. As part of his duties he journeyed throughout the empire's distant provinces arranging for the import of supplies for Egypt's state monopolies, notably olive oil, wine, honey, figs, dates and timber. He kept careful records on papyrus of the places and people he visited on his extensive travels, and these archives were discovered in the Fayum region, south-west of Cairo, where he spent his years of retirement.)

Thus, as early as the middle of the third century BC, this Jewish House of Tobias was already in contact with the Egyptian court and on familiar terms with high Greek officials and with the Greek way of life. It was some years later that a member of this family of commercial and landed gentry married into the devout and priestly House of Onias, with Joseph the product of that alliance.

At this time – still under the Ptolemies – Judea was virtually self-governing. It was, in the words of the noted historian of this period, Elias Bickermann, 'an "aristocratic" commonwealth'. The ruling body was the Council of Elders, comprising both laymen and priests and headed by the High Priest. As the intermediary between the Jews and the Ptolemaic administration, and as the person responsible for exacting and paying the tribute to the monarch, the High Priest was the political head of the nation, in addition to being the highest authority for its religious life.

Joseph launched himself into the centre of Judean affairs when difficulties arose between his uncle the High Priest and the reigning Ptolemy. It appears that Onias II had refused tribute, and Ptolemy was threatening to occupy Judea. The background to the dispute was apparently a fresh outbreak between the Seleucids and the Ptolemies, and Onias may have supported the former. One probable reason was that a Seleucid victory would promote more open contact with the flourishing Diaspora community in Babylonia, with much older and stronger links with Jerusalem than the new, though growing, Jewish community in Alexandria. But there were other leading Jews who favoured continued Ptolemaic rule. Joseph was one of them, and he was no doubt influenced by his family's long business connections with Alexandria and by Egypt's control of the eastern Mediterranean coast, which offered wider scope for those engaged in commerce.

Joseph and his supporters were alarmed at the rift between Ptolemy and Onias, and he managed to persuade his uncle and the Council of Elders to let him proceed to Alexandria and pacify the king. Neither Onias nor the elders could have imagined that, as a result, Joseph would siphon off a good deal of their civil and political authority, handling the economic affairs of Judea as well as relations with the imperial power. This initial erosion of the supreme priestly office would have a grave impact on the Jews of Judea – and on the Seleucid empire – during the subsequent reign of Antiochus IV. It would open the way for the High Priest's garb to be worn by a renegade Jew. Not even Joseph could have wanted or foreseen this as he made his preparations for his journey to the royal court.

Joseph clearly had a flair for what today would be called public relations and combined it with a shrewd commercial sense. Josephus (in *The Antiquities of the Jews* XII. 180 ff) has an eloquent description of how Joseph succeeded in ingratiating himself with the royal family in Alexandria. He had prepared his path well, borrowing money from friends 'for defraying the expense of apparel, horses, carriages, plate and other necessaries for his equipage', and offering a lavish banquet to one of the royal officials who thereupon 'spoke of Joseph in such high terms of commendation that both the king and queen expressed a desire of receiving a visit from him'. At the

A Roman relief showing farmers paying their tax dues

meeting, Joseph handled himself in a manner which was 'so pleasing to the king, that he gave orders for Joseph to be provided with apartments in his palace, and to be entertained at the royal table'. Joseph insinuated himself into even greater favour at court when he showed the king how he could secure a higher return on the tax-farming services in the imperial provinces. 'A proposition so beneficial to his income could not fail to be pleasing to the king', and Joseph was granted the concession for gathering the taxes in the whole of Palestine.

It was not long before this nephew of Jewry's spiritual leader had amassed great wealth and become a worldly man of affairs. He was beginning to revel in the luxury and material pleasures of an uninhibited hellenism and was finding traditional Judaism somewhat cramping whenever he returned to Judea from his Alexandrian visits. Yet he was careful not to drift too far from his people (his children and grandchildren would feel no such restraints) for he knew that however engaging his charm and however welcome his additions to the royal coffers, his principal value to the king was his virtual civil leadership of the Jews of Judea, and he could be trusted to keep them in check.

He almost forfeited that leadership in a weak moment, when he became infatuated with a courtesan and almost married her. The colourful story is told by Josephus, and whether or not it is accurate in detail, it captures the atmosphere in which some Jews of prominent priestly families could stray from the rigid patterns of their society and end up by opting for hellenistic assimilation – thereby contributing to the subsequent events at the village of Modi'in.

It appears that on one of his visits to Alexandria, Joseph, by then a married man and father of seven, was accompanied by his brother, Solymius, who had come 'to find a Jew of rank' among the Alexandrian community 'proper to marry his daughter' (who was also with them). Arriving in the capital, Joseph left them and went off to a banquet at the palace, and there he 'fell in love with a maid who was dancing to entertain his majesty. Communicating his secret to his brother, he requested that since he could not lawfully espouse the maiden of whom he had become enamoured, he [Solymius] would contrive to introduce them privately to each other.' Solymius was alarmed, but he saw that Joseph was in no mood for argument.

Thereupon he readily promised compliance, but put his own daughter to bed with Joseph, instead of the other virgin; and he having drunk freely, the deception was not discovered. The same artifice was repeatedly practiced, till Joseph, becoming violently enamoured, he lamented to his brother that he was risking his life for a dancer whom the king would perhaps not allow him to have. Solymius told him he had no cause of uneasiness, saying, he might take the woman as his lawful wife; and after explaining all the particulars of the stratagem he had put in force, added that he had chosen to dishonour his own daughter rather than see his brother fall into disgrace. Joseph commended him for his brotherly love, and in a very short time married the daughter, who bore him a son that received the name of Hyrcanus . . . (*Antiquities* XII. 186–9).

Some of the ingredients of this story by Josephus are doubted by modern scholars. What is true, however, is that Joseph *did* have a son named Hyrcanus; he was the youngest; he was his father's favourite; and he was hated by his brothers. This hatred was passed on as a legacy to their offspring. It is also true that Hyrcanus inherited Joseph's role – and favours – at Ptolemy's court, and this may have helped drive his brothers into the pro-Seleucid camp. These political differences were also inherited by their descendants. Hyrcanus lost out when the Seleucids, under Antiochus III, gained control of Palestine. (He fled to Transjordan and is thought to have committed suicide some years later.) From then on the families of his brothers – the remaining 'Sons of Tobias' – were the ones who were favoured by the royal court, now the Seleucid court at Antioch.

A fashionable Greek lady of the 3rd century BC

# 2 Intrigue in Jerusalem

The High Priest in Jerusalem when Antiochus IV reached the throne
was Onias III, a pious man in the devout tradition of his predecessors. The hold of the high priesthood on temporal affairs, which
had been weakened by Joseph the Tobiad, had not been regained;
but its spiritual primacy had never been challenged, and both the
majority of the Jews of Judea and the large Diaspora communities
in Babylonia and Alexandria held Onias III in great respect and
regarded him as their sole leader.

His distant cousins, however, the descendants of the fashionable
Joseph, were by now very much assimilated, displaying an open
admiration for the hellenistic mode of living and mingling mostly
with Seleucid notables, officials, traders and agents, with whom
they felt they had more in common than with their fellow-Jews.
They belonged to the pro-Seleucid hellenistic party in Jerusalem,
which was led by the brothers Simon, Menelaus and Lysimachus,
and there is a strong suggestion in the historical sources, though no
unequivocal assertion, that these brothers were Tobiads. Some
historians go so far as to say that they were the elder sons of Joseph
and thus more closely related to Onias III.

Though removed from the ways of their own people, this group
still wielded considerable economic influence in the Jewish community. Simon, indeed, even held the position of administrator of
the Temple, much to the chagrin of the High Priest. They enjoyed
little popular support, but drew their political power from their
close association with the imperial régime. However, they recognized that their status with that régime rested ultimately on the
backing they received from, or at least the capacity to manipulate,
their own community. They considered that they could best dom-
inate their people if the highest communal office were held by one
of their nominees.

A 1st-century BC bronze
statue of a pugilist, one of
the contestants at hellenistic
games

27

Raphael's painting, now in the 'Heliodorus Room' in the Vatican, of the unsuccessful attempt by Seleucid minister Heliodorus to seize the treasures of Jerusalem's Temple. Note the *menorah* at the right of the vaulted hallway

These, then, were the men who now intrigued against High Priest Onias III, with the daring aim of securing his deposition and gaining the appointment for one of themselves. They had begun their manoeuvres shortly before Antiochus came to power, while his brother Seleucus IV was still on the throne. It is alleged that Simon had 'laid information' with the Syrian administration that Onias was pro-Egyptian; and furthermore that he had hidden in the Temple treasury 'untold riches – indeed the total of the accu-

mulated balances was incalculable and . . . he suggested that these
balances might be brought under the control of the king' (II
Macc. 3:6).

The immediate outcome of this move was a Seleucid attempt to
appropriate the Temple treasure. It failed, as the principal Seleucid
minister (Heliodorus) who had come to investigate – and seize the
treasure – was refused entry to the sacred Temple precincts. (The
Second Book of Maccabees 3:24–8 ascribes the failure to a dramatic

miracle.) But it exposed Jerusalem to reprisal action and endangered the position of Onias. He therefore decided to proceed to Antioch in order to explain to the king that no insult had been intended – it was simply that the Temple was sacrosanct to the Jews – and also to clear himself of Simon's charges. He had just reached the Seleucid capital when Seleucus was murdered, and he was still there when Antiochus IV was enthroned.

Onias' rivals in Jerusalem quickly took advantage of his absence. They found a ready listener in the new monarch, who was bound to be receptive to men sharing his feeling for hellenistic culture, able to show that they had led the pro-Seleucid group in their province and undoubtedly safer politically than the incumbent High Priest. The next we hear is that Onias was deposed (he was apparently given shelter by the Jews of Antioch) and his brother Joshua (whose name was hellenized to Jason) was appointed High Priest by the king.

It is not easy to tell from the historical records whether Jason had intrigued against both his brother and the hellenists to secure the office for himself, or whether he did so with the connivance of the hellenistic leaders Menelaus and Lysimachus. (Brother Simon drops out of the record after the death of Seleucus IV.) It seems likely, in the light of subsequent events, that the hellenists backed Jason for the moment, with the intention of ousting him later. Their reasoning is not difficult to fathom. Jason, though son and brother of a High Priest, had turned his back on religious orthodoxy and joined their group. He was not as rabid a hellenist as Menelaus, but he could be relied on to press their policy and aims. His blood relationship with the High Priest would make his appointment more feasible to the king and more acceptable than that of an outsider to the Judean populace. Moreover, the elevation of Jason would break the hereditary tradition of the high priesthood, since Onias III had a son (albeit still a minor). This precedent could be exploited later for the appointment of one who was not even a member of the priestly family. The Second Book of Maccabees (4:7–10) offers simpler reasons for the king's appointment. Jason offered a higher tribute to the coffers of His Majesty – always welcome to the cash-hungry imperial court to finance its campaigns – and outlined a programme which would virtually turn Jerusalem into a hellenistic city.

[There is scholarly controversy over the extent of Jason's hellenistic aim. Victor Tcherikover argues that he had in mind the conversion of Jerusalem into a full-fledged Greek city (*polis*) to be called 'Antioch', the name adopted by several hellenistic cities throughout the Greek world. Elias Bickermann opts for the more limited hellenistic 'corporation' (*politeuma*), constitutionally distinct from the city of Jerusalem, with the hellenized Jews, 'the Antiochenes' of Jerusalem (II Macc. 4:9,19), establishing a Greek quarter of the city.]

Why would Jason make such a proposal? It would be in keeping with the character of a man like Menelaus – as we shall see – who was brought up in a family atmosphere of hellenism, whose estrangement from his own people was more complete, who sought acceptance as an assimilant by Greek society and whose crowning ambition was to become a Seleucid satrap. But Jason had been nurtured in a pious Jewish household, and though he had developed a taste for hellenism, he was still concerned with the welfare of the Jewish community. Why then had he succumbed to the overtures of his brother's rivals, joined them in their intrigue, acquiesced in the move against his brother and taken his place?

In so doing, he may have thought he would provide benefits for the Jews of Judea. The way to prosperity lay in economic integration within the empire. If the Jews of Jerusalem, the capital, were allowed to establish a hellenistic centre, whether it was a *polis* or only a *politeuma*, they would enjoy wider privileges, including the possible right to their own coinage, and this would enlarge their commercial scope.

However, the action he was taking also entailed cultural integration with its built-in religious forms. To gain hellenistic status, a city had to establish a 'gymnasium' and an 'ephebeum'. The gymnasium was a sports stadium where games and physical contests were held, mostly track racing, jumping, throwing the discus, wrestling and boxing. To the Greeks of old, however, athletics were a way of life; they followed a special ritual. All participants had to appear naked, and gala sports contests were preceded by sacrificial offerings to the gods. The ephebeum was an early Athenian

An Athenian relief of wrestlers at athletic games, an integral part of the hellenistic culture which the Seleucids introduced into Jerusalem

Athlete depicted on a Greek vase (*ca.* 540 BC)

*opposite* A 15th-century French illuminated manuscript of Josephus' *Wars of the Jews* describing the plunder of the Temple by Antiochus IV

institution, organized under state control, where young men were given training in arms and were prominent in stadium games. They, too, had to take part in pagan festivals.

These institutions were widely established throughout the Middle East under the Ptolemies and the Seleucids and exercised a powerful attraction to the young manhood of the subject peoples. They served the imperial purpose of promoting hellenism, and the gymnasiums expressed, as the historian Edwyn Bevan has pointed out, 'fundamental tendencies of the Greek mind – its craving for harmonious beauty of form, its delight in the body, its unabashed frankness . . . The gymnasiums . . . were the social centres in which the life of a Greek youth got those interests which go with companionship, the spur of common ambitions, and esprit de corps . . . '

But the Jews of Judea had achieved their own unique *esprit de corps* through quite other means – loyalty to their austere faith, laws and customs – and they viewed these extraordinary practices with gross repugnance. Nevertheless, Jason saw only the economic handicaps of isolation as against the material advantages which assimilation would bring to his people. Thus were the gates of Jerusalem opened to hellenism.

Except for the small hellenistic group, the Jews were stunned. They had been shocked by the deposition of their High Priest. The king may have considered it within his rights to decide who should hold such office, just as he could dismiss at will the local governor of any other of his local provinces; but the Jews rejected this royal right over their priesthood. The High Priest was their spiritual leader, and therefore beyond the authority of any human agency, certainly an agency outside their community, be it even the imperial monarchy. True, the High Priest also exercised civic authority, however much it had been weakened. But this was because the very quality of the Jewish way of life was governed by the spirit and the ordinances of the Jewish religion, so that the High Priest was their guide in all things. Moreover, the succession was from father to son, and Jason, quite apart from his estrangement from the faith, was a brother.

What shocked them most of all, however, was the introduction into their very midst of the gymnasium, with its naked exercises and its associations with paganism. For a thousand years the Jews had preserved their special identity precisely because in every generation they had resisted the tempting appeals to conform to the customs of their idol-worshipping neighbours. They had kept their religion intact and survived as a nation by virtue of their refusal to be swayed by the reasoning which informed the minds of the

Jasons. They spurned material benefits if the price was religious abdication. And thus they had remained Jews. Now, in the city of Jerusalem, pagan institutions were rising in the very shade of their holy Temple.

But Jason had the backing of a mighty king, and the Jews of Jerusalem felt helpless. For the moment, there was no rising. They bore their opposition with sullen passivity. Many left the city, going out into the country hamlets which were as yet unblemished by an abhorred hellenism.

One of them was Mattathias. He took his family from Jerusalem and went back to his native village, where they could continue to to live as Jews. The village was Modi'in.

Jason lasted in office for three years. He paid his tribute punctually to Antiochus, honoured the king with a torchlight procession when he visited Jerusalem and behaved as a dutifully submissive vassal. It would appear from the ancient records, however, that he made no great advances towards the hellenizing of Judea. He established a gymnasium in the capital, but it is not known whether he gained any of the expected privileges therefrom, such as the right to strike his own coinage and the expansion of Judea's commercial horizons. While athletic exercises in the stadium became part of the Jerusalem scene – shameful enough in the eyes of the populace – there was no coercion on the community to join the hellenistic ranks and no ban on their following the traditional Jewish laws and customs. Jason also respected the sanctity of the Temple.

The impatient and ambitious hellenist diehards, led by Menelaus and his brother Lysimachus, resolved that the time had come to put into operation the final phase of their plan. Jason had served them well. He had accepted the king's appointment, breaking with high priestly tradition, and had made a start in hellenizing Jerusalem. But he had not gone far enough or fast enough to make it a favoured, kindred imperial 'city of Antioch'. He was still tied to his priestly family roots, showed compassion for the Jewish traditionalists and permitted religious seperatism. He had to go; and they conceived a simple method to effect his removal.

It was Jason's practice to send his annual tribute to the king in Antioch through Menelaus. A conventional ceremony accompanied such transactions in the royal palace. The monarch would graciously receive the representative of his tributary, accept the renewed pledge of fealty and make polite inquiries as to the state of his subject people. When Menelaus paid his visit in the year 172, it was not difficult for him to assure Antiochus that 'all was well, but . . .' Judea would be a more reliable province under more forceful leader-

A 4th–3rd-century BC laurel wreath of gold with which the winner of the games was crowned

ship; the Seleucid cause would be pursued more vigorously and the hellenizing process advanced. He even persuaded the king that this was what the people themselves wanted, but they were restrained by Jason. Having induced the appropriate mood in the emperor, using the refinements of diplomacy to twist the dagger in Jason's back, he volunteered a proposal (similar to the one Jason had made in his day to secure the leadership) which could not fail to tempt Antiochus. If he, Menelaus, were to be made High Priest, he would raise the prosperity of Judea, and its tribute would be correspondingly higher. As an earnest of his conviction, he was ready to add a substantial sum to the amount he had brought on behalf of Jason.

The king needed to hear no more. He promptly ordered the dismissal of Jason and the appointment of Menelaus in his place. Although he accepted his visitor's assurance that the local population would be with him, Antiochus despatched an army unit under the command of a certain Sostrates to ensure a smooth take-over – and to see to it that the promised additional tribute was raised and remitted to him forthwith. Jason fled across the Jordan, and Menelaus, backed by the garrison of Seleucid mercenaries under Sostrates, was installed as High Priest in Jerusalem.

If the appointment of Jason had been a shock to the Jews, the appointment of his successor was shattering. Jason, at least, had been the son and brother of High Priests, whereas Menelaus had no such close priestly association. (According to certain versions of the Second Book of Maccabees, he was not even a member of the priestly tribe of Levites. But if he was in fact a descendant of Joseph the Tobiad, as some historians suggest, he could claim a high priestly association through Joseph's maternal grandfather.) An equally stunning blow was his extreme hellenism, and they knew that traditional Judaism was now gravely threatened. Unlike Jason, Menelaus would not tolerate religious seperatism, and he would seek actively to impose foreign practices upon the community. But again they felt themselves powerless to act. Menelaus was too well protected by the mercenaries.

Hellenization now proceeded with redoubled vigour. For the Jews it was offensive to see the occupying troops openly practising their heathen rites in the Holy City; and it was humiliating to be subjected to their taunts and flagrant contempt for Jewish customs. Far worse was the sight of young Jews, including young Jewish priests, persuaded by Menelaus to enter the gymnasium for training in Greek games. Since it was Menelaus' hope that they might participate in the imperial athletic meets, where they would have to appear naked, they sought to eradicate the sign of circumcision

Athenian stone relief of Greek troops at pagan worship, reminiscent of the practice of Seleucid occupation forces which so angered the Jews of Jerusalem

by undergoing the painful operation of 'drawing forward their prepuce' (I Macc. 1:15), extending the foreskin. Nothing could be more abhorrent to the community than this arrant toadying to strangers by young fellow-Jews and their engagement in so shameful a treachery to their own people and to their time-honoured laws – and all with the blessing of one bearing the title of High Priest! It seemed that the only consolation during the first two years under Menelaus' rule was that he took no overt action against the traditionalists, and it was still possible for the main body of Jerusalemites to follow the Jewish commandments. He also made no changes in Temple procedures and worship.

Then came his first major clash with the community, bringing bloodshed to Jerusalem. It was touched off by two simultaneous incidents. In his second year as High Priest, Menelaus found that the price he had offered Antiochus for this office was proving beyond his capacity. He had taxed his people heavily, but he was still in arrears with his tribute. An angry monarch summoned him to Antioch. Leaving his brother Lysimachus in charge, he proceeded to the Syrian capital, taking with him some of the holy vessels of gold from the Temple as a propitiatory offering to his irate master.

Upon arrival in Antioch he was relieved to find that the monarch had been called away to deal with a troublesome issue in his western province of Cilicia. At this point in the ancient records, Onias III reappears on the scene. The deposed High Priest had lived in hiding in a suburb of Antioch since his dismissal. To the traditional Jews of Judea and the Diaspora communities, he was still the true High Priest. (The reference in the Book of Daniel to 'the one who is anointed shall be removed with no one to take his part' [9:26] is

Holy vessels of the Jerusalem Temple as conceived by the illustrator of the 13th-century Hebrew Bible of Perpignan

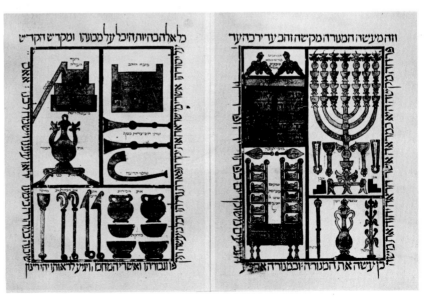

believed to be to him.) To the renegade Menelaus, he was a living reproach. Now, while Menelaus was also in Antioch awaiting the king's return, Onias was drawn by a ruse from his place of refuge and done to death. Menelaus was implicated in the murder.

Meanwhile, in Jerusalem, Lysimachus had made a further raid on the precious vessels in the Temple to help pay the tribute. This unheard-of sacrilege was also held to have been committed at the instigation of his brother. The Jews of Judea discovered the violation of the Temple treasury at the same time as they heard the news of Onias' murder, and they rose in angry demonstration against the hellenistic group. Lysimachus, his followers and the Seleucid troops tried to hold them back. In the *mêlée* that followed, with mercenary spears and swords against civilian stones and sticks, Lysimachus was killed.

The Jews then petitioned Antiochus to remove Menelaus, for how could a man who was responsible for such outrages continue to hold priestly office? It was not difficult for Menelaus, who was still in Antioch, to persuade the king that the petition and the uprising were inspired by a small minority who were moved by pro-Egyptian and anti-Seleucid sentiments. Antiochus re-established Menelaus in office and provided him with military protection. It is unlikely that thereafter he gave Judea much serious thought – until his humiliating encounter with the Roman legate Popilius on the outskirts of Alexandria in June 168 BC.

The news Antiochus heard from Jerusalem while retiring with his armies northwards along the coastal road of Palestine after submitting to the Roman ultimatum was that Jason, the High Priest he had dismissed four years earlier, had emerged from his Transjordanian retreat, crossed the Jordan and marched on Jerusalem to drive out Menelaus. The report added that he was receiving the support of the populace, which was now in open rebellion against the royal appointee, and therefore against the emperor himself.

This report was true. What was not true was another report which had sparked the rebellion. The treatment of Antiochus at the hands of the Romans was a wondrously dramatic story which quickly made the rounds of the Middle East, receiving embroidered furbishings in the retelling. When it reached Jerusalem – and Jason – the punch-line of the tale was that Antiochus had been killed or had died of shock. In any event, he was dead, and this 'fact' gained credibility by the retreating Seleucid armies – for why else would they be retiring when victory had been within their reach? It was upon this news that Jason acted, and with him the bulk of the Jews of Jerusalem; for however much they had opposed Jason's earlier

Remains of a palace wall from the hellenistic period discovered on what are believed to have been the estates of the Tobiads in Transjordan

appointment, he had never been as bad as the monstrous Menelaus.

Thus, they joined the rebellion of Jason, who proceeded to avenge himself on the hellenistic group. Menelaus took refuge with the Seleucid troops, but these by now had become soft with the luxury and idleness of an unchallenged occupation force, and they were content simply to maintain a holding operation in defence of their garrison. Signals were sent to Antiochus for reinforcements. The king, smarting under his bitter encounter with the Romans, was incensed, and he promptly despatched one of his generals, Apollonius, to Jerusalem with drastic instructions to restore order.

There are certain discrepancies of detail in the accounts in the First Book of Maccabees, in the Second Book and in Josephus. For example, the despatch of Apollonius is recorded in the Second Book of Maccabees (5:24) but not in the First Book of Maccabees, where he is referred to simply as 'the officer of the Mysians' (1:29). One account sets Jason's attack in the previous year, at the close of Antiochus' *first* campaign. Another records that it was Antiochus himself who rushed to Jerusalem and sent in Apollonius only several months later. However, whether it was the king himself or his general, the historical fact is that a Seleucid force, fresh from the Egyptian battlefield, entered Jerusalem. They chose to do so

on the Jewish Sabbath, having heard that the Jews respected it so scrupulously that they would not take up arms even in self-defence on this day. The troops turned on them, carried out an indiscriminate slaughter, took many survivors captive to be sold into slavery, razed houses and parts of the city walls, broke into the Temple treasury, stole the funds and more of the precious holy vessels and re-established Menelaus as High Priest.

They also constructed a new fortress on the western hill opposite, and partially commanding, the Temple and separated from it by the central valley (later called the Tyropoeon Valley, which filled up over the centuries). It was elaborately fortified with stout walls and towers, and it is referred to in the Greek texts as the Acra, or Citadel. It was intended partly to give them some strategic control over the Temple compound and partly to safeguard the hellenistic group who were expecting to establish a regular Greek quarter in this western area. Stationed in this fortress as a permanent garrison were a considerable force of mercenaries, commanded by a Phrygian general named Philip, who was also installed as governor. He and his military unit were to play a focal role in enforcing the harsh laws against the Jews which Antiochus was about to introduce. The scene was set for the crucial clash.

A 15th-century miniature depicting Antiochus directing the massacre in Jerusalem, from Jean Fouquet's illustrated manuscript of Josephus' *Antiquities*

# 3  The Decision

Back in his Syrian capital after the retreat from Egypt and the events in Jerusalem, Antiochus undertook a reappraisal of his imperial prospects and policies. The effect on Judea would be disastrous. His prevailing mood was one of black depression. It was not simply the abasing encounter with the Roman legate which sent him into despondency, but its grim implications. It was now evident that he had little hope of restoring the mighty empire which Alexander the Great had created and which had crumbled so soon after. Between Antiochus and his ambition stood the power of Rome. True, there could be an upheaval in Rome – kaleidoscopic changes had occurred in the eastern Mediterranean in his own lifetime, with nations rising and nations falling. But as he viewed developments in the region, he was forced to conclude that this was unlikely. Rome was still on the rise, and, as a realist, he had to admit, not without envy, that she had acquired the art of acting like an aggressive great power. She had denied him Egypt, and there was small chance in the immediate future, if ever, that he would be able to incorporate it within his realm. Rather was it probable that Rome would incorporate it within hers – and then embark against his own. He may well have suffered the sobering thought that if anyone were to match the conquests of Alexander, it would more likely be Rome.

The result of his analysis now led Antiochus to a grave resolution: he would have to abandon his policy of expansion and pursue instead a policy of consolidation, bracing the territories he already ruled, welding his subject peoples together, unifying his empire. Unity would give it internal strength. Vigorous and compact, it should be capable of exploiting the opportunity offered by changes in the region, and of deterring – and if necessary resisting – invasion by Rome. This meant keeping a tight rein on his imperial provinces,

A bronze bust believed to be that of Antiochus IV because of the resemblance to his portrait on coins

43

A 2nd-century BC relief of a family sacrificing to Zeus and Athena

especially those on the borders, and particularly Judea because of its proximity to Egypt.

The instrument of unity would be hellenism. All Seleucid possessions would now follow the Greek way of life. There would be no exceptions.

The idea of hellenizing his empire was not new to Antiochus, though up to now its purpose had been social and cultural. Ever since he ascended the throne, he had cherished the aim of bringing the glories of hellenism, as he conceived them, to his subject people, 'civilizing the primitives' by exposing them to the culture and religion of Greece. This programme had not been enforced, but mere exposure had been enough to achieve much success with the inhabitants of all his provinces – except Judea. The others were pagans, and they could enjoy Greek pagan festivities in addition to their own and add Greek gods to their pantheon without any crisis of conscience. The Jews, however, with only a few exceptions, had clung to their traditional monotheistic ways. Antiochus had hoped to bring them round by appointing hellenistic Jews to high office in Judea. But it was evident from the troubles and insurrections in Jerusalem that his nominees had made little headway. The bulk of the community was clearly unmoved by the temptations of his hellenistic blessings. This had caused him little disquiet, for Judea had hardly been a factor in his grand strategic plans. But now that those plans had come unstuck through Rome's 'diplomatic' intervention, the province closest to Egypt became of considerable moment.

In accordance with his resolve, the hellenization of the empire would now be pursued not only for religious and social ends but for an important political purpose. It would therefore be imposed by force on any recalcitrant. Judea would no longer be permitted to follow its separatist course.

Although the records are not explicit, Antiochus appears to have concluded that allowing the Jews religious latitude had been a political error. To him, the latest rebellion in Jerusalem had sprung not from purely religious motives but from a prevailing pro-Egyptian mood in Judea, and these political sentiments had been given dangerous expression precisely because the Jews, alone of all his people, had sought and been allowed a large measure of religious separatism. Attempted political separatism had been the result. This, he decided, would be stopped. The Jews of Judea would have to toe the line. They would be made to conform to the cultural and religious patterns of the rest of the empire, stop being a distinctive entity, merge smoothly into the imperial landscape. Judea would then cease to be a potential danger to Seleucid interests, and the empire would be strengthened by a more cohesive unity. This radical policy would be carried out with a firm hand, so that never again would the Jews dare rise up against the monarch. They would learn to fear, respect and submit to his authority.

The Acropolis in Athens, the city where Antiochus spent part of his youth

When he thought at all of the peoples in his realm, the imperious Antiochus, schooled in the sophistication of Athens and Rome, did so with contempt. For the Jews he had a special distaste. He could not understand them, nor would he wish to; but from what he had seen and heard of them, they were a strange people. They professed a curious faith and followed outlandish customs. They believed in a single God, and this God was invisible. Unlike the temples with which he was familiar, the Jewish Temple in Jerusalem, their holiest shrine, contained no tangible deity, no material shape or image of the God they worshipped. It had a Holy of Holies, but this sombre chamber, he had heard, held only the 'spirit of the Lord'.

Three goddesses depicted
on a gold finger ring
believed to be from
Alexandria (1st century BC–
1st century AD)

These people also indulged in novel practices and adopted odd prohibitions in accordance with their queer religious laws. They circumcised all male infants on the eighth day after birth. They set aside one day in the week which they called the Sabbath, and on that day they did no work of any kind, treating it as a holiday, dressing in their finery and attending special services in the Temple. Even on the other days of the week they spent much time in prayer. They had scrolls of parchment inscribed with the strange letters of an unusual language, and these were accounted holy. They followed a special bathing ritual. And they had phobias about certain foods – calling them dietary restrictions imposed by their laws – so that the pig, for example, was regarded as an 'unclean' animal which they were forbidden to eat.

There was no accounting for such bizarre tastes and customs which, Antiochus understood, had been practised by this people for hundreds of years. Well, he would put an end to all this. Having taken the political decision to complete the hellenization of all his provinces, his fervent enthusiasm for Greek civilization lent it wings. This passion was to be the driving force behind his subsequent actions in Judea.

Antiochus' zeal for all things Greek had been acquired as a youth, having been born in Athens and brought up with the consciousness that no nobler civilization existed. Later, during his hostage years in Rome, where hellenism had taken root, he naturally gravitated to that section of society which professed a warm admiration for hellenistic achievements in literature, scholarship and science, philosophy and rhetoric, art and architecture. He was particularly attracted by the Greek language, the worship of Greek gods (with the pomp and pageant of its attendant festivities and with its licentious pagan rites), the athletic games, the organization and training of young male groups, Greek political skill, Greek dress and Greek drama.

When he became king, Antiochus adopted the title 'Epiphanes'. The ordinary meaning of this Greek word is 'Illustrious'; but it bore a special meaning, for he intended it as an abbreviation of 'Theos Epiphanes' ('God-manifest'), which was the title taken by his distinguished predecessor, Alexander the Great. Under this title he claimed divine honours and laid particular stress on the religious content of Greek culture. 'In the sacrifices he furnished to cities', wrote Polybius, 'and in the honours he paid to the gods, he far surpassed all his predecessors'.

The madness of Antiochus is mentioned in all the history books. In his early years on the throne, he could indeed be capricious, so

Street musicians depicted in a 3rd-century BC mosaic from Pompei, reminiscent of the eccentric Antiochus, who would descend upon a private party 'quite uncere-moniously with a fife and a procession of musicians'

much so that shortly after he assumed his divine title of 'Epiphanes', he became better known by the contemptuous nickname 'Epim-anes', which is Greek for 'the madman'. Polybius says that he 'gained the name of Epimanes by his conduct . . .'

Escaping from his attendants at court, he would often be seen wandering about in all parts of the city . . . He was chiefly found at the silversmiths' and goldsmiths' workshops . . . He used also . . . to drink in the company of the meanest foreign visitors to Antioch. Whenever he heard that any of the young men were at an entertainment, he would come in quite uncere-moniously with a fife and a procession of musicians, so that most of the guests got up and left in astonishment . . . In consequence all respectable men were entirely puzzled about him, some looking upon him as a plain simple man and others as a madman. His conduct too was very similar as regards the presents he made. To some people he used to give gazelles' knucklebones, to others dates, and to others money. Occasionally he used to address people he had never seen before . . . (*Histories* XXVI.1).

It was, however, less for his eccentric social behaviour than for his frenzied hysteria in Judea that the appellation stuck. His resolve to hellenize the Jews developed into a mania, and he now embarked on a nightmare course of brutish savagery which was to have the strangest possible consequences for the nation he victimized – and for his empire.

Jews were put to death for studying the Torah. Sacred scrolls were torn to shreds and put to the torch. Women with babies newly cir-cumcised were publicly paraded round the city, their infants cling-ing to their breasts, and then hurled headlong from the battlements.

Scene from a Greek cup showing a Greek soldier killing a woman (*ca.* 450 BC)

Copper etching from an early 19th-century French Bible depicting Jewish mothers with babies newly circumcised – despite the Seleucid prohibition – flung headlong from Jerusalem's battlements by occupation troops

Their families were also slain. A Seleucid mercenary ran his sword through a Jew who refused to taste the flesh of a pig. Jews at worship were burned alive when their secret prayer chamber was discovered and set on fire. Others were struck down for failing to worship a pagan deity. These were the scenes of horror in Jerusalem within weeks of the emperor's decision to make the Jews conform.

By his declaration of war on the Jewish religion, with the explicit aim of stamping out Judaism, Antiochus IV Epiphanes became the first leader in history to engage in religious persecution. Not that oppression was unknown in his age or in previous epochs of cruelty. But heretofore the grounds – if indeed there were any, beyond mindless hate and sheer sadism – were said to be political or military. Now, for the first time, the target was specifically religious.

A royal decree went out from Antioch ordering all Jews in the Seleucid possessions to renounce the laws of their God and to offer sacrifice to the Greek deities. It thus applied not only to the Jews of Judea but also to the Diaspora communities under Antiochus' rule. However, the initial thrust was directed at the Jews of Jerusalem, though the policy soon affected the rest of the Jews in the

שי מאל ואאברהב הישריקה נגיב שריק כי ילרתי בן לוקנון ויגדל הילד וינאל ויעש אבדה אשתיר גדול ליזב יזב ל

אניהב את יצחק בני בן שמנת יבים באשר שיה אתו אלהיב ואבריהב בן מאת שנה בהלד לו את יצחק בנ

empire. Additional officials were appointed to aid the local governors in implementing the regulations.

It was now prohibited for Jews to congregate in prayer, observe
the Sabbath and the religious festivals, be in possession of their
sacred writings, carry out circumcision or respect the dietary laws.
The penalty for infraction was death. This was also the penalty
for failing to follow idolatrous hellenistic practices – the worship
of Greek images and partaking of the monthly sacrifice in honour
of the emperor – and for refusing, upon demand, to eat the flesh
of animals prohibited by Jewish ritual as 'unclean', particularly
swine. The itemized injunctions were cunningly devised to strike
at the very roots of Judaism and to extirpate those religious
rites which outwardly distinguished the Jew from the heathen. To
obey any one of them would be an act of renunciation. Moreover,
evasion was excessively difficult. The evidence of circumcision,
when investigators freely entered Jewish homes, could not be concealed. Ordered to join in a sacrificial pagan ritual, a Jew could
either comply or face death. There was no third course.

Adherence to the laws of the Torah and the age-honoured

Circumcision scene from
a 13th-century illuminated
Hebrew manuscript
known as the 'Regensburg
Pentateuch'. Antiochus
ordained the death penalty
for any Jew respecting the
'Covenant of Abraham'

customs of his people was (and is) part of the very soul and fibre of the traditional Jew. To disavow them, especially under the compulsion of conversion, was unthinkable treachery. 'Never before', wrote Elias Bickermann, 'and never thereafter was the spiritual existence of Israel so imperilled.'

The Seleucid officials at first tried cajolery to get the Jews to conform. It did not work. None could contemplate idol worship (a breach of the First Commandment), desecration of the Sabbath (a breach of the Fourth), or abandoning circumcision (a breach of the Covenant of Abraham); and none could imagine that the threatened penalties would indeed be exacted. The officials quickly showed that they could, and the slaughter began. Particularly cruel forms of torture and execution were devised to serve as an example (II Macc. 6:10).

This ruthlessness undoubtedly had its initial effect on many Jews, driving them to outward compliance, though with an inner prayer to the Lord for forgiveness and the hope that the dark shadow would pass and they would be able to resume their traditionalist ways. Many others, however, chose death. A number, like the pious Hasidim (the 'righteous'), who also knew they would never submit, fled from Jerusalem to the hills and the desert and found refuge in caves. Pursued, discovered and challenged to conform – the Seleucid mercenaries usually surprised them on the Sabbath, knowing that they would not desecrate its holiness even to defend themselves – the Hasidim calmly accepted death.

Thus, in those early months of terror, there was no active resistance. The Jews were too stunned to think of any other course but to hide when they could and submit to the executioner's sword or flames when caught. They felt themselves too weak, collectively, to fight the imperial might of Antiochus, yet not too weak, individually, to surrender their lives. However, that, too, was a form of resistance which was soon found to be charged with dramatic potency.

The mounting horror unleashed by the authorities to cow the community into submission gradually had the reverse effect. It produced martyrs, and they set an example which carried an incalculable power and impact: their self-sacrifice fired the people to active resistance.

These Jews were the first religious martyrs in history. What moved them to behave as they did? Upon what profound moral source did they draw to keep their spirits intact while their bodies were being broken? Their martyrdom, after all, occurred more

The numerous caves in the desert south-east of Jerusalem were natural hide-outs for the persecuted

than 2,100 years ago, an age when few peoples in this region, if they could understand the phenomenon at all, would have thought it anything but the most monumental absurdity to give one's life for an idea or a custom. Moreover, each victim could savour the thought that he was not being asked to betray another but only himself. One could persuade oneself that obeisance to a pagan god was but a meaningless gesture. One could postpone the circumcision of a babe beyond the statutory eight days with the secret promise to conduct the rite when the danger passed. One could pray in the privacy of one's chamber and not in congregation. One could conceal the holy scrolls until such time as they could safely be retrieved. In short, one could promise to conform outwardly to hellenism and trust that God would understand the true conviction of the heart. The rationalizations, when the flesh is seared by fire, are limitless. Why, then, did these Jews forswear such escape? Why, when caught and asked to comply, did so many refuse and maintain their tenacious refusal to the bitter end? How did they find the strength of will to preserve their spirit from disintegration?

The fact is that the Jews of the second century BC, unlike their neighbours – and their oppressors – already possessed a unique code of laws and ethics, the terms of their covenant with the Lord, which had been engraved on the collective soul of the nation for more than a thousand years. The history of their people throughout that long period in the land where they themselves now dwelt was also as familiar to them as were the happenings of yesterday. Both the commandments and the history were recorded in their sacred writings, which they had studied from childhood and read over and over again – the Five Books of Moses, Joshua, Judges and others (which were to form the basis of the Old Testament canon some 250 years later). Also written in their sacred scrolls and studied and read at their regular prayer services were the books of the giant Hebrew prophets, notably Hosea and Amos, Isaiah and Jeremiah and Ezekiel, with their powerful exhortations to righteousness and justice and to the scrupulous observance of their religious laws and customs. In this way, each generation kept the collective memory of its people fresh. Thus, most of the Jews under Antiochus' rule could recite by heart (as can the children of today's Israel) the deeds of their national leaders of old and the sublime appeals to the spirit by their prophets.

Commandments, annals and prophetic teaching, inalienable components of their faith, exerted an influence upon them that was without measure, just as they had influenced earlier generations. This is what had preserved the unique identity of the Jewish people throughout all their vicissitudes. This is what the Jews of the

Michelangelo's 'Daniel', in the Sistine Chapel. The biblical Book of Daniel is believed to have been written during the period of Seleucid persecution

second century BC understood and were determined to sustain. This is what Antiochus and his pagan subjects would never understand.

When other peoples had been vanquished, they had eagerly accepted the gods of the victors because these were clearly more potent than their own. The more powerful the deity, the more worthy was he of their worship. The Jews were different. They clung to their faith in success and adversity – indeed, stirred by the voice of their prophets, they were even more devout in catastrophe. When they lost a battle or a campaign – even when they lost their land and were driven into exile – they blamed not God but themselves, for not living up to the Covenant of Moses in Sinai. The path to recovery after disaster, therefore, lay not in embracing the religion and culture of their conquerors but, on the contrary, in affirming their faith with even greater fervour. True, there were always those, like their own hellenists, who were drawn to assimilation. But the bulk of the people had held fast to their identity. Only a short time before, a bare four centuries, the nation had suffered its most momentous tragedy, Jerusalem and the Temple destroyed and the survivors exiled to Babylonia. In exile, where they could have assimilated with ease, they adhered more firmly than ever to their precepts, yearning for their return to Jerusalem and the restoration of their central shrine. In their hearts the Temple continued to live, and all hopes were centred on its resurrection. It was 'by the waters of Babylon' that they uttered their cry which is heard to this day, but was heard with a more poignant urgency by the Jews oppressed by Antiochus: 'If I forget thee, O Jerusalem, let my right hand forget her cunning.' Less than fifty years later, their conquerors were themselves vanquished, and the Jews returned to Judea and rebuilt the Temple and walls of Jerusalem.

All this was known to the Jews of the second century, strengthening their conviction that however grievous the suffering – and nothing could have been more devastating than the loss of Jerusalem and exile – their fortunes would eventually be reversed if only they remained loyal to their creed. The words of the prophets which had sustained their exiled forbears in the sixth century – and which had proved true so dramatically – fortified them too. They also had living in their midst the author of the Book of Daniel. (Most modern scholars agree that he was a contemporary.) Elias Bickermann writes:

A book has come down to us from this period of persecution, the biblical Book of Daniel. In the midst of these afflictions a seer perceived the significance of the ancient prophecies concerning the world empires, their wars, and the tribulations of the holy people. To him, these prophecies seemed to speak of his own time, and thus he interpreted them for his contemporaries, suiting them to the events during the persecutions of Epiphanes.

Thus it was that when Antiochus inflicted his cruel choice upon the Jews of Judea, while some chose physical survival, many resolved to depart not one hair from the injunctions of the Torah, convinced that the last thing they should do was to turn their back on God. That way lay doom. It was the weighty historical and prophetic baggage in their spiritual knapsack which encouraged them now, in their hour of agony, to save themselves from betrayal. By their act of martyrdom, passive though it might seem, they would be fighting for the survival of the nation.

They were right. Soon stories of Jews who had elected to die rather than deny their faith began to reach communities throughout Judea and the empire, stiffening their resolve to hold out against hellenization. The mounting effect of these reports of individual heroism was eventually to rouse a family in the village of Modi'in to transform the communal mood from unresisting endurance into armed struggle.

# 4 The Martyrs

Two stories in particular, gruesome but moving, are credited with having sharpened the Jewish mood of defiance in the early months of persecution. They were of crucial relevance to the times (and, alas, to later times), for they showed how pious reasoning steeled the martyrs to bear the sufferings of the flesh. One concerned Eleazar, a venerable old sage. The other told of a mother and her seven sons.

The stories have come down to us in the Second and Fourth Books of Maccabees. The Fourth Book was written as a work of religious edification at least a century, and possibly a century and a half, after the Second Book and contains an ornate elaboration (in fourteen chapters) of the comparatively brief version (less than two chapters) which appears in the earlier work. The intellectual and literary artistry of the later author is much in evidence in the Fourth Book, particularly in the well-rounded phrases of the dialogue. There are also certain discrepancies of detail between the two books. But scholars agree that despite the embellishment in the retelling, the substance of the narrative is true, the stories are rooted in historical fact and they faithfully reflect the mood of the times, the deeds of the persecutors and the spirit and behaviour of the victims.

The background to the two episodes was Antiochus' impatience with the sluggish advancement of his hellenization programme. The killings proceeded apace, but conversions were few. His officials then suggested that perhaps the choice of victims had been too haphazard. Stray Jews had been snatched from alleyways, families rounded up at random from their dwellings, pious groups caught in their caves of refuge. But the fate of these victims had not boosted the conversion rate. Since they could not fathom the Jewish mind, the persecutors ascribed their failure to the undistinguished

Fragment of a 1st-century AD Roman bas-relief showing the ceremonial sacrifice of a pig

standing of the men and women they had trapped. What was needed, they told the king, was a Jew of influence among the traditionalists. If such a personality could be persuaded to embrace hellenism, many would follow. The king agreed and they thereupon sought Eleazar, a learned, friendly, warm-hearted man who was respected by the community and who had hitherto been quite well regarded even by the Seleucids. To him they put their demand. He refused.

They then decided that he could serve their purpose even better. He would be coerced into compliance; and if his followers also sought the touch of torture to salve their consciences before submission, this was a happily acceptable course. To gain the maximum effect, a public recantation ceremony would be held in the presence of the emperor. Eleazar would be taken first.

So it came about that 'the tyrant Antiochus, sitting with his counsellors upon a lofty place and surrounded by his soldiers under arms', surveyed the crowd of Jews who had been 'seized and corralled' like cattle and then commanded that the ceremony begin. The Jews were to be haled before him one by one and ordered 'to eat of swine's flesh and of meat consecrated to idols; and those who refused to eat of the contamination he ordered to be broken on the wheel and killed.'

If it seems odd to the modern reader that the command to eat pig should figure so prominently in the coercive practices against the Jews, it should be recalled that to the surrounding population the Jewish prohibition against tasting this animal's flesh was perhaps the most conspicuous mark of difference between them. Most of them, including Antiochus, were unfamiliar with the extraordinary Jewish code of ethics and regulations covering most aspects of human behaviour which were set out in the Ten Commandments and the Covenant Ordinances and enshrined in the Torah. The fundamental religious and ethical principles of the Commandments were to influence what was to become known as Western civilization only in subsequent centuries. In the second century BC, however, they were almost unknown to any but the Jews. The Jews, not being a proselytizing people, had no interest in making their sacred books known to others, and these books (canonized later as the Bible) were preserved in their original tongue, Hebrew, which was read and written only by the Jews. (In the previous century they had been translated into Greek [the Septuagint], but this had been done primarily to enable the younger generation of the Greek-speaking Diaspora Jewish community in Alexandria to read and understand their holy works. Few outside that community had read them.)

Thus, the Gentiles, Antiochus included, knew nothing of the essence of Judaism. To them, the commonest image of a Jew that came to mind was one who abhorred pork. This is what made him 'different'. The abstinence from eating pig accordingly became for both Jew and Gentile almost symbolic of Jewish 'separateness', which Antiochus was so determined to destroy and the Jews to uphold. Moreover, forcing them to eat pig could be directly associated with pagan worship. It had therefore been chosen as the central spectacle in the public ceremony over which Antiochus was now presiding.

The 'first of the herd' to be brought before him was Eleazar,

a priest by family and an expert in the Law [the Torah], advanced in age, and known to many of the king's court because of his philosophy. When Antiochus saw him, he said, 'Before I commence inflicting torture upon you, graybeard, I would give you this counsel: eat of the swine's flesh and save yourself. I respect your age and your hoary head; but I cannot think you a philosopher when you have so long been an old man and still cling to the religion of the Jews. Why do you abominate eating the excellent meat of this animal which nature has freely bestowed upon us?' (IV Macc. 5:4–8).

He continued in this vein, and ended by suggesting with a malicious smile that even if there existed 'some power that watches over that religion of yours, it would pardon you for a transgression arising out of extreme compulsion'.

'When the tyrant had in this fashion sought to urge him on to the eating of forbidden flesh', Eleazar made reply:

We, Antiochus, who out of conviction lead our lives in accordance with the divine Law, believe no constraint more compelling than our own willing obedience to the Law; and therefore under no circumstance do we deem it right to transgress the Law. Nay, even if our Law were in good truth, as you suppose, not divine, and we merely believed it to be divine, even so it would not be possible for us to invalidate our reputation for piety. And do not regard the eating of unclean flesh a small offence; transgression is of equal weight in small matters as in large, for in either case the Law is equally despised. You mock at our philosophy ... Yet it teaches us temperance, so that we rule over all pleasures and desires; and it inures us to courage, so that we willingly endure any difficulty ... I shall not violate the sacred oaths of my ancestors in regard to keeping the Law, not even if you cut my eyes out and burn my entrails. I am neither so decrepit, nor so ignoble, that reason should lose the vigour of youth in the cause of religion. So make ready your torturer's wheel, fan your fires to a fiercer heat ... You shall not defile the sacred lips of my old age ... Unsullied shall my fathers welcome me ... (IV Macc. 5:14–36).

Engraving from an 18th-century French Bible showing Eleazar the martyr spurning Antiochus' order to eat pig's flesh

The king made a simple motion with his hand, and the guards seized Eleazar, stripped him, bound his arms 'and scourged him with whips, while a herald who faced him cried out "Obey the bidding of the king!" ' Eleazar could only shake his head in refusal.

With his head raised high to heaven the old man suffered his flesh to be torn by the scourges; he was flowing with blood, and his sides were lacerated. He fell to the ground, when his body was no longer able to endure the torment; but his reason he kept erect and unbent. With his foot one of the savage guards struck his flanks to make him rise up when he fell; but he endured the pain, despised the compulsion, prevailed over the torments, and like a noble athlete under blows outstripped his torturers . . . With his face bathed in sweat and his panting breath coming hard, his stoutness of heart won the admiration even of his torturers (IV Macc. 6:6–11).

Thereupon, some of the courtiers who had known Eleazar earlier approached him and suggested how his life could be spared without his having to transgress Jewish law. They would arrange for him to be brought meat that it was proper for him to eat but he would pretend that he was 'eating the meat of the sacrifice ordered by the king. Thus he might be saved from death and . . . obtain courteous treatment.' Eleazar disdained their offer. The voice was weak, but there was no weakness in the words. How could he go through with this pretence? If he did so, 'many of the youth [would] think that Eleazar in his ninetieth year has changed to heathenism. They, because of my pretence and for the sake of this short span of life, will be led astray through me . . . ' It would be a shameful act, and 'we should become ludicrous in the eyes of all for our cowardice, and earn the tyrant's contempt as ignoble

Painting on a Greek cup showing Greek soldiers torturing a prisoner

by failing to protect our divine Law unto death'. Better to set an example 'to the young men . . . of how to die happily and nobly on behalf of our revered and holy Laws'.

He was then taken to the rack and after that his maimed body was brought to the fire, 'and there they burned him with evilly devised instruments . . . and into his nostrils they poured a noisome brew', and in the midst of these torments he expired.

It had been an entertaining spectacle for the emperor and his party, but that was only part of the objective. The other part, persuading their victim to adopt their faith, had not been gained. Surprisingly, Eleazar had failed them, and now the rest of the Jewish 'herd' would probably prove equally stubborn. But they could discern a glimmer of hope. Eleazar had been an old man, nearing the end of his days. With little to lose, he could afford to be brave. The order went out to choose some young men, with all of life before them.

Within minutes, seven lads were seized by guards and paraded before the king. They were brothers. With them, though she had not been bidden, was their mother, Hannah. [She appears anonymously, simply as 'the mother', in the Books of the Maccabees. But she was given the name 'Hannah' in an early sixteenth century edition of the tenth-century *Book of Josippon*, a narrative history in Hebrew of the Second Temple period, which draws directly on the Second Book of Maccabees for its account of Jewish martyrdom under Antiochus Epiphanes. This late edition of *Josippon* received wide currency in subsequent generations, and it is as 'Hannah and her Seven Sons' that this story is now known.]

The sons were 'handsome and modest and well-born and in every way charming', and the emperor was taken with them.

Hanna and her seven sons depicted in a 1427 German illuminated manuscript, the 'Hamburg Miscellany'

The 'Martyrdom of the holy Maccabees', an engraving from a 1580 Latin version of Josephus Flavius' works

Young men [he said], with right good will do I admire you . . . and because I pay high honour to such beauty and such a numerous band of brothers, I not only counsel you against raging with the same madness as that old man who has just been tortured, but I urge you further to yield to me . . . Renounce your ancestral Law . . . Share in the Greek way; change your mode of life; take pleasure in your youth. If by your intransigence you rouse my anger, you will force me to have recourse to terrible punishments, and to destroy you with torture (IV Macc. 8:5–9).

To show them what he meant, he gave a sign, and 'the guards brought forward wheels and instruments for dislocating joints, racks and wooden horses . . . and caldrons and braziers and thumbscrews and iron grips and wedges and bellows; and the tyrant then resumed, and said: "Lads, be afraid; the justice which you revere will be indulgent to transgression under duress"' (IV Macc. 8:13–14).

The eldest brother replied for them all, saying that they were ready to die rather than transgress the commandments. 'You seek to terrify us by threatening us with death through torture, as if you had learned nothing from Eleazar a short while ago. But if old men of the Hebrews have died for the sake of their religion, and persevering through torture have abided by their faith, it is even more fitting that we who are young should die, despising the torments of your compulsion, over which our aged teacher triumphed . . . ' (IV Macc. 9:1–7).

There follow in the ancient writings ghoulish descriptions of scourging, maiming, limbs hacked off, burning, scalping, as first one and then the second was put painfully to death while the remaining brothers 'with their mother encouraged each other to die nobly', and hurled defiance at the king before they expired. When six had died and the turn came of the youngest son, the emperor summoned the mother and urged her to advise her son to save himself. Hannah's response was to lean over the boy and, 'jeering at the king', she spoke 'in the Hebrew tongue' and said: 'Do not be afraid of this executioner, but show yourself worthy of your brothers'. He was then dealt with 'worse than the others', and 'after her sons, the mother died also' (II Macc. 7:29–40).

Accounts of both these episodes had reached the ears of Mattathias and his sons in Modi'in, pushing their thoughts in a particular direction. But it was the next episode that was to lead them to fateful decision.

A 4th-century BC bronze statuette of Zeus holding a thunderbolt. Antiochus desecrated the Temple and converted the Jewish sanctuary into a pagan shrine, complete with images of the Greek deity installed above the sacred altar

Thwarted by their stubbornness in his efforts to 'civilize' the Jews, Antiochus now struck his most grievous blow. He desecrated their Temple in Jerusalem. During the Hebrew month of Kislev (December) in the year 167 BC, Seleucid mercenaries, at the express orders of the emperor, entered Jewry's most hallowed shrine and carried out a series of vile profanations, one more abhorrent than another. Their very entry was a sacrilege, for access was prohibited to Gentiles, and certain chambers and cloisters were forbidden even to most Jews, being open only to the priesthood. One chamber, the Holy of Holies, was open to one Jew alone, the High Priest, and even he was allowed in on only one day in the year, the solemn Day of Atonement (Yom Kippur).

Forcing their way into the Temple precincts, Antiochus' troops proceeded systematically to remove or rip away whatever precious and sacred appurtenances had escaped the heavy hand of earlier Seleucid pillaging and to tear down all signs of Judaic association. Then, under the guidance of an elderly Athenian philosopher, edifice and courts were prepared for the ritual that was to follow: the formal conversion of the Jewish sanctuary into a pagan hellenist shrine. (The Athenian – some records say he was a 'noble Antiochan' – was well versed in Greek ways, and he had been brought to Jerusalem by Antiochus for this express supervisory purpose.) The Temple of the Jews was now to be dedicated to Olympian Zeus, and an image of this Greek deity was installed above the altar. (It is suggested in one of the ancient records that Antiochus arranged for it to be fashioned in his likeness.)

On the twenty-fifth day of the month, the dedication was solem-
nized by the sacrificial offering of a pig to this pagan image. Not
content with defiling the Jewish altar, the desecrators also sprinkled
some of the hog's blood in the Holy of Holies. The sacred scrolls
found in the Temple were bespattered and then burnt. Thereafter,
sacrificial ceremonies, with pigs, became a regular feature of the
polluted Temple scene, while the mercenaries and their courtesans

Sacrificial pig near the
altar at a pagan ceremony,
as depicted on a Greek
bowl (*ca.* 500 BC)

performed licentious pagan rites in the courts. 'For the heathens filled the Temple with riotous revelry: they took their pleasure with prostitutes and had intercourse with women in the sacred enclosures' (II Macc. 6:5).

It was the blackest day for Jewry since the destruction of their Temple four hundred years earlier. In one way it seemed more agonizing. Though nothing could have been more disastrous than destruction, at least the shattered stones had remained undefiled by impure sacrifice, had served no heathen deity, no pagan purpose. Now, however, though the walls of the Temple still stood, so that its life, so to speak, endured, it was a living death – and, converted from the House of God to the House of Zeus, a living lie. It was the grossest affront to the Jewish faith, which was precisely what Antiochus had intended.

This national catastrophe was felt by every Jew within the hellenistic world. For by now, the second century BC, the Temple had become more than the central shrine of the Jewish community. It was also the symbolic centre of the nation, the focus of their existence as a people.

The original edifice had been erected by King Solomon in the tenth century BC, and in the following centuries it had figured prominently in the lives, activities and utterances of the kings and prophets of Judea as recorded in the sacred annals. It had been destroyed in 587 BC by Nebuchadnezzar, who had carried off the Jews to Babylon, and had been rebuilt with the miraculous return of the exiles a bare fifty years later. In the course of this long period, and particularly in the centuries since its dramatic reconstruction, the Temple had become invested with a singular mystique. As much as the geographic landmark of Jerusalem, it was the spiritual landmark in the soul of the nation, the fount both of its religion and its hope for renewed freedom and restored glory. Thus, the three Pilgrim Festivals, Passover, Pentecost and Tabernacles, when all Jews in the land journeyed to Jerusalem to worship at the Temple (in accordance with the biblical injunction in Deuteronomy 16:16). had acquired a national significance.

Pilgrimage now was not only a religious rite; it had also become an expression of Jewish national solidarity. By now, too, it was not only the Jews of Judea who gathered at the Temple at festival time. The Jews in the Diaspora, from Babylonia, Alexandria and Antioch, also journeyed to Jerusalem for these occasions. If they could not come three times a year, they came once a year; and those with meagre means scrimped and saved and tried to come at least once in a lifetime. If even this was beyond them, they hoped that upon their death they might be brought to Jerusalem and buried within sight of the Temple. Each Jew, wherever he lived and whatever his station, made every effort to send his annual Temple dues to Jerusalem. This practice was followed even by those who had drifted away from pious devotions but who regarded it as an act of Jewish identification. The Temple, because of all it had come to represent in their dramatic history, was central to Jewish thought and emotion. Now, Antiochus had turned it into 'the abomination of desolation' (the phrase is taken from the Book of Daniel 9:27 and the First Book of Maccabees 1:54).

What of Menelaus and his hellenistic Jewish supporters? How did they view the violation of the Temple? The records are not explicit, but it is most likely that they deplored this deed. They had gained power, through obeisance to Antiochus and bitter conflict with the traditional Jewish leadership, in the hope not of destroying their people but of weaning them from their ancient ways and introducing them to the more worldly hellenistic patterns. This, they believed, would enable Jerusalem to qualify as a 'Greek city' and enjoy the economic and social benefits accruing therefrom. Menelaus would be the provincial ruler with considerable authority over a semi-independent Judea.

But Menelaus and his supporters had misjudged the character and mood of their community, and both were now paying the price for the error. The hellenists had not thought that the traditionalists would be so defiant, or that Antiochus would be so merciless. They were now trapped, wholly committed to the Seleucid side, forced to collaborate with the persecutors of their people – and profiting in no wise from the treacherous association. Their dreams of power and wealth had dissipated, for far from becoming a prosperous, semi-autonomous province of the empire, Judea had become a crown colony, teeming with troops and officials – and these were now bent on destroying it and slaughtering its inhabitants. Menelaus and his friends had become powerless liegemen of Antiochus and of less and less use to him as developments moved towards crisis point.

When the news of the Temple disaster reached Modi'in, which was still untouched by active official interest, Mattathias and his sons, following the traditional ritual for a bereavement, tore their garments, donned sackcloth and went into mourning. This was the climax to mounting tragedy. First the restrictions, then the tortures, the killings and now the Temple desecration. It was too much.

And so they sat in silent mourning, Mattathias, scion of the distinguished House of Hashmon (Hasmoneans), and his five sons, 'Johanan (John, called Gaddi), Simon called Thassi, Judah called Maccabee, Eleazar called Avaran, and Jonathan called Apphus' (I Macc. 2:2–5). Each was wrapped in his own thoughts. Occasionally the old man heaved a sigh and gave utterance to his misery.

Oh! Why was I born to see this
the crushing of my people, the ruin of the holy city?
They sat idly by when it was surrendered,
when the holy place was given up to the alien.
Her temple is like a man robbed of honour;
its glorious vessels are carried off as spoil.
Her infants are slain in the street,
her young men by the sword of the foe . . .
She has been stripped of all her adornment,
no longer free, but a slave.
Now that we have seen our temple with all its beauty and splendour
laid waste and profaned by the heathen,
why then should we continue to live?      (I Macc. 2:7–12)


The last line suggests despair; but it held a special meaning, one which went well with the bitterness of line 3 – 'They sat idly by . . .' This meaning was to become evident in the remarkable episode that occurred only a few weeks later.

Antiochus considered that he had done well in Jerusalem by cutting out its Judaic heart and investing it with the trappings of hellenism. But he still found himself far from his goal, for the Jews remained as uncooperative as ever. While many were killed, and there was no core of active resistance, more and more were escaping the terror – and paganism – by fleeing the city. The next step was clearly to trap them and also to move beyond the environs of Jerusalem and ensure that his decrees were applied rigorously to the whole of Judea. Army commanders and officials were now ordered to proceed systematically to all the main villages in the province to enforce the regulations, while other detachments were to increase their patrols and ambuscades of the refugee hideouts.

In the villages, the inhabitants were to be assembled in the central square and their renunciation of Judaism and induction into the culture and religion of hellenism was to be formalized at a sacrificial ceremony upon an altar to Zeus.

Thus it was that Apelles, his bodyguard and the pig came to the village of Modi'in.

# 5  The Deed

We are back in the market-place of Modi'in. Apelles has just called on Mattathias to 'be the first to come forward and carry out the order of the king' to take part in the sacrifice of the pig to the god Zeus and to taste of the sacrificial flesh. He awaits the answer of the old man. The villagers wait too, tense and uncertain. No such uncertainty is apparent in the eyes of Mattathias; and whatever his inner tautness, it is given no visible expression. His face is calm, and so is his voice as he addresses himself to Apelles:

Though all the nations within the king's dominions obey him and forsake their ancestral worship, though they have chosen to submit to his commands, yet I and my sons and my brothers will follow the covenant of our fathers. Heaven forbid we should ever abandon the Law and its statutes. We will not obey the command of the king, nor will we deviate one step from our forms of worship (1 Macc. 2:19–22).

Mattathias ended his words, but his eyes continued to hold the officer's in challenge. Tension in the market-place was now at snapping point, every villager aware that the moment of supreme crisis had struck. Something was bound to happen in the next few seconds, something violent. They had heard enough of Seleucid behaviour to know how Apelles would react to the patriarch's defiance. But what of Mattathias? He had uttered resolute words, but what would he *do*? And what would they themselves do? This was perhaps the most urgent of the thoughts that must have gnawed at their tormented minds as they awaited the climactic eruption. Husbands and wives drew their children protectively closer.

Suddenly the spell was broken. There was movement – but it came not from the protagonists. One of the Jews had stepped forward into the centre clearing and was walking slowly past

Scene of the drama in the market-place of Modi'in, as conceived by the monks of St Gallen, Switzerland, in their 10th-century illuminated manuscript of the Books of Maccabees

the mercenaries towards the altar. The villagers watched him with wonder – what was he about? – and relief. Here was a respite from decision, if only for a few moments. The Jew walked on, and now Apelles and Mattathias turned from each other to follow his progress. He stepped up to the altar and announced, to the surprise of his fellow villagers, that he was willing to make the sacrifice. The officer and his troops must have been equally surprised, and also relieved: there would be a ceremony after all, and it could now begin. They could relax. Mattathias would be dealt with later.

There is now a gap in the ancient records; but it is reasonable to suppose, in the light of what followed, that a couple of the soldiers, at a sign from their officer, hoisted the pig onto the altar and prepared it for sacrifice. Everyone would be watching, villagers, soldiers and Apelles himself, his attention now on the altar and the compliant Jew and away from Mattathias and the crowd. The soldiers, too, would be off guard, curious about the unexpected altar scene, eyes riveted on the new principal character and not on the populace, sensing no danger. The Jew was handed a knife and he approached the pig.

The records tell us what happened next. 'The sight stirred Mattathias to indignation; he shook with passion, and in a fury of righteous anger rushed forward and slaughtered the traitor on the very altar.' He no doubt did so with the sacrificial knife. He then turned upon the astonished Apelles and killed him too. Before the troops could take in what was happening and pull themselves together, the sons of Mattathias and their friends, spontaneously aided by the rest of the villagers, had rushed upon them and slain them.

(To understand how even a small unit of well-armed soldiers failed to hold off a larger group of unarmed civilians, it is well to recall that these mercenaries, though crack troops on the battlefield, had been spending the last few months living soft as an occupation force in Judea, enforcing the royal decrees, by coercion or killing, upon submissive men and women. Before their visit to Modi'in, they had encountered no active resistance, and they had expected none now. They were therefore not as vigilant as they had been trained to be, and were taken completely by surprise.)

It was all over in minutes, and everyone was flushed with the dramatic turn of events. They were alive; they had not betrayed their faith; and the representatives of the tyrant lay dead. But they were quickly sobered by the question: what next? The old man and his sons had the answer, though they, too, shared some of the surprise of their fellow-villagers. True, they had known what they would do, but they had not foreseen the outcome, for they had not envisaged the possibility of a renegade in their midst and could not have anticipated how they would react. They had known only that Mattathias would reject Apelles' demand; that Apelles would doubtless order his men to cut him down; and that he and his sons would do battle. They accounted their chances of success as meagre. They fully expected to go down fighting – and that was what Mattathias had meant when he said 'why then should we continue to live?' Others had submitted passively to the executioner's sword, and the less stalwart had 'sat idly by'. They, however, would set a new example. They would assuredly be killed, but they would sell their lives dearly.

If they were alive now, it was largely because of the diversion created by the renegade Jew. It is thus unlikely that they had devised a detailed contingency plan in the improbable event that they would survive Apelles' visit. But it mattered little, for they had such a plan in broad outline. They had long known that at some time the very crisis they had just met was inevitable, and they had discussed often enough the course to be followed if they were spared to fight another day.

There was thus no need to convene a formal village council to decide what to do next. Mattathias simply moved to the centre of the market-place and addressed his people, the Seleucid dead lying where they had been killed. It was evident, he told them, that they would have to leave Modi'in without delay. There would be search parties, probably within a day or two, when the authorities registered that Apelles and his men had failed to return, and anyone found in the village would be given short shrift. Nor, he advised them, could they expect to find refuge in another hamlet, for every Judean habitation was now the target of the emperor's decrees. He, for his part – and he could speak also for his sons – did not seek 'refuge'. Escape, yes, but not in order to spend the rest of their days cowering in some miserable hiding hole. They had struck at the enemy that day. With God's help, they would strike again, and continue this pattern until their last breath.

Mattathias then called upon his people to do the same. They would make for the hills, organize themselves and, if caught, give battle. They would not, as others had done when trapped, forfeit their lives without a struggle. He ended his talk with a simple appeal: 'Let everyone who is zealous for the Law, and would maintain the covenant, follow me.'

The villagers agreed, though all were now conscious of the agonizing implications. In the space of a few shocked minutes, their normal world, the village world of pious, hard-working farmers, had come crashing down. They would be forsaking their

One of Gustave Doré's wood-engraved illustrations of the Bible (1866) of Mattathias rousing his people to revolt after the incident at Modi'in

The Gophna hills, site of the Maccabee guerilla base. The hills were thickly wooded at that time, but were denuded by conquerors in subsequent centuries

homes and their lands, and few imagined that they would ever return. Ahead of them lay the life of outlaws, with no permanent shelter, no certainty of sustenance, constant danger and with their wives and children forced to share their hardships and perils. It was a bleak and poignant prospect. But as Mattathias had indicated, they would go forth with straight backs, bowing to neither man nor idol, and fight for their faith and their lives.

Thus was the banner of revolt raised against Antiochus.

There was no time to be lost. While the young men tore down the altar, stripped the uniforms from the dead troops – there might be a use for them later – and removed their weapons, the villagers were instructed to gather essential belongings (including portable farm implements) and victuals (dried dates, dried figs, raisins, oil, flour) and to be ready by sundown. Mattathias, his sons and some of the village elders then sat down to decide on a suitable retreat. They were not looking for a place of refuge, but a base of operations. It should therefore be somewhat reasonably close, difficult of access to columns of regular troops, affording good cover and commanding all-round visibility. All were familiar with the surrounding terrain, and after a short while they decided to make for the hills above Gophna (as modern scholars believe), just beyond the Judean border in southern Samaria, some 13 miles north-east of Modi'in.

[Our designation of Gophna as the site they chose is simply a hypothesis. No one can be certain of the exact location, for no place-name is given in the Books of Maccabees or in any other contemporary source. The First Book of Maccabees simply says that Mattathias and his sons 'took to the hills' (2:28). But from certain references in Josephus, though in another context (after the encounter at Beth Zechariah, 'Judah retreated with the remnant to the province of Gophna', *Wars of the Jews* 1.45); from studies of the terrain surrounding Modi'in; and from features of the first major battles fought by Judah as described in the early texts, scholars have concluded that the most likely retreat to which the Modi'inites proceeded were the Gophna hills; and this will be our assumption throughout the book.]

By the appointed time, all were gathered in the market-place, enacting an exodus scene but vividly reliving every stark detail of the terrifying tableau they had witnessed only a few hours before. The heavier bundles of belongings, equipment and provisions were being loaded onto asses and carts. Each family would carry what it could. The villagers were then divided into five contingents, headed by Judah, Johanan, Simon, Eleazar and Jonathan. All was now ready. With Mattathias at their head and Judah at his side to serve as guide, they strode off into the gathering dusk – and into history.

The going was slow. There were the children and the aged. There were the goats and the sheep. And there was little light from the stars and a crescent moon; but it had been considered safer to get away quickly and exploit the shield of darkness, lest they encounter a Seleucid patrol. They had not far to go, however; unencumbered, and in daylight, they could have walked the distance in four hours. Still, it was past midnight when they left the plain and began the climb, and they were still on their slow move, still climbing, when they were caught by the dawn. By then they were well protected from hostile observation by the oak, terebinth and pine which covered the slopes. Shortly after midday they reached the summit of the central hill in the Gophna group, exhausted and hungry, and there they bivouacked.

It was a small beginning to an epic adventure that was to bring down an empire and preserve a nation.

# 6 The Guerillas

The first few days in their Gophna retreat were crucial. The villagers were weary, shaken, unorganized. They were few, numbering perhaps two hundred souls. Of these, not more than forty to fifty were males, able-bodied but with no military training. A determined assault by a platoon of regular troops could have wiped them out. (The reflection is inescapable that had this happened, Antiochus might well have succeeded in stifling the Jewish religion in Judea, and there would have been no dramatic crucifixion of a Jew in Jerusalem two hundred years later!)

That they were not attacked was due to vision and luck; and once the band from Modi'in survived that first week, the resistance movement which had burst into existence was to grow in strength, and become more difficult to suppress, with each passing day.

They were lucky not to have been intercepted by a patrol *en route* or attacked soon after reaching their base. The chances are that Seleucid headquarters in Judea would not have discovered where their prey had flown until much later. The search-party would have arrived at a deserted Modi'in, come upon the corpses of their men, together with the destroyed altar – and a roaming pig which had escaped sacrifice. They would have interrogated the neighbouring hamlets and got little for their pains. After killing a few inhabitants in vengeful reprisal, they would have left. They would not have wasted time on a meticulous search for the tracks of the escapees, concluding that they had either fled to the usual Judean hideouts – the wilderness caves south-east of Jerusalem – or taken refuge in scattered Judean villages. Either way, they would not long evade capture: all villages would be visited in any case for the erection of altars to Zeus; and the wilderness retreats were routine targets of assault.

Even if the authorities had known about Gophna sooner, several

Caves in the wilderness of Judea, where the Jews found refuge from Seleucid tyranny before the Maccabees raised the banner of revolt

75

factors would have dissuaded them from energetic pursuit. Mattathias and his sons had chosen their retreat with political and military
foresight. It lay just north of the boundary of the Judean sub-district.
This put them within the area ruled by the Seleucid governor of
Samaria, and although Judea came under his administrative control,
it was the local Judean commander who was in immediate charge
of enforcing the hellenistic decrees, and he concentrated his operations within Judean territory, which held the bulk of the country's
Jews. Furthermore, even if he had wished to extend his operations
northwards, he would have hesitated to plunge into some 20 square
miles of forested hills where the quarry could prove most elusive
against a small routine unit. To comb the area thoroughly would
require a considerable force, and this was wasteful against a handful
of malefactors who would anyway expose themselves sooner or
later in search of food. Moreover, a large-scale military action in
this region could not be mounted without the reasons becoming
known to the governor of Samaria, and possibly to the court in
Antioch, and the Judean commander would have been reluctant
to draw attention to his humiliating failure in Modi'in. The incident
could pass unreported, and the death of Apelles and his few guards
'written off' by slipping them into the casualty list without a
detailed explanation.

However, perhaps the weightiest reason why no immediate
action was taken was also the simplest: it never occurred to the
authorities that the men of Modi'in were, or could be, dangerous.
They were expected to behave, at best, like all the other subject
peoples within the empire, or, at worst, like their fellow-Jews who
had fled to the desert not to create trouble but to avoid it. Trouble
from an occupied people at that time was rarely envisaged by
occupation troops. A popular rising was highly unusual. A vassal
king might rebel against an imperial monarch, usually in alliance
with other vassals and mostly with the backing of a rival imperial
power. War would then follow, with opposing armies in regular
array confronting each other in set battles. Whoever won would
occupy the conquered territories, and the peoples therein would be
subservient to their new masters. The masters might change with
new turns of the wheel, and station new occupation troops; but the
subservience would remain. The troops would be installed largely
to 'show the flag'. Their presence alone was sufficient to keep the
people in check. They rarely encountered resistance, and never
organized resistance, from the populace. It was the political leaders
and the generals who initiated rebellion, never the people.

Thus, the Seleucid authorities in Judea, though irked by the
Modi'in incident, could have foreseen no possible peril from a

bunch of Jews from this obscure village, led – if they were led at all – by someone who was totally unknown and therefore unimportant. They erred in their judgement of Mattathias and his followers, and they failed to gauge – being ignorant of their history – the temper of the Jews. By the time they were to discover their mistake, it would be too late.

Whatever their reasoning (the records are silent on this point) it seems that the Seleucid authorities in Judea left the group at Gophna unmolested for about a year. It was a year well used by the rebels. They set themselves four main objectives: to train in guerilla warfare; to rouse the spirit of resistance among their people in Judea and recruit as many as possible to their ranks; to restore, in the words of Mattathias, a respect for the Law and the 'maintenance of the covenant' wherever this had been weakened by the hellenistic process; and to give battle whenever they encountered the enemy, but not to initiate military action until they were ready.

The rebels spent the first week organizing their hill-base, getting to know every inch of the surrounding wooded terrain, marking appropriate ambush spots in the event of assault and staking out pickets who kept wary watch on all the approaches night and day. It is probable that only thereafter did they venture out to establish contact with their fellow-Jews, no doubt choosing one of the villages near Modi'in where they would be known and which would be easy to reach, with time to return to base, during the hours of darkness. Because the initial meeting would be decisive, it was presumably one of the brothers, perhaps Judah, who would have led the first mission, starting down the hillside after sundown with one or two companions and making for the homes of trusted boyhood friends and erstwhile neighbours.

Subsequent events offer a clue as to what must have transpired at this bizarre midnight meeting. Judah, or whichever brother it was, gave an account of the episode at Modi'in and reported on their resistance aims. These reports were to be spread by relay from village to village throughout Judea to hearten the community and condition them to future action – and probable Seleucid reprisals. The friends, who would assuredly have wished to join the group at Gophna, were to remain and establish a 'rear-echelon' base to serve the Gophna 'front', organizing an intelligence network, supply system and messenger service. They would arrange for reliable contacts in all villages to gather information on the size, movement and likely intentions of occupation troops in their areas and funnel the intelligence to a message centre to be located within night-reach of Gophna. Rear-echelon would also approach trust-

An Etruscan pottery vase (*ca.* 500 BC). The soldier slaying his bearded adversary is Greek

worthy villages to furnish food and equipment to maintain the Gophna base, for the reserves brought from Modi'in would not last long. Supplies and messengers would move only at night.

The friends must have done their work well, for it was not long before most of the Jews had heard the Modi'in story, and here and there – at the beginning they were few – young villagers volunteered to join the rebels and were passed from one village contact to the next until they reached Gophna. The news even reached the Jews who were hiding out in the hills and wilderness of Judea, and all made their furtive way to the Gophna base. Most of these were Hasidim, many of whose members had been killed when caught by troops in their caves of refuge on the Sabbath day.

All, particularly the Hasidim, 'stalwarts of Israel' (1 Macc. 2:42), were warmly welcomed by Mattathias and his comrades – with one reservation. It arose out of the manner in which so many of the Hasidim had lost their lives. When they had fled from Jerusalem and gone into hiding in the wilderness, a unit of

the king's officers and the forces in Jerusalem . . . went quickly after them, came up with them, and occupied positions opposite. They prepared to attack them on the Sabbath. 'There is still time,' they shouted; 'Come out, obey the king's command, and your lives will be spared.' 'We will not come out,' the Jews replied; 'We will not obey the king's command

or profane the Sabbath.' Without more ado the attack was launched; but the Israelites did nothing in reply; they neither hurled stones, nor barricaded their caves. 'Let us all meet death with a clear conscience', they said . . . So they were attacked and massacred on the Sabbath, men, women and children, up to a thousand in all . . . (1 Macc. 2:32–8).

The Hasidim joined the Maccabee struggle and fought as 'stalwarts of Israel'. On the eve of Israel's independence in 1948, pious Jews fought in the ranks of the Jewish underground in the defence of Jerusalem

When Mattathias had heard this at the time, he was stricken with grief, and said to his friends: 'If we all do as our brothers have done, if we refuse to fight the Gentiles for our lives as well as for our laws and customs, then they will soon wipe us off the face of the earth.' It was then that he decided that 'if anyone came to fight against them on the Sabbath, they would fight back, rather than all die as their brothers in the caves had done.'

This is what Mattathias now put to the Hasidim who had joined him at Gophna, and they agreed. 'Every one of them [became] a volunteer in the cause of the law.' They would defend themselves if attacked on the Sabbath (though not even Mattathias would initiate an attack on that day).

This decision was revolutionary for its time. The Fourth Commandment was observed by traditionalists with scrupulous regard to the tiniest detail, and it was naturally understood that one would not desecrate the Sabbath by blocking up a hiding place even to save one's life. Only some three hundred years later, in the second century AD, did the rabbis ordain that 'the Sabbath is given to man, not man to the Sabbath', and so the preservation of life now takes precedence in Jewish law over observance of the Sabbath.

At the time, then, Mattathias was taking it upon himself to re-interpret the traditional law. This function had hitherto been vested in the High Priest and his council, who were now Menelaus and his hellenist supporters. Thus, says Elias Bickermann:

> When Mattathias, a man previously unknown, one priest among ten thousand, resolved . . . to infringe upon the prerogatives of the High Priest, he raised himself, perhaps without intending to do so, to the position of an opposition government. Hence his resolve constituted a turning point in Jewish history. His measure immediately gave him the authority of a leader. The 'community of the pious' [Hasidim] . . . and . . . those who had abandoned their homes in order not to depart from the law . . . were united by that very measure which infringed the Torah for the Torah's sake.

As soon as the Gophna base had been organized, the sons of Matta-thias began training their men – and themselves – as future guerillas. Judah was put in charge. Some of what they learned would be put to immediate use – mostly how to steal through the enemy lines in order to show their presence in Jewish villages and how to defend themselves if attacked *en route*. Much of their training, however, if they were given a long enough respite by the enemy, would be applied only after they had grown in strength, numbers and skills and could initiate military action.

Judah's overriding principle – what might be called his guerilla strategy – which determined the tactical training of his men, was to turn their own inadequacies into assets and the enemy's advantages into handicaps. Simple as this may seem to us today, the very enunciation of this principle in the circumstances and context in which it was uttered was an expression of unusual courage and deep faith in the success of their cause. It was being presented in the year 166 BC by a young villager to a handful of bedraggled civilian refugees beneath a clump of trees on a Samarian hillside, preparatory to challenging a mighty empire which seemed to be suffering from no military handicaps whatsoever.

Indeed, the mere listing of Seleucid assets might well have shaken Judah's listeners: a huge army, battle-trained and battle-hardened, comprising heavy and light infantry, heavy and light cavalry, camel units, elephant units, chariots, regiments of 'artillery' (oper-ating ballistas), sappers (for building roads and bridges), as well as intelligence and service units. These troops wielded an immense array of weapons: swords, javelins, spears, bows, slings, ballistas (engines for hurling huge stones) and battering rams (though the last two types of arms were used only in attacks on walled cities). The only weapons possessed by the Jews were the mace (a primitive instrument consisting of a short wooden handle topped by a stone or metal head), the sling (devised by ancient shepherds to scare away predatory animals) and their farm implements, the scythe, sickle and pitchfork, adapted for combat. Backing the Seleucid force was a powerful administration with immeasurable resources. The Jews of Gophna began with no resources and no administration; they lived from hand to mouth. How, then, could they think of even denting so strong a military host?

There are crevices in the most formidable mountain, and the mightiest army has its chinks. Judah showed his men where these might be found among the enemy forces. Seleucid superiority in manpower and arms was overwhelming, but the Jews had read in their sacred books how Gideon with three hundred men had routed the Midianite army of thousands, and how David had defeated

Detail from a Greek bronze vase of a manned war-chariot and a foot-soldier

*left* A 5th-century BC bronze figurine of a Greek foot soldier
*right* David and Goliath, detail from a stone relief on a 10th-century Armenian church near Lake Van (on the Turkish-Russian border). Judah encouraged his Maccabee comrades – outnumbered by Seleucid forces – by recalling David's triumph over the Philistine giant

Goliath. The armies of Antiochus were well trained, but for the set battle; the Jews would avoid the set battle. They were well organized, but in conventional formations, fighting in conventional ways; the response would be unconventional stratagems. There were other enemy weaknesses. Their size and weight of arms limited their mobility; a small group with few weapons could move quickly. They were mostly foreign auxiliaries, unfamiliar with the terrain; the Jews were natives. They were unused to fighting after dark; the Jews would strike at night. They could expect no support from the hostile population; to the Jews, the local inhabitants were brothers. Above all, they were mercenaries who fought for their living; the Jews would be fighting for their lives.

Judah accordingly laid down the guidelines of future action against this powerful foe when the resistance force would be larger, stronger and properly trained – guidelines which in our own day have become standard principles of guerilla warfare: Desist from open battle. Choose the time and place of your encounters, don't leave it to the enemy. When he attacks, melt. When he shies from fighting, assault. When he halts, harass him. When he flees, pursue. Use the night as your shield. Strike and run. Behave like a phantom. Make him fear danger from every side. Give him no rest.

Judah of course knew that no single guerilla action could be decisive; but mounting harassment and attrition might induce the enemy to reconsider his policies. If compulsory hellenization proved too costly, made no progress and resulted in loss of Seleucid prestige, perhaps the Jews would be left free to worship their God and follow their traditional customs. Offensive action, then, would be initiated when they were ready. Meanwhile they would undergo intensive training, avoid the enemy if they could, but pay surprise visits to the villages in Judea to keep aloft the banner of Judaism.

In the early months, therefore, there was instruction in guerilla tactics by day and the movement of supplies, contact with intelligence messengers, and sporadic operations at night. Judah and his brothers would slip out of their Gophna base after dark, each at the head of a small guerilla band, and proceed to villages where the authorities had erected a pagan altar. They would enter these villages, destroy the altars, deal harshly with any who had collaborated with the hellenizers (probably killing them), arrange the circumcision ceremony for male infants who had been left uncircumcised and rouse the men of the village to join them.

If the villages were too distant for a night's return march, they would stay in some 'safe' hamlet or hide-out and return to base the following night. If they observed the approach of a strong enemy contingent, they would scatter; but if they encountered a small patrol, and the tactical conditions were favourable, they would strike, carry off the weapons of the dead troops and hide their bodies in the scrub to delay discovery – and reprisal.

For the villages it was a time of torment. They bore the brunt of Seleucid retaliation when a hellenizing unit was wiped out nearby, a pagan altar was torn down, or infants were found to have been circumcised. There was a good deal of bloodshed. More painful was the discovery in their midst – and execution by the rebels – of a collaborator. Not everyone was strong in heart. Quite a number were simple folk concerned largely with survival, and they may well have seen themselves caught between the imperial troops and the rebels. However, the bulk of the community were zealous traditionalists who were aware of the vital issues which confronted them in that dark period but who had been confused as to what to do until Mattathias had shown them the way. They rallied to the cause of active resistance, knowing the possible price and prepared to pay it. The arbitrary slaughter in Seleucid reprisals was heavy to bear; but sorrow merged with anger, and anger fuelled the resolve to fight back. Volunteering swelled, and the populace, though hard-hit, faithfully kept the rebel base supplied with food.

In this first year, the rebels limited their activities to the Judean countryside. At no time did they venture into walled Jerusalem, headquarters of the occupation administration and army. They were not yet geared to breach so formidable a bastion.

Mercenary depicted on a 3rd-century BC tombstone uncovered in Sidon

It is unlikely that the activities of the Judean rebels during this first year were known to the court at Antioch. By Seleucid army standards they were trivial, and the local commanders would hardly have thought them worth more than a sentence in their reports. To them the guerillas were a nuisance, but certainly not a serious military threat. For that very reason no major force had been sent to engage them.

To the rebels themselves, however, this was a year of great importance. They had survived – on their feet and not on their knees. They had lived hard and trained hard. As farmers they had an eye for terrain, as hunters they could move with stealth, and they made natural soldiers. The Judean hill-country, which they knew intimately, lent itself to guerilla action, and they had met the foe – albeit in minor skirmishes – and emerged as victors. Each small success, even the ambushing of a half a dozen troops, which was of little account to the Seleucid army, was of great account to them and fired them with a prodigious faith in their capabilities. They now considered themselves a force of significant potential harassing power. Their supply lines were organized and they no longer had to live from hand to mouth; they were adequately maintained by the Jewish villages, and their ranks were continually strengthened by fresh volunteers. From their original nucleus of forty or so fighting men, they had now grown to many hundreds. They realized that they would soon be facing action on a larger scale, action for which they had trained and to which they looked forward. They were confident that they would successfully cope with that, too.

Their guiding spirit had been the venerable old Mattathias, wise, practical, gifted with inspired leadership and blessed with five remarkable sons who served as his principal lieutenants. Each had shown special qualities of command during this first year at Gophna. (Each was to prove himself through individual achievement in the years that followed, and all were to die a violent death.) Without these five, it is doubtful whether Mattathias' idea of active resistance would have been given practical shape. Mattathias had listened to them in counsel and watched them in operation and had formed a shrewd judgement of the capacities of each. He had decided in his mind which of them would replace him as leader.

Now, a year after his dramatic act in Modi'in, Mattathias felt his days running out, and it was time to name his choice. Gathering his sons to his tent, he first gave them his parting testament: continue with the struggle and go from strength to strength. He then recalled the great heroes in Jewish history, with whose exploits in adversity they were familiar from their sacred books, and urged them to maintain this noble tradition so that they, too, would make history:

Be zealous for the Law and give your lives for the covenant of your fathers. Remember the deeds they did in their generations . . . Did not Abraham prove steadfast under trial . . . Joseph kept the commandments, hard-pressed though he was . . . Joshua kept the Law . . . David was a man of loyalty . . . Elijah never flagged . . . Follow their example; for no one who trusts in Heaven shall ever lack strength.

They were living, he told them, in 'a time of calamity and raging fury . . . But you, my sons, draw your courage and strength from the Law . . . ' (1 Macc. 2:49–64).

He then designated Judah, his middle son, as his successor, to be 'your commander' to 'fight his people's battles'. He also singled out Judah's older brother Simon as a man 'wise in counsel' who 'shall be a father to you'. The patriarch's deathbed wish was endorsed by acclamation.

Mattathias died soon after. At night, his sons and a few of the other guerilla commanders brought his body down from the Gophna hills and moved silently to deserted Modi'in. They laid him to rest in the family tomb just outside the village. 'Then Judah, who was called Maccabee, came forward in his father's place. He had the support of all his brothers and his father's followers, and they carried on the fight for Israel with zest.'

The 'Tombs of the Maccabees' at Modi'in

מכבי

ויש טוכפו בחמרית וכטור מטים התון ‏‏‎ וירח
נען כבר להחן מדוכמתיט הא יוטאו ערכב יון
מחמתכחטות ויטיוויוהת על היטי ויוזרי
ומית

הב והנ
וב אזנך
שוער ן
וב אויו
הי בקש
דלה לני
ב אביצה
הימי ן
אשר כ
יצר כנכה
אורב
ם אגן
לי ומעו

לריות מותלטוטנ מתוריך
 וות קטוין ומתעוד והטור
מטטר יהר לומי מל הח

# 7  The Test

It was with Judah that the struggle of the Jews against the Seleucid empire began in earnest. In the immediate years that followed, he was to display a rare combination of qualities which made him both a charismatic national leader and an inspired general. Though he had never soldiered before, he seems to have taken naturally to the art of warfare, devising his own principles and drawing on the skills absorbed as a country lad in outwitting animals. His early experience in stalking, hunting and trapping would have been useful to him as a guerilla private. The competence in higher commands he acquired as operations continued and as his force grew from section to platoon to company to battalion and to brigade (as the formations would be called today). By the time he was commanding a body of men the size of a division, he had already proved himself a sound and thoughtful strategist and an ingenious tactician. He was daring but not impulsive. Intrepid himself as a fighting commander, he could enthuse his men and bring out the innate bravery that is in every man. He must have had more than a touch of ruthlessness, as must all wartime leaders, and an underground resistance leader in particular, ordering actions to advance his people's aims even when they might bring down reprisals upon their heads. He must also have possessed tremendous self-confidence, which stemmed no doubt from his boundless faith in the righteousness of his cause and the unshakeable belief that God was with him. He was as devout and pious as his father had been.

Some of these qualities were assuredly evident when Mattathias named him as his successor. He had said at the time that Judah 'has been strong and brave from boyhood', and this must have been recognized also by his brothers and the other families of Modi'in. He was called Judah the Maccabee, Hebrew for 'Judah the hammerer', and the resistance forces he led were therefore known, and

Judah the Maccabee, in a 15th-century.Hebrew illuminated manuscript from Italy

87

they continue to be known up to this very day, as the Maccabees.

['The hammerer' is the generally accepted translation of 'Maccabee', deriving from the Hebrew word *makabah*, which means hammer. However, in Hebrew, the word which is pronounced Maccabee may be spelt in two slightly different ways. One means 'the hammerer', the other 'the quencher' or 'the extinguisher', and some scholars prefer the second meaning as descriptive of Judah, 'who extinguished hellenism in Judea'. Another scholar suggests that Maccabee may have been a nickname and simply meant that Judah was called 'the hammer-head' because of the shape of his cranium. A more ingenious recent theory is that the word stems from the same Hebrew root of the verb *yikavenu* used in Isaiah 62:2 and meaning 'he shall be named [by the Lord]'. Talmudists fond of word-play saw the Hebrew letters that make up Maccabee as an acronym for the Hebrew of Exodus 15:11: 'Who is like unto thee, O Lord, among the gods?' which occurs in the song sung by Moses after the successful crossing of the Red Sea. Whatever the original derivation of the term, it signified at the time, and has been so held by the generations of Jews ever since, the leader who, under divine guidance, hammered and smote his foes and so kept Judaism alive.

It may seem strange that the man who fought so determinedly against hellenism should be commonly known by the Greek form of his name, Judas Maccabaeus. This is because the First Book of Maccabees, originally written in Hebrew, failed to qualify for the Old Testament canon, established at the end of the first century AD, and therefore ceased to circulate in its Hebrew version. It was, however, one of the sacred books which had been translated into Greek for the Septuagint and was included in the Apocrypha. The Apocryphal texts, which centuries later were adopted by the Christian canon, have therefore come down to us not in their original Hebrew but in their Greek version; and other translations, including the English, followed the Greek style of Judah's name.]

When Judah returned to base after the burial of his father, he took stock of his assets and prospects. The rebel group he now commanded was a more sizeable and experienced force than it had been a year earlier. They had all come a long way in the few miles they had journeyed from Modi'in to Gophna. They had succeeded in their primary objective of forging an instrument of potential resistance by concentrating on military training (which included a number of skirmishes), inducing a mood of active rebellion among the villagers – and avoiding heavy encounters with the enemy. Yet

it was only by such encounters that they would gain their resistance
aims. Judah was anxious to come to grips with the adversary, to
move from the phase of preparation to the phase of operation. He
had confidence in the combat-worthiness of his men; but they were
still comparatively few. And he may well have doubted whether
the military apparatus he had helped to construct and which he
had just inherited, geared as it was to the training phase, would
serve the new stage equally well.

As to aims, it is doubtful whether at this stage Judah had any idea
of restoring Jewish sovereignty over the whole of the original
territory of the kingdom of Israel. His purpose was to enable the
Jews of Judea to uphold their faith and pursue their traditionalist
ways. In military terms, this meant first disrupting Seleucid rule
in rural Judea, rendering the countryside unsafe for occupation
troops and guaranteeing the villagers freedom from molestation.
With this accomplished, he should be in a position to tackle Jerusalem, regain the Holy Temple from the pagans and rededicate it
to the Lord.

After much reflection, Judah must have recognized that to do
this would require revolutionary changes in the size, location and
maintenance of his force. He would need more men to undertake
action on the scale he envisaged, the scale necessary to achieve their
new objective. They would begin to suffer casualties – these had
been minimal so far – and continuous replacements were essential.
The kind of numbers he expected to recruit to his ranks could not
all be permanently stationed, sheltered and fed in Gophna, even if,
unlike the original group from Modi'in, they came alone and not
with their families and cattle. Moreover, Gophna could not play
its old role in the new phase contemplated by Judah. It had been
ideal as a retreat, training centre and an operational base for the
minor forays that had been undertaken in the first year. But it would
no longer be wise or effective, even if it were possible, to station
the entire guerilla force in this one location. Advance bases would
need to be established – closer to the areas of proposed action. It
would be best to station small concentrated units in the different
districts throughout rural Judea. Each could operate in its own
region, yet be ready to augment another force for major action
anywhere else.

It is reasonable to suppose that these considerations led Judah to
the concept of a militia, for it is clear from subsequent events that
the fighters of Judea must have followed the pattern of underground
militiamen. One can imagine that Judah now devised a scheme
whereby Gophna continued for the time being as the base for the
main core of his force, his general headquarters and the principal

guerilla training centre. Volunteers would henceforth proceed in the usual clandestine way to Gophna, where they would undergo basic training. Their wives, parents and children would stay behind to tend the fields and ensure a steady supply of produce. Upon completion of their training, the volunteers would return to their villages, conceal their weapons and resume their farming; but they would come under the military command of one of Judah's officers responsible for their district, who had probably had his underground headquarters in one of the villages. They would be on permanent call by this local commander, either for an operation on their own or with other units, and would return from an engagement to the life of a farmer.

In this way Judah would have his men stationed throughout Judea; camouflaged as innocent farmers, they would be 'invisible' as guerillas to the occupation troops; and they would maintain themselves, thereby relieving general headquarters of the arduous problems of food, shelter and the movement of supplies.

Between battles, the watchful Maccabee farmer-militiamen tilled their land. Spring plowing today in a farm village between Modi'in and the Gophna hills

The militia system would also provide more eyes and ears for Judah's intelligence network. Each militiaman would be a one-man intelligence unit, able to file his report quickly to the nearby district commander, and intelligence, in the new operational phase, was of key importance. Heretofore, when they were dodging action, the rebels needed information on the general movement of enemy troops so as to know which areas to avoid. Now that they would be initiating action, they needed to plan each operation, and for this they required intelligence on the whereabouts of enemy units and patrols, their strength, their likely routes of march, the times of their moves and their purpose. Certain tactical intelligence of the simplest kind, by ordinary observation, would now be gathered and passed on by militiamen. For example, from their fields they might notice in the distance the movement of a Seleucid unit consisting of so many men and heading north-east. The news would be passed by runner, or by a system of flag-signals, to the militiamen in the next village, and from there to the next until it reached the district commander. Other militiamen in villages along the enemy's route would file similar reports. From the collection of such intelligence messages, general headquarters might discern a pattern to enemy movements and plan appropriate ambuscades. Or the district commander might undertake a quick operation of his own if the intelligence suggested it was feasible.

It is clear from his military record that Judah set great store by intelligence, and the subsidiary services of his militiamen were, of course, only a link in his intelligence chain. Strategic intelligence – information on the enemy's overall designs, intentions and plans – was more difficult to secure, but much seems to have seeped through to Judah's headquarters. The centre in Judea where such information was available was Seleucid headquarters in Jerusalem. There is little doubt that Judah had established contact with trustworthy Jerusalem Jews, men whose hearts were with the rebels, who continued to practise traditional Judaism, but who, perhaps through close family relationship or friendship with hellenistic Jews, remained un-molested by the Seleucid officials. They would be in a position to pick up intelligence items of importance to Judah, and there were ways of passing them on. Travel was still possible, and such 'pro-tected' Jews would have no difficulty in visiting a nearby village and contacting its militiamen. Or reports might be carried back by trustworthy village women who had brought their produce to Jerusalem. It is possible, too, that some of his own militiamen might have used captured Seleucid uniforms to secure access to forbidden places. The waylaying of Seleucid runners and the interception of messages they carried was another means of supplementing the rebels' information. Intelligence gathering was assuredly easier for the rebels, backed as they were by the population, than it was for the occupation authorities.

Later, Judah apparently succeeded in obtaining strategic intel-ligence from Samaria, which was Seleucid headquarters for the entire region of southern Syria, and even from Antioch itself, making contact with travellers and merchants who were well received in these centres but who were prompted either by greed or by hatred for Antiochus. Later still, Judah would be in touch with far superior intelligence sources – with Rome and other countries ill-disposed towards the Seleucids. But this was some years away.

To get his militia system started, Judah, his brothers and his prin-cipal lieutenants must have undertaken an intensive recruiting campaign, visiting between them every village in Judea, explaining to the men at urgent midnight meetings the new proposals and plans and showing them how they would now be able to farm and

fight, thus intensifying the struggle with less disruption of village life. District commands were probably established soon after, officered by local men, veteran volunteers who had proved themselves at Gophna.

Within a day or two new volunteers would be on their way to Gophna for a crash training course, and within weeks the militia system would have been well under way. In that time, too, the communications systems must have been improved and tested. Simple messages, such as a general alert or a summons to district commanders for a night rendezvous at a pre-arranged spot, could be flashed from general headquarters by a combination of different coloured flags and reach every village in Judea within the hour. It is possible that torch-flares and smoke signals were also used – with discretion. A more complicated message which would need to be sent by a runner or a relay of runners could get to general head-

Village women taking produce to the Jerusalem market served as Maccabee couriers to trusted friends. The peasant in this terracotta statuette is trying to steady a faltering donkey laden with grapes for the city market

A unit of the Israel Defence Forces moving into the very ambush positions in the Judean hills taken by the Maccabees more than twenty-one centuries ago

quarters from the most distant Judean village in five or six hours.

Judah's force was expanding. His intelligence system was working. Enough items would have come in on the daily movements of enemy patrols within the first few weeks to enable him to detect a pattern. He could thus start planning operations on a new scale and go into action upon completion of the training course for the first of the new militiamen.

There is nothing in the ancient records on this intermediate phase of Judah's activities. But we know that they led directly to a critical confrontation with the enemy, and there is much original information on the tactics he employed on that occasion. It is thus possible to offer a reasonable conjecture on the nature of the operations he now launched, using surprise, mobility, night cover and local numerical superiority to discomfit the enemy. As to this last factor, manpower, the armies of Antiochus might outnumber Judah's force by the crushing ratio of a hundred to one; but at the very local level, a lone Seleucid patrol, for example, of perhaps thirty-two men operating in the Judean countryside could be tackled by a fifty-man rebel unit. In this and other ways, Judah's planning of each operation would be designed to neutralize the enemy's objective advantages.

We can envisage some of the early incidents. Intelligence reports show that half a dozen Seleucid patrols move out each day from Jerusalem. They proceed in different directions to show the flag in the various districts of Judea. They follow one set of routes on Mondays, another set on Tuesdays and so on. They stick to main roads and well-defined tracks. (They seldom ventured cross-country as there had been no need.) Judah decides to pick off three patrols simultaneously. He and two of his brothers will command the three assault units, each probably of fifty to sixty men.

Two nights before the day set for the attack, small reconnaissance teams of the three units move out to choose suitable ambush sites along the expected patrol routes – a coppice, a mound whose reverse slope would be hidden from the road, or a defile with a sharp-angled turn. (Judea's terrain is such that any road or track which the troops would have taken ran close to a wood or low hill at some point.) The reconnaissance men return to Gophna and rest up during the day. Late that night they lead their units to the selected attack points and shortly before dawn take up concealed positions – ideally, on both sides of the track. They wait. An hour passes. Two hours. Suddenly they see a cloud of dust in the distance. As it comes nearer they get ready, the slingers reaching for their jagged stones, the storming detachments clutching their daggers. The unsuspecting troops come ambling along. As they get abreast of the rebels, the slingers let fly, sending them into confusion. A moment later, the rest of the Maccabees fall upon them in close combat. The soldiers have no time and no space to wield their swords, javelins or spears. (Patrols would normally have no archers to cover them.) Taken by surprise and outnumbered, they are slain. It is all over in minutes. The bodies are dragged into the woods, or behind the hill, stripped and buried. Their weapons and uniforms are taken. The rebels tend their wounded and carry back their own dead for burial in their villages.

That evening, when the three patrols fail to return to their Jerusalem garrison, the Seleucid commander is only slightly worried. He concludes that his men have probably been held up by trouble in one of the Jewish villages and have bivouacked for the night. They will surely be along by noon next day. But by noon they fail to appear, and by dusk they are still missing. He decides to send another three patrols the following morning to follow the routes taken by those who have vanished. Judah may have anticipated the reasoning of the enemy commander and laid ambushes at the same locations. The new patrols meet the fate of their predecessors. They, too, fail to return to their Jerusalem base. Their commander is now baffled.

He cannot continue the usual patrol routine, for he will soon have no men left. His supply is not inexhaustible. He has a fixed number in his garrison, its complement prescribed not for battle but for occupation duties, which are to maintain order in Jerusalem, protect its hellenists and be on hand in the villages to enforce the royal decrees. No serious fighting is expected. The troops are there largely as a symbol of Seleucid power, and their presence alone is normally enough to keep the populace submissive. They have encountered little trouble so far – except for that vexatious episode in Modi'in more than a year ago, and some slight skirmishing since, in which they suffered a few casualties. But now the situation is grave, and the commander is in an unenviable position. He has already lost a significant portion of his force, and he does not quite know how, which makes his problem acute and its solution elusive. His obvious course is to send large forces along all three mystery-ridden routes, to search for traces of his vanished units, interrogate the villages in the area and find out what is going on. But to do so, and maintain his other patrols, will dangerously deplete his Jerusalem garrison, and the city is his one stronghold, which must be kept secure. He can appeal to Samaria for reinforcements, but it is too soon to make so drastic a confession of incompetence. He decides perhaps to send out fewer patrols and double the strength of each.

Judah waits and watches. Within a few days the reports from his militiamen observers come in and he grasps the enemy's design. The mercenary units are larger and more heavily armed. They also

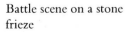

Battle scene on a stone frieze

appear to be more vigilant, no longer marching as though they were on a routine outing, casual and bunched-up. They move like combat troops on their way to battle through hostile territory, with reconnaissance scouts ahead and pickets on the flanks. Judah decides to halt action for a while, ordering his militiamen to remain in their villages and try and observe where the troops stop for rest and food. After perhaps a couple of weeks, when these new enemy units, unmolested, also settle into a routine and become less wary, he orders a guerilla attack in strength on one of their resting places. It is unlikely that all enemy troops are killed. Several are bound to get back to Jerusalem to tell their pitiable tale.

The Jerusalem commander now knows that he has a rebellion on his hands. His next probable move is to establish a base in the heart of rural Judea from which his units will fan out each day instead of

Hand-to-hand fighting depicted on a Greek vase from the 5th century BC

returning to Jerusalem each night, comb every village in search of rebels – and keep an eye on Gophna. He will have concluded by now that Gophna must be the principal rebel hide-out. He had avoided it in the past, believing it to be an innocuous place of refuge and not worth the cost of a major action. He now knows that it is worth the cost; the men it hides are not refugees but fighting rebels. But he has not enough troops to venture up the forbidding, thickly covered slopes, so protective of the hunted, so hostile to the hunter. He may, however, set up a few small outposts at the foot of the Gophna hills in the hope that if he cannot venture up, he may perhaps dissuade the rebels from venturing down.

Judah and his men stay put during the day. At night they easily elude (or demolish) the enemy outposts, and, knowing every inch of the area, they reconnoitre the new Seleucid encampment. This is an easier target than a morning ambush, and the prize is greater. During the next few nights Judah assembles a strong force at Gophna and relays to it the dispositions for attack which he has worked out. On the night fixed for the operation, the men move down the hillside, light-footed and without a sound, and make their stealthy way towards the enemy base. They surround it, taking up positions a short distance from its perimeter, and wait. At a nudge from their section officers, teams of two creep forward and silently throttle the sentries. The rebels then rush the encampment from all sides. They lose some men. The enemy loses more. Survivors escape in the darkness and make their way back to Jerusalem. The base is set on fire, after weapons and equipment are collected to augment the Maccabee arsenal.

Whether or not it was precisely such operations which marked the opening of the Maccabee's new military phase, they are in keeping with what we know from the records of the Seleucid occupation pattern and of Judah's later tactics. Yet if our description of these actions is speculative, there is nothing speculative about the fact that action was taken and it had far-reaching results. The ancient texts show that Judah carried out wide-ranging attacks which soon made it impossible for the imperial mercenaries to move freely in rural Judea. The countryside was under the effective control of the Maccabees. Seleucid rule in Judea was confined to Jerusalem alone. Officials and troops were virtually bottled up inside the city walls. The Jerusalem garrison was cut off.

In this parlous predicament, the Jerusalem commander could no longer hide his failure, humiliating because his adversary was not a regular army force but a poorly armed bunch of rebels. He was compelled to send a report of his plight to General Apollonius, head-

quartered in Samaria, the governor and commander of Seleucid forces in the region. Even the report could not be sent by direct route through the mountains due north of Jerusalem. The messengers had to descend westwards to the plains, then north along the coastal highway past Jaffa and cut in eastwards near today's Netania to reach Samaria. The report was accompanied by an assessment of the military situation – including the acknowledgement that the populace of Judea had revolted and an intelligence estimate that the main rebel concentration was believed to be Gophna – and a call for reinforcements.

Apollonius decided that more than reinforcements were needed. His subordinates in Judea were clearly nincompoops. They had gone soft with occupation living. How could men who had once known battle fail to subdue a gang of civilian bandits? He would show them

Remains of a hellenistic tower in Samaria, the starting point of Apollonius' march to fight Judah

what it was to be a Seleucid soldier. He would crush the rebellion himself.

Judah and his Maccabees were about to face their most critical test since Modi'in.

The quickest route from Samaria to Jerusalem is the one that runs due south. Modern scholars agree that this is almost certainly the route which Apollonius took, though the fact is not recorded in the ancient documents. (The First Book of Maccabees 3:10,11 simply says that 'Apollonius now mustered the heathen, with a large contingent from Samaria, to fight against Israel', and that when Judah 'heard of it, he marched out to meet him'. It then reports the outcome. Nor is the route mentioned by Josephus or other ancient historians. But from certain clues contained in documented details of later developments, it is possible, by inference, to deduce the movements of Apollonius and Judah.)

The direct Samaria–Jerusalem route has several straight stretches where the gradient is gentle; but parts of it wind through the hills in steep ascent. It passes close to Gophna. One cannot know, therefore, whether it was Apollonius' intention to march directly on Gophna, crush the rebels and then proceed to Jerusalem, or to go straight to Jerusalem, demonstrate to the occupied population the power of Seleucid authority, stiffen the morale of his garrison in the Acra Fortress and organize from there the pacification of Judea.

The core of the Seleucid mercenary army was the phalanx, a powerful tactical formation consisting of heavy infantry drawn up in close order which advanced upon the enemy in line of battle and in a tight mass, the troops in each rank shoulder to shoulder and almost on the heels of the men in front. The Seleucids followed (with certain variations) the military pattern of their hero, Alexander the Great, who had developed the Macedonian phalanx from the earlier Greek model. The basic unit in Alexander's phalanx was a 256-man body known as the *syntagma*, comprising sixteen ranks with sixteen men in each rank. They were armed with a spear (sarissa) said to be 21 feet long. When moving into action, the first five ranks held their spears horizontally and the remaining eleven vertically until ready to engage, and they would then press towards the enemy with inexorable tread.

On open, level ground they could change pattern into a V-formation or wheel to the left or right. They were protected on the flanks by cavalry armed with swords and lances. Lightly armed slingers and archers often went ahead of them for preliminary skirmishing, and these would retire to the rear, joining the auxiliary

Enamel plaque of Judah the Maccabee as conceived by a 16th-century French artist

units, when heavy battle was about to be joined. Then the phalanx would thunder forth, crushing all before it when the enemy was weak and meeting a foe of comparable strength in a mighty head-on clash. Four *syntagmae* formed a *chiliarchia*, just over one thousand men, and the smallest sized phalanx used in a battle of moderate dimensions would probably consist of two *chiliarchiae*. They would form up in battle array only when approaching the battleground or when they entered hostile territory and expected to be attacked. On the march, they would move in columns, and the number of files would vary. Columns of four were usual.

The phalanx possessed the great advantage of might – so long as it kept its tight formation. For this it required flat, open country. In hilly or rocky terrain it was unwieldy. Its rigid pattern was jolted. The mailed fist became a flabby open hand. What was a solid block of offensive power disintegrated, and its components, the individual soldiers, found themselves engaged in hand-to-hand combat where the long spear proved an encumbrance.

We cannot know for certain what was the size of the force used by Apollonius in his march on Judea; but it is estimated that of the units under his general command, he selected two *chiliarchiae*. To get these two thousand men on the move would have taken a few days – a regular army follows fixed procedures – with staff officers working out the operational plan and the order and route of march, organizing supplies and ensuring that each unit was up to establishment and each mercenary equipped according to regulations. Those few days between Apollonius' decision and its implementation would have been sufficient for Judah to have acquired enough intelligence on the size, route and possibly the purpose of the enemy expedition to enable him to devise his course of counter-action.

The plan which Judah conceived was the product of tactical reasoning which probably followed these lines: the Seleucid force that was about to move into Judea was larger and more formidable than any he had encountered so far. Whether it was coming to attack him in Gophna – and it was large enough to comb the area systematically – or whether it was making directly for Jerusalem, he had the alternative of giving immediate battle or of 'vanishing' – melting into the countryside by dispersing his men among the villages. If he took the second course, he could emerge later to harry the enemy, for in order to crush the scattered rebels the Seleucid troops would perforce need to operate not as a single formation but in small vulnerable units. Six months earlier, this is precisely the action Judah would have taken. Not now. As he studied the intelligence reports, reviewed in his mind the country through

Detail of a Greek vase painting (*ca.* 640 BC) depicting hoplites, heavily armed foot-soldiers who formed the phalanx and fought in close formation

which the enemy would be passing and tried to anticipate Apollonius' thinking, he saw in an immediate engagement enormous opportunity.

If the enemy were taking the direct north–south route through the hills, it showed Judah that they were ignorant of the military situation in Judea or that they were over-confident. Either way, it meant that they foresaw no danger, and unwary troops are easily surprised.

Their self-assurance would have been understandable. They would know that the Jewish rebels could never match their own strength in numbers and weaponry. They would thus assume as a matter of course that the initiative would always be theirs – theirs to decide where and how they would engage the miscreants who had dared defy the authority of Antiochus. Here was Judah's first opportunity to spring a surprise: he would be the one to decide where the forces met – and how.

Judah would select ground which would neutralize the enemy's advantage of numbers and deny them the chance of exploiting the tactical power of the phalanx. They needed flat, open terrain; he would attack them in a defile. They would expect a set battle; he would assault them on the march. They would anticipate little opposition while proceeding through Samaria and their level of vigilance would be low. He would surprise them before they reached the Judean border. They would then be far from their base – and from their reinforcements; he would be close to his, close enough to make his dispositions in a few hours. It would be a daylight action; but he would prepare his emplacements under cover of night. This time, it would be no pin-pricking, harassing engagement on the run. This time it would be a serious battle, with the object of stopping the enemy in his tracks, destroying his force and collecting a maximum of his heavy weapons.

Where was such an ideal site to be found? A survey of the terrain shows that the area satisfying almost all the conditions suited to Judah's tactical requirements is a defile some 4 miles north-east of the centre of the Gophna hills. This is now generally held to have been the battleground chosen by Judah to meet Apollonius. It lay along Apollonius' line of march, roughly midway between the city of Samaria and Jerusalem.

The route south from Samaria broadens into a comparatively wide valley some 7 miles north-east of Gophna. It continues for about 2 miles along fairly level ground and then enters a narrow defile which winds uphill for more than a mile. It must clearly have been Judah's idea to set up ambush positions at key points covering this defile, allow the enemy troops to enter, wait until they were all in and then launch simultaneous attacks on all sectors.

The Seleucid troops would usually march only by day and halt for the night. Proceeding from their Samarian base, they would have to make one night-stop before reaching the Gophna area. Judah would know when they started, and during the night hours when they were bivouacking he could move his men to their ambush stations.

Night reconnaissance would have confirmed what Judah had no doubt recalled from his general familiarity with the terrain – that the ground near the projected battle site gave cover to only a limited number of attackers. It is estimated that Judah therefore used in this engagement a force of no more than seven or eight hundred. They would have been picked fighters, no doubt veterans who had been with him from the beginning, supported by a few militiamen. Leaving a reserve at Gophna, he would probably have sent the rest back to their villages to remain on emergency alert – and to continue the Maccabee struggle if anything went wrong and he and his men suffered defeat.

The day of battle approached. Word came through to Judah that the Seleucid force had left their Samarian base and were on the march. At dusk that evening, Judah led his men from Gophna to take up their attack positions. While they waited through the hours of darkness, a few scouts would have been sent further northwards into the hills to observe the enemy at their night halt and the resumption of their march next morning. They would have reported to Judah that Apollonius was indeed continuing along the anticipated route and that his mercenaries were proceeding in their conventional formation. Judah would have been able to estimate the time of their arrival and alert his units.

He had split his force into four, according to Eitan Avissar (former major-general in the Israel Defence Forces) in his excellent

reconstruction of this engagement given in his Hebrew book *Milhamot Yehuda Hamaccabi* ('The Wars of Judah the Maccabee'). (Avissar, incidentally, sets this action in Nahal el-Haramiah, some 3 to 4 miles north-east of Gophna, while historian and archaeologist Michael Avi-Yonah says [in *A History of the Holy Land*] that it probably took place at 'the ascent of Lebonah', about $2\frac{1}{2}$ miles further north.) Judah posted one unit in concealed positions along the eastern side of the defile, one along its western side, and one at its southern exit. The fourth unit was held a short distance north of the first, also on the eastern side, ready to be rushed to the northern entrance of the defile as soon as the entire enemy force were within, and thus complete the trap.

The spearhead of the first Seleucid *chiliarchia* came marching into the defile in columns of four. Between this thousand-man body and the second *chiliarchia* of mercenaries rode the commander, Apollonius. The formation, as usual, was compact, each man almost bumping into the man in front. The only gap was that between the two *chiliarchiae*. The men in ambush waited silently. They allowed the enemy to proceed through the defile until the leading troops had almost reached the southern exit. Then came the signal to attack.

Judah's sealing unit at the southern end sprang forth from their ambush positions and rushed through the narrow exit to fall upon the surprised enemy vanguard with slings, daggers, farm-sickles and a few swords captured in earlier skirmishes. The leading troops fell before they had the chance to use their spears, and those immediately behind them were driven back. But the main body further in the rear, ignorant as yet of what was happening, kept pressing forward, squeezing their already crowded comrades into an almost immoveable mass. And still they came, each file bumping into the

The level part of the north–south route from Samaria (to the right) towards Judea (to the left) taken by Apollonius in the first major battle with the Maccabees. The route begins to wind uphill (at the left) and reaches the positions where the Seleucids were ambushed by Judah's forces (shown on page 108)

The defile (left centre) a few miles north-east of Gophna where the regular military formations of Apollonius were routed by the Maccabees

halted file in front. Soon, almost the entire first *chiliarchia* was brought to a standstill, pressed in front by Judah's sealing unit, in the back by their rear files and on either side by the banks of the gully.

This was the moment for the ambushers on the east bank to let fly with their slings, sowing confusion and chaos among the astonished, wedged-in troops. While some may well have succeeded in turning laboriously to meet this fresh threat, they were subjected to a surprise assault in their rear from the ambushers above them on the west bank. The ambush units now followed up their sling attack by falling upon the enemy with their short, light but lethal weapons. The mercenaries were helpless, weighed down with their heavy arms and equipment, with no room to manoeuvre into the phalanx formation and little enough room for the individual soldier to wield his spear. They were like a powerful jungle beast suddenly attacked on all sides by a swarm of death-dealing insects.

Apollonius, hearing the cries of battle and concerned at the halting of his first *chiliarchia*, tried to press forward to learn the

The Seleucid commander led his men on horseback. This 4th-century BC tomb-painting is from Alexandria

reason. A few moments later he was dead, killed by one of Judah's men. While the news was being rapidly whispered through the Seleucid ranks, adding to their disarray, Judah's fourth unit was racing round to the northern end of the defile to deal havoc to the rear of the second *chiliarchia*.

The troops of Apollonius were routed. Not all were killed or wounded. A number managed to evade the small attacking force and straggle back, northwards, to their Samarian base. Not all of Judah's men survived. They had suffered severe casualties in the fierce hand-to-hand fighting. But they had come through a crucial military test with victory on the battlefield.

The First Book of Maccabees, which starts its report of this engagement with Judah's marching out to meet Apollonius, ends by recording that Judah 'defeated and killed him. Many of the Gentiles fell, and the rest took flight. From the arms they captured, Judah took the sword of Apollonius, and used it in his campaigns for the rest of his life' (3 : 11,12).

# 8 The Battles

The Jews of Judea were understandably heartened by Judah's victory, and there was rejoicing in all the villages. For the first time since Antiochus had launched his campaign to uproot the Jewish religion, they could glimpse the hopeful prospect of survival as Jews. They had willingly supported the resistance movement as the only alternative to surrender, but most of them had inwardly doubted its chances against so powerful an empire. They expected to go down fighting, upholding their faith but losing their lives. Now, after what they considered a stunning feat of arms by the Maccabees, there was hope that they might preserve their lives too. Even those who had been hesitant, unable to share Judah's confidence, came to believe that the weak and the helpless, given the will and the faith, could indeed prevail over the strong and the mighty. The defeat of Apollonius was a proof – and a sign.

Judah and his combat commanders were more restrained in their rejoicing. They were of course gratified with the outcome of their most serious battle to date. They could take satisfaction in having outwitted a redoubtable, battle-hardened, Seleucid general; in having beaten a much larger force of well-trained, combat-experienced imperial troops; in having proved their own skills as tacticians and fighters. They could be pleased that, apart from Jerusalem, they now controlled Judea more firmly than before. And as for Jerusalem, the Seleucid garrison was bottled up, cut off, helpless, unable to venture beyond the city walls, and Menelaus and his hellenistic Jewish group of collaborators must be in despair. Judah and his colleagues could find comfort in the solid support they now enjoyed from their people, in the wave of volunteering which had swelled after their latest victory and in a better stocked arsenal of heavier and more sophisticated weapons and equipment which they had captured on the battlefield.

Detail of a battle scene from a 1581 wood-cut illustration in a German edition of Josephus' works

III

They knew, however, that their victory, however formidable to them, was by no means decisive. It was but the end of one phase in the resistance struggle and the beginning of a new, the start of a tough military campaign which would be fought at an escalated level of battle; for Judah was certain that Antiochus would not reconcile himself to his latest setback. He would send in another force, and, if that failed, yet another, until he, or whoever succeeded him, decided that it was more expedient to come to terms with the Jews than to go on fighting them. Until such decision, if it should ever be taken, the Jews, to survive, had to win every battle, and Judah had thus to school and condition his Maccabee fighters to meet the new dimension of challenge.

Members of the Jewish
underground in the pre-
Independence days of
modern Israel were also
poorly armed, and the ac-
quisition of a light-machine-
gun was as important to
them as was the capture
of a bow to the ancient
Maccabees

The next invasion force would assuredly be larger and more determined than that commanded by Apollonius. Judah would need to introduce new training methods to match the new combat conditions. He would need to keep his military mind supple to conceive new ingenuities, for he would always be outnumbered and out-armed. He would need to train his men in the new weapons which had come into their possession, the swords, the more sophisticated slings, the javelins, the spears, the bows; and he thought these would best be employed not in the conventional manner followed by the enemy but in accordance with the tactical demands of the guerilla patterns he had fashioned.

He could not know where military developments would take him a few years hence, if he lived that long; but for the immediate future he assumed that the battlegrounds would be confined to Judea; and the hill-country of Judea was his country. None knew better than he how to exploit it to military advantage. The attacking troops from Antioch would have to come up from the lowlands and negotiate one or other of the passes to reach the Judean heights. If they came in overwhelming numbers – if, that is, the emperor were prepared to put forth his full power – they could, of course, crush the Maccabees. But Judah by now had familiarized himself sufficiently with affairs in the empire to know that Antiochus had other imperial commitments which, at this stage, he would consider of more immediate urgency than bringing Judea to heel. Judah felt confident that he could deny entry to the kind of formation the emperor would permit himself to detach for action in Judea. Sound intelligence would inform him of its size, nature and route, which would enable him to devise his stratagem. Interior lines of communication would afford him swift movement to cover any pass selected by the enemy and to rush to the focus of danger.

In Antioch, the news of Apollonius' defeat was disconcerting, but no one would have deemed the event disastrous. None would have considered – as did the people of Judea, and as subsequent developments showed – that it could have a significant impact on the fortunes of the Jews and of the Seleucid empire, and indeed on the history of the region. At Seleucid army headquarters it would have been regarded as a minor, though irksome, local mishap whose effects would soon be remedied. At the imperial court, however, Antiochus would have been piqued by the rout of one of his units. He was contemplating a major campaign in his eastern provinces to strengthen, and in some areas to restore, his authority there, and he could leave in better heart if his southern provinces were trouble-free. Even a slight defeat was politically burdensome, a blow to his military prestige and bad for the morale of his troops.

His advisers would have sought to mollify him by dismissing the engagement as of small importance. The less generous among them would have attributed the setback to the ineptitude, carelessness and inadequacy of the commander, being as scathing about Apollonius as Apollonius had been about the commander of his Jerusalem garrison and assuring the emperor that they would pick a better general next time. The more charitable would have judged that it was Apollonius' unfortunate death in battle which had led to the collapse of his units, and he had no doubt been the victim of a chance shot by the rebels, which could happen to any soldier. None would have ascribed his defeat to the skill of the Jewish resistance fighters. No one in Antioch as yet considered them to be of any military consequence. True, they had just been successful; but any bunch of bandits could have a run of success for a time, until the authorities got tough – and they would get tough now.

Thus, neither Antiochus nor his counsellors accounted the event serious enough to warrant a fresh evaluation of the military and political situation in Judea. What was required was not a change but a reaffirmation of policy, not a questioning of the wisdom of the anti-Jewish hellenistic decrees but firm and speedy action against those who rejected them.

The man entrusted with the task of restoring law and order in Judea was General Seron, commander of the Seleucid forces in Coele-Syria, the western and southern portions of the empire. (Coele-Syria was the official Seleucid name for those parts of Palestine and southern Syria which Antiochus III had captured from the Ptolemies of Egypt in 200 BC.) Seron set forth without delay from his northern headquarters probably at the end of 166 BC or early in the year 165.

Again, the ancient records give no details of the size of his force; but they cite the figure of his casualties. This clue, plus the fact of his superior rank and the known magnitude of the units under his territorial command, have led to the scholarly estimate that his expeditionary force was double that of Apollonius, numbering some four thousand men mustered in four *chiliarchiae*, a formation known as a grand phalanx.

He had evidently given much thought to the selection of his route south from his base to Judea. He could save time by taking the direct road to Jerusalem, but this would have brought him, from Samaria onwards, along the very track where Apollonius had been ambushed. He accordingly decided on the alternative route, longer but easier and safer, which ran through the Mediterranean coastal

The track to 'the pass of Beth Horon', site of Judah's victory over General Seron in the second major Maccabee battle

plain. In this way, he could bypass a considerable stretch of the insecure and rough-going mountain country and turn up into the hills only when he was close to his target. We learn from the First Book of Maccabees 3:16 that he made for 'the pass of Beth Horon'. This had long been one of the main passes through which one climbed to the Judean capital from the coastal plain. It lies only 10 miles north-west of Jerusalem. Seron must therefore have marched southwards almost as far as Jaffa, then wheeled south-east, passed through Lod (site of today's international airport), proceeded along a slow gradient to the foot of the hills and then begun the steep ascent to the pass of Beth Horon.

[In the evening of 5 June 1967, six hours after Jordan's Arab Legion launched their surprise attack on the Jewish quarters of Jerusalem, an Israeli army reserve force of mechanized infantry, in a topographic switch of history, took the very route which General Seron had taken twenty-one centuries earlier in his drive against their forebears, the Maccabees. Dashing up the ascent to Beth Horon, the Israeli unit overwhelmed the enemy forces trying to hold the pass, while a reserve armoured brigade made the main breakthrough further to the south-east in a series of tough, uphill, night battles, pressing eastwards to capture the main north-south road from Samaria to Jerusalem – the very route Apollonius had intended to take. The armour then turned south and reached Mount Scopus, overlooking the Old City of Jerusalem, early next morning. This, coupled with the paratroop successes in the bloody night fighting on the mounds and in the suburbs just beyond the north city wall, and with the actions of the Jerusalem Brigade in the south, effected the encirclement of Jerusalem and set the dramatic stage for the storming of the Old City by the paratroopers on the morning of 7 June.]

It was Seron's intention to reach Jerusalem, free his garrison and, with the city as his base, move out into the countryside, crush the rebels and re-establish Seleucid authority in the villages. It was Judah's aim to prevent him from getting even within sight of Jerusalem.

While Seron was marching down the coast, enough intelligence on the size, purpose and broad directional aim of his force would have reached Judah to enable him to prepare a rough plan of action. Seron at some point would need to leave the plain and enter Judea through one of the passes broad enough to take his large formation. It was Judah's resolve to attack him while he was negotiating the pass. But which one would Seron select? It is possible that Judah's intelligence service would have provided this information early on. But if not, he would have known it was Beth Horon as soon as the

The Jerusalem scene during the Six Day War – taken from Mount Scopus – as viewed by the Israeli unit which reached it after moving up the ascent to Beth Horon and fighting its way through the Judean hills

The strategic pass of Beth Horon (right to Latrun and Tel Aviv, left to Jerusalem), one of the main approach routes to Jerusalem from the coastal plain

Seleucid troops had moved through Lod, no doubt setting up camp for their final night halt shortly thereafter. With his small compact force, Judah could have rushed from his Judean base to cover any pass within a few hours. In the event, he had ample time to make his dispositions behind the protective boulders and scrub near the top of the Beth Horon pass and along the sides of the defile leading up to it.

Seron's force struck camp early in the morning and began the last stage of their march. If all went well, they should be in Jerusalem by evening. Now that they were about to enter the hills, they were put on alert, with scouts sent ahead and protective units posted on the flanks of the main body. An hour or so later, the point *syntagma* of the lead *chiliarchia* was beginning its climb up the long, winding, uneven ascent to the pass. It was hard going, uncommonly laboured

for troops, weighted down with heavy weapons and equipment, who had grown accustomed in the preceding weeks to the easy swinging, regular pace of the daily march along the flat plain. There was also less freedom from anxiety, for they now found that, apart from their imminent confrontation with the enemy, the security precaution of flank protection was rendered unworkable by the narrowness of the ascent.

'When he [Seron] reached the pass of Beth Horon, Judah advanced to meet him with a handful of men' (1 Macc. 3 : 16). Judah had split his estimated force of about a thousand into three units. One had been posted during the night near the head of the pass and the other two in concealed positions along each side of the ascent. Now they waited silently, watching the long column of troops trudging uphill over the broken ground. When the leading enemy files had

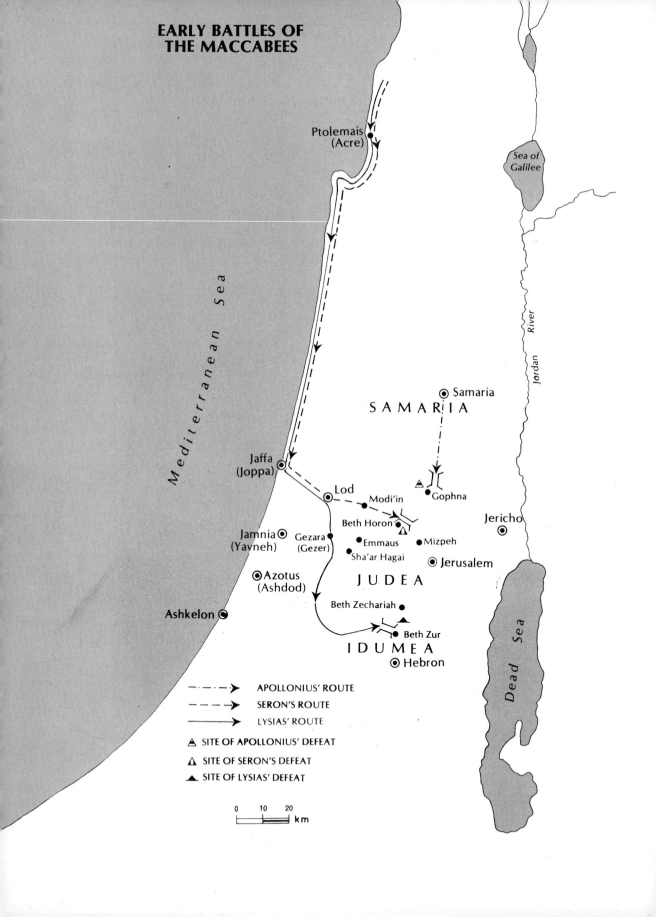

# EARLY BATTLES OF
# THE MACCABEES

Ptolemais
(Acre)

*Mediterranean Sea*

*Sea of Galilee*

*Jordan River*

⊙ Samaria

S A M A R I A

Jaffa
(Joppa) ⊚

⊙ Lod

Modi'in ●

● Gophna

Jericho
⊙

Jamnia ⊙
(Yavneh)

Gezara ●
(Gezer)

Beth Horon ●

● Emmaus
● Mizpeh

Sha'ar Hagai ●

⊙ Jerusalem

⊙ Azotus
(Ashdod)

J U D E A

Ashkelon ⊙

Beth Zechariah ●

● Beth Zur

I D U M E A

⊙ Hebron

*Dead Sea*

--·-→ APOLLONIUS' ROUTE

-- -→ SERON'S ROUTE

——→ LYSIAS' ROUTE

△ SITE OF APOLLONIUS' DEFEAT

◭ SITE OF SERON'S DEFEAT

▲ SITE OF LYSIAS' DEFEAT

0    10    20

⊢—⊢—⊣—⊣ km

almost reached the top, Judah gave the signal, and his sealing unit, at the head of the pass, went into action. Archers and slingmen, using weapons captured from Apollonius, killed or wounded the enemy point-men and sent the oncoming files staggering back on their comrades. The rest of the sealing unit, wielding handy swords, then rushed upon the teetering foe, claiming further casualties and thrusting those behind back down the slopes. With the lead column off balance, each soldier seeking desperately to retain his footing before he could even consider using his weapon, Judah signalled his units posted along the flanks. They, too, opened their assault with arrows and slings and followed it up with a simultaneous close-quarters attack from both sides. The main body of the leading *chiliarchia* were utterly at their mercy, and as they fell, their comrades in the rear turned and fled down the hill, encountering the other Seleucid units who promptly did the same.

Judah, seeing the break-up of the enemy formation and the troops running helter-skelter down the hill, gave the order for pursuit. And 'they pursued them down the pass of Beth Horon as far as the plain; some eight hundred of the enemy fell, and the rest fled to Philistia'. Josephus, recording that 'the Assyrian army was totally routed', adds that 'Seron, the general', was among those 'slain in the field of battle' and 'the survivors were pursued towards the sea' (*Antiquities*, XII.10). Seron was probably with his lead units and his death within the first few minutes would have contributed greatly to the demoralization and collapse of his army and would explain why the surviving forces failed to rally and stage a counter-attack.

At the Seleucid court in Antioch, the report of Seron's defeat was received with the utmost gravity, for it brought the authorities to the sudden apprehension that they had been wrong in their assessment of the troubles in Judea. They realized now that what they were faced with in that province was a major rebellion. The failure of a distinguished general, the rout of a powerful formation and the heavy losses in men and equipment could not be dismissed as a minor mishap or the chance triumph of a gang of hoodlums. This was clearly the work of a skilled and well-organized force which could operate only with mass local support. Indeed, if army headquarters in Antioch had underrated the significance of previous engagements, they may well have exaggerated the scale of this one, for the straggling survivors, in their debriefing reports, would have multiplied the strength of the Maccabee units to rationalize their own discomfiture. This did not mean that anyone at the imperial court considered, or dared to suggest, a re-examination of the policy which had provoked the rebellion. It was generally agreed that if the writ of the emperor were to run in Judea, the province had to be treated as a hostile state and an appropriate expedition mounted to subdue it.

This latest misfortune could not have come at a worse moment for Antiochus, wholly preoccupied as he was with his imminent eastern campaign. As we have seen, he had been contemplating such a campaign for some time in order to re-establish Seleucid control in his eastern territories. By now he had assembled a huge force and was about to set forth on the long march to do battle beyond the Tigris and Euphrates. The principal danger came from Parthia, a considerable kingdom stretching from the Caspian in the north to the centre of Iran in the south. It had been neutralized by Antiochus III some forty years earlier, when he had also recovered the eastern provinces of the Seleucid empire. But Parthia had later regained its strength, and the local Seleucid satraps in the adjacent territories, notably Persia and Media, were now showing signs of separatism. They had withheld their tribute to Antioch, and their next step could be secession. Antiochus felt this to be the gravest threat to his empire, for the eastern provinces were its backbone, and if he lost those he would be losing more than the considerable revenues they provided and more than prestige. He would risk losing even the dwindled imperial territory left to him, and with it his throne; for each loss, which weakened him, strengthened his enemies. His contracted empire could well fall prey to expansionist Parthian designs in the east, while Rome, watching hopefully, might welcome the opportunity of striking him in the west.

It was a grim prospect for a king who had started his reign with the ambition to emulate the success of Alexander the Great. At the very least he had expected to match the gains of his own father. Now, he seemed hard put even to maintain the status quo. To stop the fragmentation of his empire, Antiochus deemed it essential to reassert his authority in the east, ensure the flow of revenues from his tributaries and blunt the Parthian menace. He resolved to take personal command of so crucial a military mission.

He appointed a certain Lysias, 'a distinguished member of the royal family', to serve during his absence as viceroy of the western and southern portions of his realm, the territories between the Euphrates and the Egyptian frontier. Lysias was also to act as 'guardian of his son Antiochus [the future Antiochus V Eupator] until his return' (1 Macc. 3:33).

His preparations completed, Antiochus IV was ready to leave when the news arrived of General Seron's defeat. It was a hard blow, but not reason enough to delay his departure. Judea was important,

A 2nd-century BC bronze figure of a Parthian prince found at Shami, Persia, where Antiochus was campaigning while his forces in Judea were being repulsed by the Maccabees

An early Greek statuette of a mounted warrior. The Maccabees faced the well-equipped mercenaries of the powerful Seleucid army

but far less so, in his mind, than his eastern provinces. Nevertheless, he had to be certain, while campaigning in the east, that his rear was secure. He was always conscious of an opportunistic Rome, which had stymied his hopes to annex Egypt and might now take advantage of his absence – and of a rebellious Judea – to land in Palestine. He accordingly ordered an all-out effort to make Judea trouble-free.

He placed a large body of men at the disposal of Lysias so that Judea could be crushed quickly. (The First Book of Maccabees 3:34 says that 'he transferred to Lysias half the armed forces' for the Judean action. Though 'half' is thought to be an exaggeration, it is generally agreed that a considerable force was assigned to this task. Antiochus was therefore able to take with him fewer troops than he had planned, and the Judean fighting may thus be seen to have had a direct impact on the fortunes of his eastern campaign.)

The emperor was so incensed with the rebellious Jews that he decided to exterminate the entire 'population of Judea and Jerusalem', and he left with Lysias precise instructions as to what was to be done with the province. Lysias was to 'uproot and destroy the strength of Israel and the remnant of Jerusalem, to blot out all memory of them from the place, to settle strangers in all their territory, and allot the land to the settlers' (I Macc. 3:35,36). Having issued this command to his viceroy Lysias, never doubting that it would be successfully executed, the emperor departed with his troops for the Euphrates.

Lysias chose three generals (according to the First Book of Maccabees 3:38) to lead the expedition against Judea. They were Ptolemy the son of Dorymenes (who is believed to have been at this time the governor of Coele-Syria), Nicanor and Gorgias. (Beyond registering his appointment, the account of the battle makes no further mention of Ptolemy, which suggests that he had overall responsibility but was not the field commander. This bears out the Second Book of Maccabees 8:9,10 that 'Ptolemy immediately selected Nicanor' to command the expedition, and sent with him 'Gorgias, a general of wide experience'.) The year was 165 BC.

There is a contradiction in the ancient records over the size of their force. The First Book of Maccabees 3:39 gives the figures as 'forty thousand infantry and seven thousand cavalry'; but the 'twenty thousand troops of all nationalities' noted in the Second Book of Maccabees 8:9 is held to be a truer record of the enemy's strength.

The commanders were determined not to repeat the mistakes of their predecessors, not to get trapped in the Judean mountains while on the march, not to make straight for Jerusalem. They would take their army down the coastal plain, set up their base near the foot of the hills, do their preliminary reconnoitring and then move up in battle array to engage the rebels. They would then proceed to Jerusalem, join up with their garrison and set about the task of systematic massacre and destruction in accordance with the orders of the emperor.

The place they selected for their base camp was Emmaus (today's Imwas, adjoining Latrun) in the lowlands, close to the Valley of

The wooded hillock (centre) is the site of ancient Emmaus, where the third battle of the Maccabees took place. The Valley of Aijalon, where the enemy fled, is in the foreground

Aijalon where Joshua bade the moon stand still. It lies 10 miles south-east of Lod and 15 miles north-west of Jerusalem. Here they were joined by troop reinforcements from Idumea (Edom, on the southern borders of Judea), Azotus (today's Ashdod) and Jamnia (today's Yavneh) in the coastal plain. They were also joined by another group – slave dealers who had been invited by General Nicanor to make their bids even before the start of the battle. Nicanor was so certain of a quick victory that he had planned to carry out only partially Antiochus' annihilation order. Instead of killing all the Jews of Judea, he would spare a number and raise a tidy sum by selling them as slaves. Accordingly, on reaching Emmaus, and while the camp was being prepared, 'he at once made an offer of Jewish slaves to the coastal towns, undertaking to deliver them at the price of ninety to the talent' (II Macc. 8:11). The response was enthusiastic. 'The merchants of the region, impressed by what they heard of the army, took a large quantity of silver and gold, with a supply of fetters, and came into the camp to buy the Israelites for slaves' (I Macc. 3:41).

From Emmaus, the commanders no doubt sent messengers at night to make contact with the garrison in Jerusalem and bring back chosen scouts, men familiar with Judea's hilly byways; for the records relate that in the subsequent engagement the Seleucid 'guides were men from the citadel' (I Macc. 4:2), the Acra Fortress in Jerusalem. It is probable that among them were also hellenistic Jews who had been pressed into service as intelligence agents for the Seleucid garrison. Their first task would have been to accompany small reconnaissance units on intelligence patrols, and a battle plan would have been devised on the basis of the information they gathered on terrain, routes, and above all on the whereabouts and movements of the Maccabees.

By that time, the Maccabees had been fashioned into a more formidable force and were well advanced in their counter-preparations. Their victory over Seron had given pride and relief to the villagers of Judea and there was hardly an able-bodied man not yet mustered who did not yearn to join the fighting rebels. Judah, with every reason to be exhilarated by the success, had nevertheless remained the sober realist, his mind more on future danger than on past victory. The enemy reaction to Seron's defeat was bound to be the despatch of another attacking force. Judah reasoned that it would be more powerful than anything he and his men had yet encountered, for the Seleucids would escalate the warfare at a geometric rate of progression. While his confidence was unimpaired, and while

Slave dealers joined the
camp of the confident
General Nicanor on the eve
of battle to bid for the
Maccabees upon their
expected defeat. A
hellenistic-period bronze
figurine of a bound slave

his own people now thought their warriors invincible, he was alive to their current limitations. He had triumphed so far with a small force, using guerilla tactics, battling on terrain which he had selected. Could he do the same against an army outnumbering his own not by three or four but twenty to one? If, as he suspected, Antioch might now launch a full-scale military operation to wipe him out, could they not surround him, overwhelm him, crush him by sheer weight of numbers? Guerilla devices would enable him to inflict heavy casualties on the enemy. But the object of the Maccabees was not simply to sell their lives dearly but to ensure the survival of their people. It was clear to Judah that he needed to enlarge his fighting force and put it through rigorous training in new forms of warfare. Fortunately, the surge of volunteering and the weapons captured in battle solved his manpower and armament problems. He was also aided by the high morale both of his men and of the civilian population.

In the same way as he had set about organizing a guerilla force at Gophna he now applied himself to the organization of an army. He raised the strength of his force, and appointed 'officers over thousands, hundreds, fifties and tens' (1 Macc. 3:55), comparable, though the counterpart units were of a different size, to the battalions, companies, platoons and sections in a modern brigade. In addition to basic guerilla instruction, the Maccabees now received special training in the deployment of larger formations and in the handling of heavier weapons.

Judah's assessment of probable imperial action was soon confirmed by his intelligence reports. Even if he lacked sources in the Seleucid capital, he would have known the size of the formation being sent against him as soon as it had begun the southward march from its base. He immediately assembled his men and, in accordance with biblical custom, 'he ordered back to their homes those who were building their houses or were newly wed or who were planting vineyards, or who were faint-hearted'. He then took a force of six thousand and established a hill-base at Mizpeh, 5 miles north-west of Jerusalem and midway between Jerusalem and the pass of Beth Horon. Here he waited until he knew what the enemy proposed to do. He was well placed to cover both Beth Horon, if they should choose that pass (which he thought unlikely in view of the Seron experience), and the route further south through Sha'ar Hagai (Gate to the Valley), which is the route of today's main highway from the coast to Jerusalem. From Mizpeh he sent out small patrols to watch for the enemy's approach, and so he learned at once that they had left Lod, avoided the road to Beth Horon, continued south to Gezer, turned east and encamped at Emmaus. When they remained there

and began busily preparing a fortified base, complete with breast-works and guarded by mounted troops, it was evident to Judah that they intended not to proceed directly to Jerusalem but to tackle him first. Only now could he start gathering the information he needed to devise a suitable attack plan. He split his force into four units of fifteen hundred each, put three of them under the command of his brothers Johanan, Simon and Jonathan and took personal command of the fourth.

Probing actions were undertaken by both armies, each trying to discover what it could of the other through reconnaissance missions by day and by night and through espionage agents. The Maccabees were better at this because of their loyal population and because of their familiarity with little-known approach tracks to Emmaus from Mizpeh. But the seasoned Seleucids, no longer taking their enemy lightly, also reconnoitred with care and skill and secured what they considered was enough intelligence on the Maccabee base to fashion *their* plan of attack. In the event, each side resolved to assault the other's camp.

The Seleucid command showed an ingenuity that had been absent in their earlier attacks. General Gorgias conceived the notion of taking a leaf out of the rebels' notebook and fighting them with their own tactics. He would take a large force through the hills under cover of darkness, creep up to Mizpeh, surround the Jewish

Sha'ar Hagai, 'Gate of the Valley', today's main approach to Jerusalem from the coast

camp and fall upon the Maccabees. Since it was widely known that the Seleucid army did not go in for night fighting, the Jews would be taken by surprise. Any who sought escape to the coastal plain would be caught by Nicanor's troops at Emmaus.

Judah, for his part, had prepared a similar plan for a surprise attack on the Emmaus camp, but his men had been better trained for this type of action, had a better knowledge of the terrain, could operàte more stealthily and had already carried out several night exercises, so that each knew exactly what he had to do. The only factor left undecided was when to launch the assault. Judah waited for the opportune moment.

It came one evening when he learned that Gorgias had set out from Emmaus with a force of five thousand infantry and one thousand picked cavalry and they were making their way through the hills to Mizpeh. Judah promptly seized upon one implication of this move: it meant a reduced enemy army, albeit still one of considerable size, at Emmaus. He assembled his units and they quietly left their base, making their way through untrodden wadis and across wild country until they reached a point just south of the Emmaus camp. Before leaving, Judah used a deception to prolong Gorgias' absence. He 'ordered', says Josephus, 'several fires to be made in his own camp', so that Gorgias would continue on his fruitless errand. It was still dark when Judah and his men arrived at the environs of Emmaus, and they were able to deploy without being observed or heard by the enemy. They were to attack at dawn.

Gorgias also reached Mizpeh in the early hours of the morning,

General Gorgias used 'picked cavalry' in a sortie against the Maccabees during the engagement at Emmaus. Greek cavalry on a stone frieze from the hellenistic period

delighted to see from their camp-fires that the Jews were not expecting him. Their surprise would be complete. He was in good spirit. The night manoeuvre over strange and rocky terrain, unusual for his men, had been successful. There had been no mishap *en route;* they had not lost their way through the winding tracks; they had come straight to their target; and they were ready to pounce. In a single action they would net the entire rebel force. They stole closer to the perimeter of the Jewish camp, but encountered no guards – which they put down to rebel negligence. Emboldened by this lack of elementary enemy precaution, they pressed silently forward. With weapons drawn for instant action they entered the camp – only to find it deserted.

Gorgias concluded that the rebels had somehow become apprised of his action and had fled in alarm. He immediately 'set out to search for them in the hills, thinking, "These Jews are running away from us"' (1 Macc. 4:5). He fanned out, sending patrols ahead, hoping to snare the escaping fugitives in their mountain hide-outs.

But at daybreak, the 'fugitives' were in the plain, listening to the exhortations of their commander prior to their attack. Judah was telling his men:

Do not be afraid of their great numbers or panic when they charge. Remember how our fathers were saved at the Red Sea, when Pharaoh and his army were pursuing them. Let us cry now to Heaven to favour our cause, to remember the covenant made with our fathers, and to crush this army before us today. Then all the heathen will know that there is One who saves and liberates Israel (1 Macc. 4:8–11).

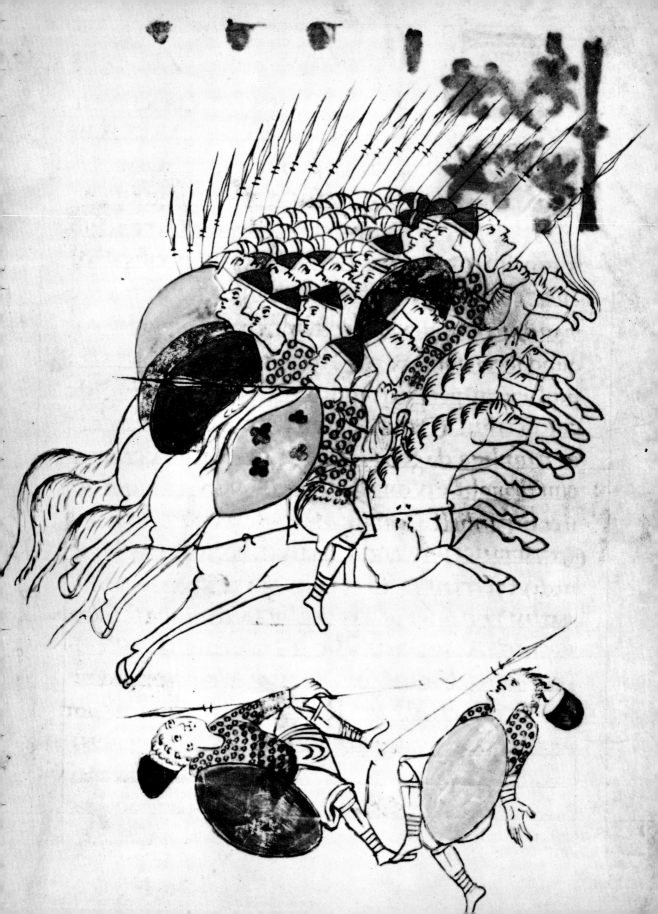

Judah then gave the signal, and the Maccabees rushed into action from their concealed positions, intending to strike the camp in simultaneous assaults from east and west. But when they emerged into the open, it was their turn to be surprised. Nicanor's forces were just coming out of their base and spotted the attackers. They were quickly ordered into the phalanx formation, ready for battle.

The details of what happened next are not given in the ancient records, the First Book of Maccabees 4:14 limiting itself to: 'The heathen broke, and fled to the plain. All the rearmost fell by the sword.' It is clear however that Judah had to make a lightning change of tactics. He would be fighting under conditions he had never met before, unaided by any of the elements which had so favoured his earlier guerilla actions. He had hoped to surprise an unwary, sleepy foe, helplessly confined within its encampment and unable to manoeuvre. Instead, he was confronting a superior force in full battle formation on level ground in open country, a pattern suited to the enemy's mode of warfare, but not to his. However, he had certain advantages. His units were lighter, more mobile and more flexible than the phalanx. It is probable, too, that the Seleucid cavalry had not yet had time to organize itself for protective duty on the flanks. It is likely, therefore, that Judah retained the direction of his attacking units, but instead of assaulting the camp, they were ordered first to tackle the disorganized flanking cavalry, and then strike at the phalanx from the sides and the rear, thus avoiding a frontal clash and forcing the compact enemy infantry to disintegrate into individual fighting units. In the hand-to-hand combat which followed, the Maccabees excelled. Nicanor's forces were routed, and they fled towards the coast. Those in the rear were cut down. 'The pursuit was pressed as far as Gazara [Gezer] and the lowlands of Idumea, Azotus and Jamnia; about three thousand of the enemy were killed.'

Judah now showed himself to be a superb commander in absolute control of his men. It was customary in those times when the battle had decisively turned for the victors to pursue the vanquished as long as possible and gather a maximum of loot and plunder. But Judah had not forgotten Gorgias. The sun was now high and Gorgias, after his fruitless night expedition in the hills, was no doubt on his way back to base. Judah accordingly ordered a halt to the pursuit, brought his men back to Emmaus, set fire to part of the enemy camp and deployed his units to meet the returning Gorgias.

It was then that 'an enemy patrol appeared, reconnoitring from the hills', one of the patrols Gorgias had sent ahead of his main force. They looked down on the plain and, as Josephus says,

An illustration of Seleucid cavalry, from the 10th-century illuminated manuscript of the Book of Maccabees in the Monastery of St Gallen, Switzerland

'perceived from an eminence the havoc made in the tents of their associates, the field covered with dead bodies, and a smoke issuing from the camp; and upon this discovery they dispersed' (*Antiquities* XII. 310, 311). The report in the First Book of Maccabees 4:21–2 adds that 'they were filled with panic as they took in the scene, and when they saw the army of Judah in the plain, ready for battle, they all fled to Philistia'.

The merchants who survived, if indeed there were any who could have kept up with troops in headlong flight, returned to their coastal cities without the 'supply of fetters' they had so confidently brought, possibly also without the 'large quantity of silver and gold' with which they had hoped to buy the Israelite slaves – and without the slaves. They may have been among 'those of the Gentiles who escaped with their lives', proceeded to Antioch with their dismal tale 'and reported to Lysias all that had happened' (1 Macc. 4:26). Lysias was 'overwhelmed with disappointment'. As viceroy, he felt answerable to the emperor for the ignominy, and he was determined personally to wipe it out. Another expedition was certainly called for, but he would entrust it to no other general. He would command it himself. Other preoccupations, however, kept him in Antioch, and not until the following year was he able to leave the capital. In 164 BC, at the head of a large force, he descended upon Judea.

They 'marched into Idumea, and encamped at Beth Zur, where Judah met them' (1 Macc. 4:29). This sentence alone contains the basic information on the route taken by Lysias as well as his tactical aim: for Beth Zur lies 17 miles *south-west* of Jerusalem. It is clear, therefore, that Lysias intended to bypass the rebels in the hills north of the capital, where they were strong, and approach Jerusalem from a direction where the rebels were weak, thus minimizing the risk of being assailed on the march. It is equally evident that he planned to reach Jerusalem and liberate his Acra garrison *before* tackling the Jewish resistance fighters. Hilly Jerusalem, strengthened by the Acra Fortress, was a far less vulnerable base of operations than the camp in open country which Nicanor had established near Emmaus. From Jerusalem, Lysias would use his large force to comb Judea systematically and quickly wipe out the rebels. This plan avoided the tactical errors of the previous Seleucid commanders. It had every chance of success.

It is reasonably certain that Lysias marched his army down the coastal plain and continued southwards in a long roundabout route beyond the Jerusalem latitude to the vicinity of Ashkelon, remaining

A painted 4th-century BC sarcophagus depicting a Greek soldier under attack

throughout in territory friendly to him and hostile to the Jews. He then turned south-east, either through Gath or Beth Govrin, towards Marisa (Mareshah) and on to Hebron, through country inhabited by pro-hellenist Idumeans. From Hebron he turned north towards Beth Zur, the Judean border fortress 4 miles away, and encamped just south of it. After the 400-mile march from Antioch, which had taken his men several weeks, he had only another 17 miles to go, through Beth Zur and Bethlehem, in order to reach Jerusalem.

The size of his army is given in the First Book of Maccabees 4:28 as 'sixty thousand picked infantry and five thousand cavalry'. Scholars consider this figure exaggerated, but they agree that it could not have been smaller than the force led by Nicanor and Gorgias, so that it may be assumed that he had under his command not less than twenty thousand men and three or four thousand horse.

Judah by then had raised his strength to ten thousand. He had had ample warning from his intelligence sources of the Lysias expedition, and simple observation by his scouts would have given him the size of the enemy formation and its route. When they had continued southwards without turning east into the hills either through Beth Horon or Sha'ar Hagai, it was apparent that they would swing round and come at Jerusalem from the south. This was unexpected. Judah's tentative plans to stop them were no longer of value. He would have to devise a new stratagem.

He had few options. He would not have sought a head-on confrontation with so large an army – Lysias was unlikely to divide his forces as Nicanor and Gorgias had divided theirs – and so he ruled out a direct attack on Lysias' camp during one of their halts. He would also have seen the grave danger of allowing the enemy force to reach Jerusalem and establish itself there. The only feasible action was to attack it *en route*, even though this meant operating in the hills south of Jerusalem, where Maccabean control was weaker than in the north and where a good part of the terrain, with gentler gradients, was less obstructive to the enemy. The questions that remained were where to strike and when.

He would easily have foreseen that the mercenaries would be aiming for the Hebron–Jerusalem road, and this would have been confirmed by his patrols as soon as Lysias turned inland from the coastal plain. Long before that, Judah would have started moving his men south, remaining within the Judean hills but keeping pace with the southward march of the enemy in the plain. As soon as they swung east, he could make his final plan. With his interior and shorter lines of communication, he would even have had time to take his officers on a reconnaissance of the battleground he had selected so that they could drill their men in the tactics he had pre-scribed. As to when the action was to be launched, Judah no doubt made his decision as soon as he heard – or saw – that Lysias had encamped between Hebron and Beth Zur.

The ancient records name the site of the battle and report its result, but they offer no further details. However, from our know-ledge both of Judah's earlier actions and of the terrain in the Beth Zur area, it seems likely that Judah posted his men at night in concealed positions on either side of the mouth of a gully on the Hebron–Jerusalem road at a point about a mile north of Beth Zur where there was good and plentiful cover for his large force. The road was too narrow for Lysias to move his army in battle array. He had to move them in column, unit by unit, and this gave Judah the opportunity, by wise choice of ground, skilful deployment and accurate timing, to tackle the enemy piecemeal, thus achieving local numerical superiority in each individual engagement.

Lysias' mercenaries had been marching for weeks without thought of danger. As they set out for Jerusalem on that last fateful morning, warned no doubt to be on the alert from now on, they marched warily towards Beth Zur. They reached it without incident and continued northwards, their confidence increasing and their vigilance relaxing with each step. As the lead unit emerged from the defile, it came under surprise attack from Judah's men. The assault was sharp and heavy and most of the unit was wiped out. Judah now had enough men to tackle several of the forward units simultaneously by enveloping them from both sides of the gully, and in a short while the lead mercenary contingents were out of action, their casualties strewn on the track. The survivors fled back in confusion, having to run the gauntlet of Maccabee ambushes, abandoning their heavy weapons to ease their flight, crashing into advancing units further back and even reaching their encampment before the rear contingents had left. 'Lysias lost about five thousand men in the close fighting' (I Macc. 4:34).

Lysias appears not to have staged a counter-attack, though he had enough men left to do so. 'When he saw his own army routed and Judah's men full of daring, ready to live or die nobly, he departed for Antioch.' This suggests both hopelessness over the poor fighting spirit of his mercenaries when faced with an unconventional army and his sudden realization that he had underrated the skill, strength and determination of the Maccabees. For the present, there was little he could do, and he accordingly retired. But he fully intended to assemble and give special training to a strong 'force of mercenaries' and 'to return to Judea with a much larger army than before' (I Macc. 4:35). The huge stocks of enemy weapons and equipment

An 18th-century drawing of antiquities (arranged as a supply train) to illustrate the military equipment in the service of ancient armed forces. Some of the weapons are similar to those captured from the Seleucid army by the Maccabees

abandoned *en route* and in the encampment were added to the growing arsenal of the Maccabees.

For the first time since they had left Modi'in for the guerilla life in the Gophna hills, Judah and his brothers could sit back for a moment and relax, giving themselves up to the relief and joy which his fighters and the civilian population had felt after each preceding success. Not that Judah thought that the latest action was his last. But it had assuredly been his most significant military encounter. It showed that his guerilla force had come of age, had adapted itself to the means and pattern of larger scale warfare and was now a fighting army, able to meet if not the full power of the Seleucid empire at least the substantial formations which would undoubtedly be despatched once again to Judea. The latest victory was also a vindication of his faith in Jewish resistance, and it reinforced his conviction that religious freedom would be restored before long to all his people throughout Judea.

The defeat of Lysias was the most shattering humiliation the Seleucids had suffered at the hands of the rebels since Antiochus had embarked on his religious persecution of the Jews, for the army had been led by the viceroy himself, and it had enjoyed weighty superiority in men and weapons. Judah recognized that there would be a repeat performance, but he calculated that it would take several months to prepare – unless Antiochus registered some startling success in his eastern campaign, and this, from Judah's political intelligence reports, seemed unlikely. (In the event, the next expedition was not sent against the Maccabees until two years later.) Judah knew what to do with this respite, now that his Maccabees were stronger than they had ever been and in full control of rural Judea. He would proceed with the aim he, his father and brothers had set themselves when they had sat in sackcloth and ashes three years earlier mourning 'the abomination', the profanation of Jewry's most sacred shrine. He would go up to Jerusalem and rededicate the Temple.

# 9  The Temple Regained

Jerusalem, its Temple desecrated, was 'the desolate city' for the Jewish faithful everywhere; but now, for other reasons, it was also a cheerless habitation for those who had wrought its ruin, the imperial garrison in the Acra Fortress and their wards, the hellenistic Jewish group led by the Seleucid appointed High Priest Menelaus. The Jewish hellenists now lived in uneasy proximity to uncouth mercenaries with whom they had nothing in common. They wielded no power and controlled no constituency, having been thwarted by the Maccabees in their promised delivery to the court at Antioch of a compliant, tribute-paying, hellenized Judea. They had little to do, and they appear even to have abandoned whatever worship they had practised in the Temple, for the Temple Mount was now a wasteland, forsaken, neglected. They were stunned by the startling turn in their fortunes, from imperial favourites to beleaguered defaulters, from potential princes of their people to loathed outcasts; and there must have been some who were anguished by the devastation they had brought to their city, to themselves and to their pious compatriots, with whom they had so sharply contended to such ill-purpose. Those with the courage to flee joined the army of Judah; the more timid felt trapped. The diehards, however, as happens when brother fights brother, developed a more pungent hatred of the Maccabees with every Seleucid defeat. Among these, according to the records, was Menelaus. He seems to have clung to his hellenistic notions and willingly collaborated with his guardians.

The troops may have suffered little more than the boredom of inactivity and irksome confinement; but the situation and mood of their officers were grievous. These warrior commanders bearing the trust of their emperor had failed in their military mission. Sent to crush Judea, they had been brought low by a rustic band

Scale-model reconstruction, by Professor Michael Avi-Yonah, of Jerusalem towards the end of the Second Temple period (located in the garden of the Holyland Hotel, Jerusalem). The white courtyard (middle right) is part of the Hasmonean palace, believed to have been built on the site of the Acra Fortress. The wall of the Temple compound was built by Herod more than a century and a half after the Maccabee revolt

of rebels, and now they could hardly venture beyond the broken walls of the city. The ramparts of the Acra Fortress alone gave them protection. They had been forced into the ignominy of calling for help, first to their commander in Samaria and then to Antioch. By so doing they had also led their superiors, the leaders of the relief expedition, into dishonour, for all had been routed. The latest had been the most disastrous, for it had been led by Lysias himself, and the rebels would now surely be tempted to march on Jerusalem. Well, the garrison commanders would preserve something of their reputation by showing Judah that Jerusalem was not Beth Horon, nor Emmaus, nor Beth Zur. The Acra Fortress had been well built; its walls were strong, and it had a well-stocked arsenal.

Judah was under no illusions about the strength of the Acra, and he was only too well aware that he lacked as yet the means to penetrate fortified ramparts. But his mind was on the Temple Mount, and he thought there was a way to reach it.

He took his army up to Jerusalem, and when they arrived at the city walls, which the Seleucids had themselves battered in an earlier rampage, they found no one to stop them, the garrison troops having elected not to leave the safety of the Acra to engage them. The Acra was only a few hundred yards south-west of the Temple Mount, on the other side of the central valley. After a quick survey, Judah decided to proceed straight to the Temple and secure his primary objective. There would be time later to tackle the citadel. But as they approached the Mount, they were assailed by arrows showered from the parapets and embrasures of the Acra. He promptly 'detailed troops to engage the garrison of the citadel', probably posting teams of snipers armed with captured bows to neutralize the enemy archers, and continued with his lead units to the Temple Mount. The sight that greeted them was one of utter desolation.

They found 'the Temple laid waste', its altar profaned, the gates destroyed, the courts overgrown and looking like thickets, the buildings in ruins. 'The deplorable situation of the place', writes Josephus, 'proved the source of great affliction to Judah and his followers'. But they wasted little time on outward expression of grief. Judah applied himself immediately to the task of cleansing the sacred shrine of all traces of idolatry and restoring it to the service of the Lord. While some of the fighting men kept the Acra inactive, others, under the supervision of 'priests without blemish, devoted to the Law, set about clearing the area, purifying the Temple, and removing to an unclean place the stones which defiled it. They took counsel as to what they should do about the altar of burnt offering, which was profaned, and rightly decided to demolish it, lest it become a reproach to them because it had been defiled by the heathen.' So they tore down the altar, stored its stones in a suitable place on the Temple Mount 'until a prophet should arise who could be consulted about them', took unhewn stones, 'according to the Law', and built a new altar on the model of the original one. They rebuilt the Temple, restored its interior, and consecrated the Temple courts.

Then, on the twenty-fifth day of the ninth month, that is the month Kislev, in the one hundred and forty-eighth year [148 in the chronology of the Seleucid era corresponds to 164 BC], they arose early and offered sacrifice according to the Law upon the newly made altar of burnt offering. On the anniversary of the day when the heathen had profaned it [the third anniversary, says Josephus], on that very day, it was reconsecrated, with hymns of thanksgiving, to the music of harps and lutes and cymbals. All the people prostrated themselves and uttered praises to Heaven that their cause had prospered (1 Macc. 4:41–55).

The retrieval of their holiest shrine from the hands of the pagan and from idolatrous worship was seen by the faithful of Judea as a miracle, the divine accolade for their unwavering religious resolve

A 15th-century Hebrew illuminated manuscript from Italy of the Mishna Torah contains this illustration of the Temple service, which was resumed after the purification and re-dedication of the Sanctuary by the Maccabees

and divine endorsement of their active fight against impossible odds to preserve their traditional beliefs and customs. The few had indeed triumphed over the many and had now wiped out the most grievous affront to the Jewish faith which Antiochus had conceived. It was the crowning glory of the Maccabean struggle and was celebrated by the community for eight days. 'Then Judah and his brothers and the entire congregation of Israel decreed that the days of the dedication of the altar should be kept with gladness and joy at the same season each year, for eight days, beginning on the twenty-fifth of Kislev' (1 Macc. 4:59). (The Hebrew month of Kislev corresponds roughly to December.)

Thus was inaugurated the Festival of Hanukkah, which is observed to this day by Jews throughout the world. 'Hanukkah' is Hebrew for 'dedication', and the name derives, as we have seen, from the First Book of Maccabees. Josephus, writing some 250 years after the event, says 'it is called the Festival of Lights', though he was not certain of the reason. This difference in terminology gave rise to much scholarly controversy. But, as Solomon Zeitlin has pointed out, 'all Jewish festivals had two names', such as the 'Festival of Unleavened Bread' for Passover, or 'Festival of First Fruits' for Pentecost, the corresponding designations referring to 'their popular character'. In the same way, Festival of Lights was probably the popular name for the Festival of Dedication, for the kindling of lights was, and is to this day, the most notable feature of the Hanukkah celebration.

In each home, lights are kindled in a special Hanukkah lamp which has eight small containers for oil or candles. (This lamp is called a *hanukkiah*, and it has varied in shape, material and decorative design from age to age and from country to country.) One wick is lit on the first evening and an additional one on each successive evening, so that all eight are alight on the final night. (This kindling procedure was codified in the first century AD after a Talmudic controversy between the rival schools of the great sages Hillel and Shammai. The School of Shammai held that 'on the first day eight lights should be lit and thereafter they should be progressively reduced'. The School of Hillel held that 'on the first, one should be lit and thereafter they should be progressively increased'. The Hillel view prevailed.) The special benedictions, songs and prayers recited during this festival recall the 'miracles and wonders' of the Maccabean victories and the recovery, purification and dedication of the Temple. In Israel today, an additional Hanukkah celebration is the running of a relay race with a lighted torch from the village of Modi'in to Jerusalem.

The lighting of the Hanukkah lamp has been associated for cen-

Aaron the High Priest lighting the seven-branched candelabrum, from the 'British Museum Miscellany' (*ca.* 1280). The Maccabees re-lit the Temple candelabrum at the rededication ceremony, and this act is associated with the eight-day miracle of the cruse of oil to explain the duration of the Hanukkah Festival and its celebration by the lighting of the eight-branched *hanukkiah*

זה המנרה ואהרן הטיב שמן בנרות"

turies with the story of a minor miracle which appears in the Babylonian Talmud to explain why this festival is celebrated for eight days. It relates that when the Hashmonaim (Hasmoneans) entered the Temple, they found that all the pure oil needed for the Temple candelabrum had been defiled, except for a single cruse which still bore the seal of the High Priest and had not been touched; but this one cruse contained only enough oil for one day. Miraculously, however, it kept the candelabrum burning for eight days. Another, later, traditional story, given in a medieval Palestinian commentary on the Jewish festivals, recounts that the Jews found 'eight iron bars' in the Temple – possibly Seleucid spears – and they 'stood them up and kindled lights on them'.

Whatever the origin of the ceremonials attending this festival, Hanukkah certainly symbolises – and continually renews – the timeless impact of the Maccabean exploits on the behaviour of the Jewish people, spurring them to cling to their traditions even under the most cruel persecution and to fight tenaciously for the preservation of their Jewish identity.

On the morrow of the dedication, the Temple services restored, Judah may well have probed the defences of the Acra stronghold. However, according to the records it continued to house the Seleucid garrison, so Judah must have judged it prudent to put off his attack, estimating that he would suffer too many casualties in tackling so formidable a bastion. The presence of enemy troops in the heart of Jerusalem was wounding to the Maccabee soul; but these troops were largely beleaguered and they posed no crucial danger. He therefore fortified the Temple Mount and left enough of his fighters in Jerusalem to blunt any aggressive move the enemy might conceivably make. His next step was to fortify and garrison Beth Zur, to protect the road to Jerusalem from the south and also 'so that the people should have a fortress facing Idumea', which had always been hostile and which had aided Nicanor and Lysias in their encounters with the Jews.

A few weeks later, the Maccabees were battling again; but this time they were fighting not for the immediate protection of themselves and their people in Judea but for the lives of Jews in distress beyond their borders. It was the first sign that their Gophna enterprise was developing into a broad movement of national liberation. Early in 163 BC, Maccabee forces led by Judah and his brothers left Jerusalem and the confines of the Judean hills and rushed to the relief of Jewish communities in the distant reaches of the neighbouring territories who were being persecuted by the local rulers. These expeditions took them east across the Jordan, north to Galilee, west to the coastal plain and south to Idumea.

Judea had long been surrounded by pagan neighbours hostile in spirit and occasionally in action, engaging in petty incursion and marauding infiltration. They had become bolder when Antiochus had started his repressive measures against the Jews, knowing that their acts of enmity would be viewed with favour by their imperial masters. The records speak, for example, of 'the tribe of Baean', who dwelt east of the Dead Sea and 'who with their traps and road-blocks were continually ambushing the Israelites' (I Macc. 5:4). Suddenly, Judah had turned the tables on Antioch, and they heard of his successes with deep concern. Judea the easy prey – feeble, passive, unarmed and the target of imperial wrath – had become strong, and a strong Judea was not what any of her neighbours wanted, or had expected. The weakling whose territory they might one day plunder and share among themselves had changed almost overnight into a potential rival who might conceive equally aggressive designs towards them. They would have to stop their predatory raids; and as for waging all-out war before Judea became too powerful, that was unthinkable. How could they hope to succeed where imperial armies had failed? Instead, they turned on the kinsmen of their Judean foes, the scattered Jewish communities who dwelt among them, men and women who followed their own strange worship of an invisible God, pursued their outlandish customs, eschewed idolatry and made periodic visits to their shrine in Jerusalem.

The persecution of their local Jews was a gesture of defiance towards Judah – made at a safe distance. It gave Judah's neighbours a reassuring posture of power and exposed Judah's vulnerability. He might be the new strong man of Judea, but he was assuredly incapable of reaching out to their provinces, powerless to save his brothers. Persecution offered additional benefits. It satisfied their xenophobia. It was also profitable: they could seize the possessions of their victims. It ingratiated them with Antioch, and enhanced their political status.

Some historians have suggested as a further reason for their oppression the fear that their local Jewish communities, encouraged by the Maccabee successes, might try to regain title to their lands; for these territories surrounding Judea had once been part of the united Kingdom of Israel. Much had happened since, including the exile to Babylon at the beginning of the sixth century BC. But fifty years after the Jews had been driven from their country, the new Persian empire had favoured their return, and in the course of the next three and a half centuries, while most of the returnees had gone to Jerusalem and Judea, some had resettled in these other regions:

Gilead (today's southern Syria and the northern part of the kingdom of Jordan), eastern and western Galilee, the coastal plain, the land of Ammon (Jordan) and Idumea. (It will be recalled, for example, that 'Tobias the Jew', mentioned in chapter 1, was a noted land-holder in 'the land of Ammon'.) These small Jewish communities had lived peaceably with their neighbours under the Persians and had begun to sense hostility only with the spread of hellenism following Alexander's conquests. But it had not been an active hostility. Liked or disliked, they had been tolerated. Now, however, they suddenly found themselves in danger of their lives. The local rulers were out to kill them and had already claimed many victims. The survivors appealed to Judah for help.

Messengers arrived from Galilee, 'with their garments torn', to report that 'Ptolemais [Acre], Tyre and Sidon . . . and all heathen Galilee have mustered their forces to make an end of us'. From Gilead came messengers with the news that there had been a rising

Young trainees of the Israel Defence Forces moving through the desert, travelling light. Judah's men likewise achieved high mobility – and surprised the enemy – when they marched through the Transjordanian desert on their rescue mission to the Jews of Gilead

against the Jews there too. Many had been murdered, and the survivors had taken refuge in Dathema, a fortress some 20 miles due east of the Sea of Galilee (on today's border between Syria and Jordan). They had also brought 'this letter to Judah and his brothers':

The Gentiles round us have gathered to wipe us out. They are preparing to come and seize the fortress where we have fled for protection. Timotheus is in command of their army. Come and rescue us from their hand, for many of our number have already fallen. All our brothers in the region of Tubias [south-east of the Sea of Galilee] have been massacred, their wives and their children taken captive, and their property carried off. About a thousand men have lost their lives (1 Macc. 5:10–13).

Judah called a 'great assembly' of the people of Judea 'to decide what they should do for their fellow-countrymen in distress and under enemy attack'. It is quite evident, however, that he had already given serious thought to the rescue expeditions and had no doubt made tentative plans with his brothers and other of his top commanders before the assembly met. He must have calculated that such military expeditions were feasible. He had the strongest, best trained and most experienced force – apart from the imperial army – in the entire western half of the empire. The local persecutors would not be expecting him, for none would think him capable of operating outside his own hilly province. Antioch would not stop him, for if Lysias were indeed able and willing to assemble quickly and despatch a force for such a purpose, he would surely have attempted another strike at Judea. Moreover, Lysias, like the hostile provincial leaders, would also be taken by surprise, hardly conceiving that Judah could take his men beyond their borders to battle in unfamiliar country after a lengthy march, for he would be thinking in the conventional terms of imperial military expeditions. Judah, however, would exploit his guerilla background. The Maccabees would not be weighted down with supply caravans, heavy weapons and bivouac equipment. They would retain their high mobility by travelling light, carrying only their weapons and minimal rations of water and dried food, living off the land, marching a longer day – well into the night – covering twice and perhaps three times the daily distance covered by a regular Seleucid unit and snatching only a few hours of sleep under the stars.

Judah and his fellow commanders thought it could be done, and when he put to the assembly the proposal that their fighting men be sent to the rescue of their distant communities, it was endorsed by popular acclaim. He accordingly entrusted his brother Simon with the relief expedition to western Galilee and put three thousand

Petra, in Transjordan, the spectacular capital of the Nabateans, who were helpful to Judah during his rescue march to Gilead

men under his command. He himself, with his brother Jonathan and a force of eight thousand, would proceed to Gilead. The rest of the militia were left to maintain a holding operation in Judea under the command of two senior officers, Joseph the son of Zechariah, and Azariah, who were given the specific order: 'Take charge of this people, but on no account join battle with the heathen until we return.'

Simon took the direct route north along the coastal plain, and although this intelligence must have reached Antioch, Lysias sent no force to engage him. Without Seleucid troops, the local tyrants were powerless against Simon's unit; and so 'Simon went into Galilee, fought many battles with the heathen and defeated them. He pursued them to the gates of Ptolemais.' He then took back with him the surviving 'Jews from Galilee and Arbatta [a settlement near today's Caesarea], their wives and children, and all their possessions, and brought them to Judea with great jubilation' (1 Macc. 5:21–3).

Judah faced a more complex operation. After extracting from the messengers of Gilead all possible intelligence on the strength, defences and location of the enemy, on routes and terrain and

possibly on the tactics of Timotheus, the enemy commander
mentioned in their letter, he decided to avoid the direct, easier and
more familiar route, which would have taken him due north and
then east. Instead, he proceeded eastwards from Jerusalem straight
to the Jordan, crossed the river and made a three day march north-
east through the Transjordanian desert. There he met the Nabateans,
the one neighbouring people who had been little affected by
hellenism, who were at odds with the Seleucids and who were
accordingly sympathetic to the Jews. Diodorus (in Book XIX. 94–7)
has a detailed account of an unsuccessful military attempt by an
earlier hellenist ruler to subjugate them.

(The Nabateans were a remarkable tribal people who had
gradually moved northwards from Arabia and began to settle in
Transjordan and the Negev at the end of the fourth and beginning
of the third century BC and who, in their brief period of glory from
the middle of the first century BC to the middle of the first century
AD, were to carve out for themselves an extensive kingdom, with
their capital at Petra. The relics they were to leave of that period,
before they were crushed by the Romans, show them to have

excelled as farmers, traders, engineers and architects. Archaeological remains of Nabatean settlement may be seen in Israel today, particularly at Avdat and Shivta in the Negev, where their amazing devices for conserving water reveal their ingenuity in coaxing crops out of arid soil.)

Judah learned from his Nabatean informants that many of his 'fellow-Jews in Gilead . . . were held prisoner in Bozrah and Bezer, in Alema, Casphor, Maked, and Carnaim – all large fortified towns; some in the other towns of Gilead.' With the exception of Bozrah, these towns or settlements were loosely grouped in an area from 20 to 40 miles east of the Sea of Galilee (just south of today's Golan Heights). The Nabateans added the intelligence that 'your enemies . . . are marshalling their forces to storm your fortresses . . . so as to capture them and destroy all the Jews in them in a single day'.

Bozrah, at the somewhat isolated eastern edge of Gilead (60 miles south-east of the Sea of Galilee and about the same distance north-east of today's Amman, which was then called Philadelphia), was closest to Judah's halting place, and he decided to attack that first. After gathering more information from the knowledgeable Nabateans on the other cities of unrest which they had mentioned, and on the best routes to reach them, he continued in a north-easterly direction and made straight for Bozrah, which he took apparently without much trouble. (Many of its armed men were probably away with the army of Timotheus getting ready to attack the Jews in Dathema.)

This had brought Judah to the rear of the main Gileadite centres, and he now switched sharply to the north-west for a night march to relieve Dathema. He thus came upon it from the south-east, instead of the more usual south-west, arriving at first light; and when dawn broke the Maccabees saw before them 'an innumerable host' engaged in 'bringing up scaling-ladders and siege engines' to seize the fortress with its beleaguered Jews. Calling to his men 'Now is the time to fight for our brothers', Judah launched a three-pronged assault, pressing the enemy against the fortress walls, destroying their manoeuverability and inflicting heavy casualties in the hand-to-hand fighting that followed. The Jews of Dathema were saved, and a jubilant 'cry went up to heaven from the town, with trumpeting and loud shouting', as 'the army of Timotheus . . . took flight before him [Judah]' (1 Macc. 5:30–4).

Judah then went on to succour the Jews in other Gileadite settlements, notably Alema and Casphor, Maked and Bezer. But while he was so engaged, Timotheus had regrouped his surviving troops, augmented them with units from neighbouring tribes and

The Hanukkah lamp has varied in shape, material and decorative design from age to age and from country to country.
*Hanging* A 19th-century brass lamp from Morocco
*top* An 18th-century pewter *hanukkiah* from Germany
*left* A 20th-century stone lamp from Yemen
*right* An 18th-century bronze *hanukkiah* from Holland
*below* An 18th-century bronze lamp from Poland

resolved to make a stand against Judah at Raphon, some 20 miles north-east of Dathema. (Raphon, or Raphana, is listed by Pliny in his *Naturalis Historia* as belonging to the [later] Decapolis, the league of ten 'Greek' cities; and Josephus also mentions it as an important city.) He assembled his army on the far side of a ravine outside the town; but this proved no serious barrier to the Maccabees, who made the crossing stealthily, appeared before the surprised Timotheus and put his army to rout. The survivors fled to Carnaim, midway between Dathema and Raphon, but Judah pursued them and sacked the city.

Judah now gathered all the rescued Jews of Gilead, men, women and children, together with their possessions, and all set off for Judea. Having civilians with him, Judah chose the quickest and easiest route back, aiming to cross the Jordan just south of the Sea of Galilee, near Beth Shean (then called Scythopolis, another of the cities of the Decapolis). This was a friendly area, and the 'Jews who lived there testified to the goodwill shown them by the people of Scythopolis and the kindness with which they had treated them in their bad times'. But to reach it, Judah had to pass through Ephron, a large fortified city east of the Jordan River opposite Scythopolis, and he sent a 'conciliatory' request for free passage. 'No one shall do you any harm: we shall only march through.' The Ephronites refused. Judah thereupon established a safe compound for the civilians and his fighting men took up battle positions near the city. It is likely that they now used the 'scaling ladders and siege engines' which they had captured at Dathema with the intention, no doubt, of using them later in Jerusalem to reduce the Acra. After a day and a night of hard fighting, Ephron fell. The Maccabees and their civilian wards passed through it, crossed the Jordan and turned south along the Jordan Valley. Throughout this march, Judah and his tough troops showed a gentle and solicitous concern for their frail civilians, and there is a special reference to it in the records (which has a contemporary ring): 'Judah brought up the stragglers and encouraged the people all along the road till he arrived in Judea' (1 Macc. 5: 53). Then Judah, his fighting men and the Jews of Gilead they had rescued 'went up to Mount Zion with gladness and jubilation' and made appropriate thanksgiving offerings in the Temple.

The rejoicing was marred by an unhappy report which Judah received when he reached Jerusalem. Joseph and Azariah, the two commanders he had left behind to maintain the defence of Judea, had ignored his order not to 'join battle with the heathen until we return'. They apparently thought they had a good chance of neutralizing the Idumean threat with the forces at their disposal by

Interior of the burial cave at Marisa

marching on Jamnia in the southern coastal plain, at the western edge of Judea. This seems to have been the site of Seleucid head-quarters in the region, for the record (I Macc. 5:59) shows that the commander there was Gorgias, the co-general with Nicanor on their luckless Emmaus expedition, and he was now 'the general in charge of Idumea' (II Macc. 12:33). The intentions of the two Maccabee officers may have been worthy, but their intelligence on the enemy's strength and movements was poor; and when they descended from the hills they found that Gorgias, apprised that they were on their way, had left his Jamnia encampment and gone out 'with his men to meet them in battle; and Joseph and Azariah were routed and pursued to the frontier of Judea' (I Macc. 5:60), suffering heavy casualties.

This Seleucid-Idumean success was likely to be followed up by enemy attacks at different points along the Judean border. Judah accordingly, after resting his men, mounted an expedition against Idumea. But instead of proceeding directly westwards to their headquarters area, he marched south, using Beth Zur as his jumping-off point, and went on to capture Hebron. From there he swung west and took Marisa. Judah could now move north-west up the coastal plain, tackling the Idumean forces from the south and reaching as far as Azotus, which he sacked before returning to Jerusalem.

Among Judah's additional military actions in the provinces bordering on Judea were his attack on the raiding tribe of Baean, east of the Dead Sea; and the burning of Jaffa harbour, with all its shipping, after learning that the local inhabitants had turned on their two hundred-man Jewish community, put them aboard boats, taken them out to sea and drowned them. Such acts restored quiet to Judea's borders and reduced the incidence of overt anti-Jewish oppression in the region.

The year 163 BC had been a remarkable one for the Maccabees. They had fashioned themselves into a first-class fighting army able to save not only themselves but also their brothers beyond their frontiers. They were now in absolute control of the whole of Judea (except for the Acra citadel). Their people were free to go about their fruitful labours in the fields, free to live their traditional life, follow their religious rites, worship at their Temple in Jerusalem and congregate there in celebration of the three Pilgrim Festivals. Their borders were safe, with no threat of attack and no marauding from their neighbours. Nor was there any sign of a move from Antioch. Judah recognized, however, that this quiescence was only temporary. He therefore retained the nucleus of his Maccabee army

Wall paintings depicting a hunting scene (above) and animals (below) from a 2nd-century BC burial cave at Marisa, which was captured by Judah in his action against the Idumeans

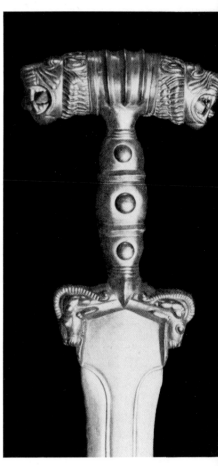

Ceremonial drinking cup and hilt from a gold treasure found in Persia. The attempted plunder of Persian temple treasures proved the undoing of both Antiochus IV and his renowned father

as a regular force and maintained his militia system, so that the men could continue at their constructive tasks yet be ready to take up arms in moments of emergency. His intelligence service, both military and political, which Judah was constantly improving, would give him ample warning of impending danger.

By contrast, 163 BC had been a grim year for the Seleucids. They were still powerless in Judea, and their failure in that year to attempt to recover their authority underscored their impotence. Nor had Lysias made any attempt to stop the Maccabee army from operating in the very territories of the western empire of which he was viceroy. He had not even rushed to the rescue of Raphon, which was much closer to his military bases than it was to Judea. Such inactivity in the face of an outright revolt was damaging to Seleucid prestige in the eyes both of the imperial provinces and of the powers in the region, notably Rome.

They were enjoying no better fortune in their eastern empire. The campaign personally conducted by the emperor Antiochus was not going well, although he had registered some initial successes. He brought back the kingdom of Armenia, which had asserted its independence after his father's death, to its tributary status. He restored Seleucid power in western Persia – in Media and in the hill-country to its south, Elymais (ancient Elam, the Iranian province of Khuzistan). In Media, indeed, its capital, Ecbatana (today's Hamadan), was renamed Epiphanea in his honour (after the title 'Epiphanes' he had assumed). But then he seems to have got bogged down, and he never did manage to engage the Parthians, the gravest menace to his eastern borders and the main target of this campaign. He ran out of money and he ran out of troops. He found that though he had re-established control in his subject provinces, he could maintain it only by armed force, for the people were in a state of incipient insurrection. Thus, instead of being able to hurry eastwards to Parthia with his full army, he was compelled to use many of his soldiers as occupation troops, which left him with insufficient forces to face his major enemy. Antiochus had expected, too, to be reinforced by the units he had left with Lysias – temporarily, he had thought – for the action in Judea, and they should have joined him in a matter of weeks. But matters had not quite worked out as he had planned, and there he was, stalemated among his sullen imperial subjects in the provinces just east of the Tigris.

The emperor had managed to augment his forces somewhat by extorting from these subjects what resources he could and recruiting more mercenaries. But funds were again low, and he remembered how his father, in a similar plight and in the same region, had once plundered a local temple. He decided to do the same, ignoring the fact that his father had been killed by the irate populace while engaged in that very act. 'As king Antiochus marched through the upper provinces he heard that there was a city in Persia called Elymais, famous for its wealth in silver and gold.' Its 'magnificent temple', says Josephus, following the account in the First Book of Maccabees 6:1, 'contained immense treasure, among which were the [golden] shields and breast-plates of Alexander the Great'. Antiochus thereupon proceeded to Elymais, drawn by the beckoning treasure and perhaps not a little by the prospect of securing, and wearing, the precious trappings of his great hero (if indeed they were there). But when he tried to seize the temple, he was set upon by the inhabitants. He had apparently thought it unnecessary to appear with more than a token force, and he only narrowly escaped with his life.

But he was now a broken man. The stalemated campaign, the harsh news from Judea, and now his ignominious flight from Elymais – without the treasure – were all too much for him. He died soon after, in Gabae (Isfahan), north-east of Elymais.

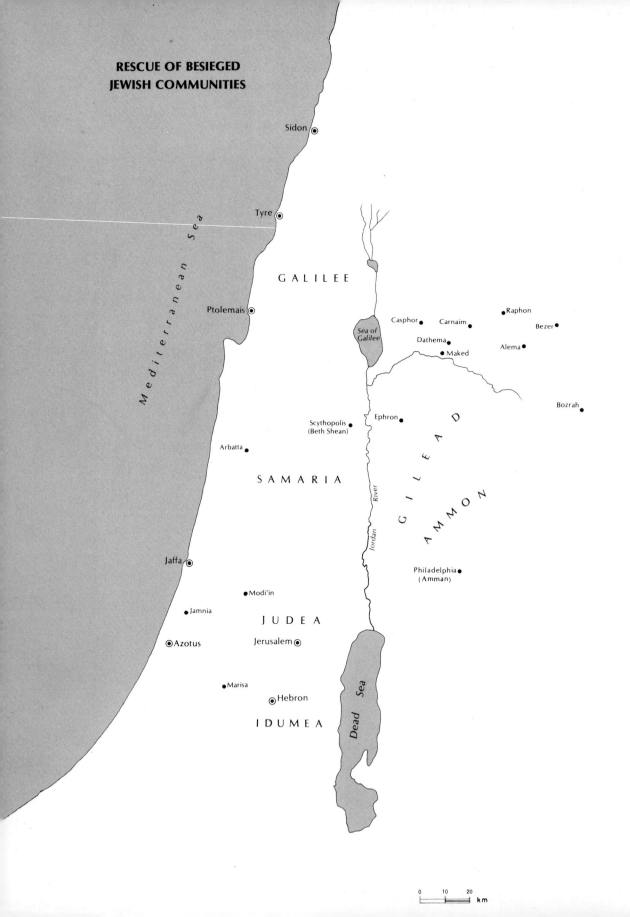

**RESCUE OF BESIEGED
JEWISH COMMUNITIES**

Mediterranean Sea

Sidon ◉

Tyre ◉

GALILEE

Ptolemais ◉

Sea of
Galilee

Casphor ● Carnaim ● Raphon ●

Bezer ●

Dathema ●
Maked ● Alema ●

Bozrah ●

Scythopolis ● Ephron ●
(Beth Shean)

G I L E A D

Arbatta ●

S A M A R I A

A M M O N

Jordan River

Philadelphia ●
(Amman)

Jaffa ◉

● Modi'in

● Jamnia

J U D E A

◉ Azotus Jerusalem ◉

● Marisa

◉ Hebron

Dead Sea

I D U M E A

0    10    20
                  km

There are varied stories in the ancient histories concerning his fatal sickness. The older First Book of Maccabees 6:8 ascribes it to the news he received of Seleucid failures at the hands of the Maccabees and adds prosaically that he 'fell upon his bed and lapsed into a lingering illness', struck with 'grief at the miscarriage of his plans'. The writer of the later Second Book allows his imagination free rein in describing the lurid details of the king's malady. He asserts that Antiochus heard the news of Judea when he was fleeing from Elymais and was so incensed that 'he conceived the idea of making the Jews pay for the injury inflicted by those [the Elymaeans] who had put him to flight'. He therefore decided to leave Persia and set out for Jerusalem, vowing that 'When I reach Jerusalem, I will make it a common graveyard for the Jews' (II Macc. 9:4). But 'the God of Israel struck him a fatal and invisible blow'. Now comes the description: as Antiochus uttered his threat, 'he was seized with incurable pain in his bowels and with sharp internal torments – a punishment entirely fitting for one who had inflicted many unheard-of torments on the bowels of others'. Then, ordering his driver to greater speed, 'he fell out of his chariot as it hurtled along, and so violent was his fall that every joint in his body was dislocated'. Worse was to follow when he was brought to bed. 'Worms swarmed even from the eyes of this godless man and, while he was still alive and in agony, his flesh rotted off, and the whole army was disgusted by the stench of his decay' (II Macc. 9:5,6,9).

The contemporary historian Polybius says that Antiochus became deranged and attributes this to the supernatural act of the goddess of the temple in Elymais he had sought to plunder. Josephus says that 'the pressure of repeated misfortunes occasioned him to fall sick' and that the principal cause of his punishing illness and death was his sacrilegious conduct towards the Jewish religion and the Jewish Temple. He has this comment on the Polybius version: 'It is surprising that Polybius, who upon the whole is deemed a writer deserving credit, should attribute the Judgement that befell Antiochus to his design of rifling the temple [in Elymais], since it surely is more reasonable to suppose that his death was the consequence of a crime actually committed in the profanation of the Temple of Jerusalem' (*Antiquities* XII. 356–9).

Did Antiochus undergo a deathbed change of heart? The Books of Maccabees and Josephus say he did. They report that when he realized he was near death, he summoned his closest counsellors and reviewed his sorry state. He had asked himself, he told them:

Why am I overwhelmed by this flood of trouble, I who was kind and well-loved in the day of my power? But now I remember the wrong I did

The death of Antiochus, an illustration from the Gustave Doré Bible

in Jerusalem, when I took all her [Temple] vessels of silver and gold, and when I made an unjustified attempt to wipe out the inhabitants of Judea. It is for this, I know, that these misfortunes have come upon me; and here I am, dying of grief in a foreign land (1 Macc. 6:10–13).

(The Second Book of Maccabees goes further, adding that one of his final acts was to dictate a friendly letter to the Jews, in which he also names his young son as his successor. The authenticity of this document is the subject of scholarly controversy.)

Some historians have dismissed such a royal reversal as unreasonable and out of character. But it is evident from the records that the emperor, though clever and able in many ways and a man of action and of ideas, both worthy and ignoble, was also given to impulsiveness and irrationality. The probability is strong that, in regretting his ill-treatment of the Jews, Antiochus had not suddenly gone mawkishly sentimental but was offering a judgement after reviewing his rule in an eve-of-death moment of truth. He had not changed his attitude towards the Jews, was not concerned for their welfare and cared not a jot about their sufferings. He was simply reflecting in his final hour that his anti-Jewish policy may well have been one of his greatest political errors and had contributed to what he could now see was the crumbling of his empire. If he had not sought to destroy the Jewish faith, he might have had a peaceful Judea. He would not have exposed himself to a series of military setbacks, loss of prestige, and waning political influence. He would also have had more troops to further his military ventures in the east. He had seriously underrated the strength of Jewish loyalty to the religion, history and traditions of their fathers. And here he was, his empire breaking up, and he himself 'dying of grief in a foreign land.'

Antiochus' last act was to appoint 'Philip, one of his Friends', as 'regent over his whole empire, giving him the crown, the royal robe, and the signet-ring, with authority to take his son Antiochus [Eupator] and bring him up to be king.' Why did Philip receive this appointment when, it will be recalled, the emperor had entrusted the guardianship of his young son to Lysias before departing on his eastern campaign? Antiochus had no doubt become disenchanted with Lysias. The viceroy of the western territories had let him down. He had lost Judea, lost battles, lost men desperately needed in Persia. One can imagine that Antiochus, the soldier in the field with the griping contempt for the rear echelon, had been sending urgent signals for troops and funds to Lysias, sitting in the comfort of the royal court at Antioch, and all he had got back were pusillanimous excuses as to why the demands could not be met. If he were not so preoccupied with the troubles in Persia, he would no doubt have replaced Lysias – although attempts at long-distance changes of personnel were risky, often resulting in a rejection, and a coup, by the dismissed leader. In any event, now that death was near, and since his son was a minor, Antiochus was anxious to ensure that the affairs of the empire would be in strong and confident hands and not in the charge of one who had shown himself to be a weakling. Philip seems to have gained his trust as a close counsellor on his eastern campaign, and it was he who was named to the regency.

This final action of Antiochus was to save Judah and his Maccabees at a critical moment in their fortunes.

# 10  The Truce

The appointment of Philip cocked the trigger for a power struggle within the House of Seleucus, heartening rivals and victims alike. To nations like Rome, Parthia and Egypt, watching from the sidelines in the west, the east, and the south, and to the recalcitrant provinces of Persia and Judea, it heralded the possible break-up of the Seleucid empire, with its obvious implications of opportunity for the rivals to strike and for the tributaries to shake off the imperial yoke.

To them, each for his own reasons, the death of Antiochus was encouraging in itself, for no one on the Seleucid scene could match the strength and ambition of this royal figure, certainly not the nine-year-old son who would follow him. True, until this boy-king came of age, the reins would be handled by a regent, either Lysias or Philip; but neither had shown any particular distinction. In any case, they would be busy sparring for position, and whoever came out on top, whether by peaceful arrangement or by combat, would find the military and political élite riven by factionalism. It was considered unlikely that either would politely give up his claim to the regency. A collision between the two seemed inevitable, with the consequent weakening of an already waning empire.

Lysias took the first step along the collision course, making it clear that he had no intention of abdicating his office. As soon as he heard that the emperor was dead, he enthroned his young princely ward as Emperor Antiochus v Eupator, with himself as regent. He was determined to keep Philip out.

Philip was equally determined to assume his title. But he was away in Persia, having taken command of the expeditionary army, and was torn by the wish to rush back to Antioch and the need to stay. Since Lysias had pre-empted the regency, Philip would need force to depose him. If he returned to the capital at the head of his legions,

Marble bust of an army commander based on a Greek model. Army commanders Lysias and Philip contended for Seleucid power on the death of Antiochus

he might well succeed, whereas delay would give Lysias time to consolidate his position. But if Philip pulled his army out of the eastern provinces at this stage of the campaign, all the military efforts expended so far would be wasted and the gains nullified. Media and Elymais would reassert their independence the moment he took his armed foot off their stubborn necks, and the menace of Parthia would loom even larger. He was faced with a fierce dilemma. He finally resolved it by deciding to stay, considering perhaps that he was the one who now commanded the bulk of the armed forces and could eject Lysias at any time. Moreover, if he returned with some impressive victories to his credit, as against the Judean failures of Lysias, he would be acclaimed in Antioch as a popular hero. And if, by pressing on with the campaign, he could establish firm enough control over his subject territories to outlast his departure, he would be ruling, when he assumed the regency, an intact and not a truncated empire.

Lysias remained in Antioch with the young king. Philip went on fighting in the east. The powers in the region watched and waited. Judah in Judea watched, but decided not to wait.

The political intelligence service of Judah was not as sophisticated as that of Rome or Egypt, but he knew in broad terms what was going on, and he judged that the coming year (162 BC) held much promise. In analysing the implications of the rivalry over the succession, he seems to have concluded that Lysias was unlikely to leave Antioch or reduce his forces there by despatching another expedition against Judea until he had met and disposed of Philip. Philip, for his part, showed no signs of returning as yet. This, then, thought Judah, was the time to act against the garrison and the hellenists in the Acra in Jerusalem.

It was Judah's first major error of political and military judgement since he had left the village of Modi'in for the hills of Gophna. It may be argued, however, that he took a calculated and warrantable risk but was dogged by mischance. Judah must have reckoned that whoever won the regency battle would be bound to act against Judea, to even greater effect, for he could then fling against the Maccabees the full force of imperial power; whereas if the confrontation took place now, it would be against a Lysias worried by what Philip might do and commanding only a portion of the Seleucid army.

Judah assembled his men and his captured siege equipment and proceeded to invest the Acra citadel. Although, as we have seen, the offensive power of the garrison was limited, the troops still retained the capacity, behind the protection of their walls, to harass the congregants on the Temple Mount by sniping. Maccabee detachments were always on the alert to counter the enemy archers, but there was constant anxiety among the worshippers and a mood of uneasiness at the Pilgrim Festivals. Moreover, the very presence of the enemy in their midst was galling to the Jews of Judea. What was most worrying to Judah was the obverse of this coin: if the Seleucid citadel was a reminder to the Jews, it was also a reminder to Antioch – of her duty to wipe out the shame of defeat, restore her authority in Judea and save the imperial garrison. If, however, the citadel fell, Antioch might perhaps accommodate herself to the situation and accept a conciliatory arrangement with the victor.

At the beginning of the year 162 BC the Jews prepared to attack the formidable Acra. They soon discovered that it was no light task. The breaching equipment which they had captured at Dathema proved ineffective against the citadel's stout ramparts. This equipment had been taken from the popular force which Timotheus had mounted to assault the unarmed Jewish communities of Gilead,

A 15th-century conception of ancient siege equipment, a design in the Alba Bible to illustrate Judah's attempt to storm the Acra Fortress

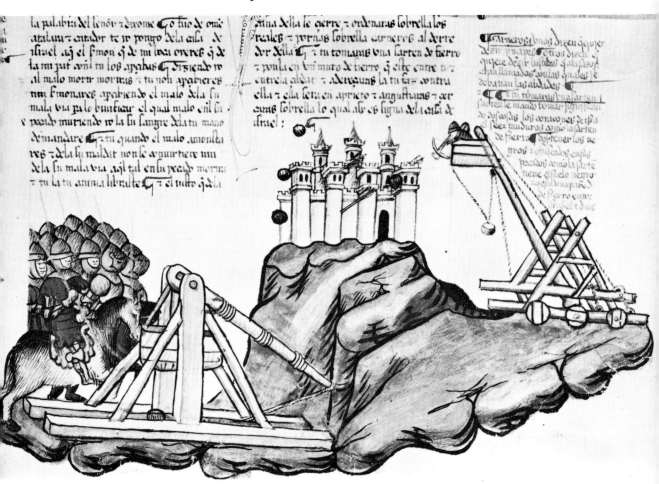

Antioch on the Orontes, the ancient Seleucid capital, as it looked in the 18th century. This engraving, made a century later, was based on a 1782 drawing by a French traveller

and it was primitive, not to be compared to that in use by the regular Seleucid army. Judah was compelled to fall back on a siege, and this was a radical departure for the Maccabees. They had been used to quick action, and here they had to 'sit it out', waiting for a surrender and unable, because of the terrain, to block every hole and seal off the Acra from contact with the outside. It is almost certain, too, that tunnels had been cut leading from the interior of the fortress to secret and camouflaged posterns beyond its walls.

Thus it came about that messengers from the citadel turned up at the court of Antioch and beseeched Lysias for help. The delegation consisted of members of the garrison and a few 'renegade Israelites'. They were very persuasive. The garrison representatives reviewed their military plight. They had been holding out for so long, a Seleucid island in a swamp of Judean rebels, frustrating all attempts to conquer them; but now they were hard pressed and they could not last much longer. They would willingly lay down their lives for the glory of the flag, but it would be a blight on the good name of the empire if they were vanquished. Only an immediate rescue expedition could save them and preserve Seleucid prestige. The hellenistic Jews added their plea. They had stood by the empire, done all they could to advance its cause, were loyal to the House of Seleucus, had faithfully followed the orders of Antiochus Epiphanes and obeyed his decrees. And what was the result? Their own countrymen had become their enemies. Many of their friends had been killed. And now, if the Acra were to fall, the Maccabees would crush them and destroy the tender shoots of hellenism which the late lamented emperor had been so anxious to cultivate among their people. Surely the noble Lysias would not countenance such reward for their faithful service.

Lysias listened. The Acra messengers had presented good reasons for him to march on Judea; but the real reasons why he decided to comply were somewhat different. His defeat by the Maccabees still rankled; he would like to lead another expedition and reverse the score. He had gained useful experience in his earlier encounter with the Jewish rebels, and now he would know how to overcome them. He would need more men; but with the old emperor gone, he was now his own master and could use all the resources available to Antioch. With his rival, Philip, in the east, he had no further supply commitments to that part of the empire. Furthermore, victory in Judea would excite favourable comparison with Philip's faltering activities in Persia. It would also restore the trust of Judea's neighbours, the targets of Judah's operations who had been irked by the Seleucid failure to intervene. And it would serve notice on Philip – and Rome, Egypt and all the fledgling vultures in the region – that he, Lysias, was now the strong man of Seleucia.

He was disturbed by only one doubt: if he left for Judea, might not Philip be tempted to hurry back and claim the regency? It was now several weeks since the emperor had died, and he had gathered from his intelligence agents that his rival, while not renouncing his claim, had decided to continue for the time being with the campaign. Lysias estimated that this would keep him in the east for some months, time enough for the army of Lysias to deal with Judea. If by chance Philip took it into his head to return sooner, Lysias would receive adequate warning, and he could get back to Antioch reasonably quickly.

Lysias accordingly set out for Judea at the head of a large force, augmenting his local units with a considerable body of mercenaries recruited from outside the country. With him was the young Antiochus V Eupator. (Appian of Alexandria, the second-century AD historian, says he was given the title 'Eupator' in honour of the valorous deeds of his father.) Lysias' army consisted of infantry, cavalry and war elephants. His use of elephants could be interpreted as an unusual gesture of defiance against Rome. Under the 188 BC Roman-Seleucid treaty of Apamea (which followed the defeat of

Antiochus III by Rome at the battle of Magnesia in 190–189 BC),
the Seleucids were forced to renounce the use of elephants in warfare.
Since then, the emperors had acquired and trained elephants, but
had so far refrained from using them in action and thus given Rome
no cause for complaint. Now, for the first time, Lysias was em-
ploying them in a military operation, in direct breach of their
treaty. Rome took note of it and would react at an opportune
moment.

It is clear, of course, that Lysias decided on the elephant unit not
to anger Rome but to achieve a quick victory over the Judeans.
Ever since Alexander the Great had experienced his first staggering
encounter with elephants at the battle of Hydaspes in his Indian campaign in the year 326 BC, all his successors, both in the Seleucid and
the Ptolemaic lines, accounted this animal as a serious fighting
weapon. As the scholar W.W. Tarn observes, they considered 'that
elephants were an arm to be obtained at any price'. Indeed, 'after
Alexander's death every one of the contending generals got all the
elephants he could'. Eventually, it was the Seleucids who secured
a monopoly of Indian elephants (the other states got theirs from

The war elephant, depicted
on this silver plate of the
hellenistic period, was much
prized by the Seleucids.
Lysias used elephants in
the battle of Beth Zechariah
against the Maccabees

The boy-king Antiochus
Eupator was given a hellenistic upbringing, and, like
the young hellenist por-
trayed in this terracotta
figurine, wore the *petasos*,
the special hat worn by
upper-class Greeks when
hunting or travelling, and
by athletes after the games

Africa), and Indian mahouts were imported to train and handle the beasts.

The idea of using elephants – even though it would incur Rome's displeasure – must have struck Lysias when planning his attack on the Maccabees. The operation had to be swift, so that he could return to Antioch before Philip, but his previous experience had shown that the Jewish fighters were stubborn and ingenious, uncowed by the phalanx, the cavalry or by superiority of numbers and weaponry, and the engagement might be protracted. The one new factor which he had the power to introduce and which would assuredly terrify them into a quick defeat, submission or flight was the war elephant. Tarn, disposing of the popular illusion that the elephant was the ancient counterpart of the modern tank, says that 'it seems as if the elephants soon lost their terrors for experienced troops, but they could be deadly the *first* time'. Lysias was banking on their terror effect upon the Maccabees, who would be facing them for the first time.

The size of Lysias' army is certainly exaggerated in the Books of Maccabees. It is put at 100,000 infantry, 20,000 cavalry and 32 war elephants in I Maccabees (6:30) and at 110,000 infantry, 5,300 cavalry, 300 chariots and 22 elephants in II Maccabees (13:2). It could not have approached anything like those figures, though it was assuredly larger than the force Lysias had commanded the first time, and scholars estimate that its total strength was in the neighbourhood of 25,000 to 30,000, with between 20 and 30 elephants. Lysias took the same route that he had taken previously, marching down the coastal road almost to its southern extremity and then wheeling east, to approach Jerusalem from the south. His first encounter with the Maccabees was thus at Beth Zur, which Judah had fortified and garrisoned and which Lysias now put under siege. Judah was forced to abandon his own siege of the Acra to meet the new threat.

The menace was grave indeed, and Judah had been searching for an appropriate response ever since he had received news that Lysias was on his way, together with alarming details of the size and unusual nature of the enemy force. He was in a quandary. He could not repeat his earlier tactics, for these were already known to Lysias. But if he abandoned his guerilla pattern, he would lose his unique advantage over a conventional force. Nor could he select the same battleground, which offered the most favourable ambush terrain between Hebron and Jerusalem; yet any other site would be less obstructive to regular troops. Since conditions suited to guerilla warfare were denied to him, Judah may well have thought that the one ingredient of surprise still left was to apply conventional

Sling 'bullet' from the Maccabean period discovered during the archaeological excavations at Beth Zur, where Lysias battled with Judah

methods, which Lysias would not be expecting, and rely on the innate fighting qualities of his men, their power of endurance and the fanatical enthusiasm for their cause to overcome the enemy. He now had enough captured sarissas, bows and arrows, swords and shields to equip at least a nucleus of what would be his counterpart to the phalanx.

As a last resort, he could, of course, do what he would have done two or three years earlier – disappear with his men into the hills, leaving Lysias with a phantom target, and reappear when the enemy had gone. But this would mean losing all he had gained and built up since the Gophna days. Jerusalem would be retaken, the Temple defiled, Judea overrun, harsh reprisals extracted and a large enemy garrison left to maintain rigorous order. As he estimated his current chances, he thought it might well come to that; but

Remains of a comparatively recent building on the site of ancient Beth Zur

before taking to the hills, he would make a supreme effort to stop the enemy from reaching Jerusalem. His men at Beth Zur would hold them up for a time, though assuredly not for long, for they would soon run out of food. (This was a sabbatical year, and the Maccabees faithfully followed the biblical injunction to leave all land fallow during the seventh year.) He accordingly decided to make a stand at Beth Zechariah, some 5 miles north of Beth Zur and 11 miles south of Jerusalem.

The Beth Zur garrison eventually surrendered. (It appears from the records that Lysias left it invested by a few besieging detachments, continued his advance, and took their surrender later.) During the night before the enemy moved northwards from the Beth Zur area, Judah disposed his forces in previously reconnoitred positions at Beth Zechariah astride the road to Jerusalem, ready for a direct frontal meeting with the army of Lysias.

Lysias moved towards the field of combat with his formations in full battle array. To the waiting and watching Maccabees, they must have been a petrifying sight. Leading the army were the elephants, the light infantry and light cavalry. Behind them rumbled the heavy infantry ready to close up into the phalanx formation with the heavy cavalry on their flanks. Attached to each elephant was a contingent of foot soldiers 'equipped with coats of chain-mail and bronze helmets' and a number of 'picked horsemen'. Each animal 'had a strong wooden turret fastened on its back with a special harness, by way of protection, and carried four fighting men as well as an Indian driver. The rest of the cavalry Lysias stationed on either flank of the army, to harass the enemy while themselves protected by the phalanxes. When the sun shone on the gold and bronze shields, they lit up the hills, which flashed like torches' (1 Macc. 6:35–9).

Lysias, a sober military commander, had learned from his previous encounter the danger of moving through defiles in hilly country without first commanding the flanking high ground; and so, as the records report, part of his army was 'deployed over the heights, and part over the low ground. They advanced confidently and in good order. All who heard the din of this marching multitude and its clashing arms shook with fear. It was a very great and powerful array indeed' (1 Macc. 6:40,41).

The Maccabees, for the first time, were about to engage an enemy from defensive positions. Judah's plan called for light units to be stationed in advance emplacements to hold up, or at least harass, confuse and delay, the enemy. If they should be overrun, the phalanxes would be engaged by the main Maccabee force deployed in the rear in compact formation. As against this, Lysias' plan was to weaken the spirits and impair the fighting capacity of the Maccabees with his elephants and destroy their advance positions with his superior light infantry and cavalry. His light units would then make way for his phalanxes, who would move up and crush the heart of the Maccabee army.

The two spearheads met. The opening battle was fierce, both sides suffering heavy casualties. But the weight of the enemy was overwhelming, and the elephants, as Lysias had anticipated, had a terrifying effect on the untried Judeans. The huge beasts lumbered forward with steady tread, shielded by their accompanying foot and horse units, driving all before them as they advanced with sedate and unwavering step, oblivious of the flashing movement of battle all around them. The leading Maccabee detachments froze at the approach of the animals, and it was under this psychological disadvantage that they found themselves moments later locked in mortal combat with the leading contingents of the adversary. Perhaps to snap them out of their terror, Judah's younger brother, Eleazar, now made a mad, sudden suicidal dash to show his comrades that the elephant, too, was vulnerable. The records give another reason, reporting that he spotted an elephant caparisoned with the royal arms, and thinking it carried the young king or the commanding general, he fought his way through its protective ranks, cutting down enemy troops right and left, until he reached it. He got beneath it, thrust his sword through its underbelly and killed it. But before he could remove his sword, the elephant fell and crushed him. He was the first of the sons of Mattathias to die.

His desperate act of valour proved fruitless. The strength and impetus of the imperial forces were too powerful, and as the way was now open for the phalanxes, Judah resolved to break off the battle and save the bulk of his army. Bitter at heart, he and his men made their way northwards, moving quickly through wadis and over mountain trails which they knew so well. Lysias pressed on to Jerusalem. There was now nothing to stop him from reaching the city.

[Twenty-one centuries later, young religious pioneer farmers would establish a group of four kibbutzim, known as the Etzion Bloc, in the very area where Judah's brother was killed and his forces suffered their grim defeat. The Jews of Etzion, too, would fight an enemy bent on frustrating Jewish independence and seeking to reach and attack Jerusalem from the south. The pious kibbutzniks would make an heroic last stand, which would delay the foe and be of crucial help in saving Jerusalem. Many would die – killed in battle or massacred. Their kibbutzim would fall – only a few hours before the proclamation of Israel's statehood on

Eleazar's suicidal attack on a caparisoned war elephant at the battle of Beth Zur, as depicted in the Gustave Doré Bible

14 May 1948. But nineteen years later, on the fourth day of the Six Day War, Etzion would be re-won, and within weeks young pioneers would be at work amidst its ruins, restoring it to life. Among them would be the sons and daughters of the defenders slain in 1948 (when, as infants, they had been evacuated on the eve of battle). In December 1967 they would re-kindle the lights at the Festival inaugurated by the Maccabees; and ever after, there would be an added dimension to the celebration of Hanukkah at Etzion.]

Josephus states in *Antiquities* that Judah withdrew to Jerusalem with his men to carry on the fight from there, but in *Wars* he says that he 'retreated to . . . Gophna'. The Books of Maccabees also record that the struggle was continued from Jerusalem, though no specific mention is made of Judah's presence. The obscurity in the

Maccabee texts and the contradiction in Josephus have given rise to speculation among scholars as to Judah's immediate movements, some holding that he proceeded to Jerusalem and others that he went to Gophna. What seems most likely, however, is that he did both: upon leaving Beth Zechariah Judah and his surviving forces made straight for Jerusalem and feverishly organized its defences. With Lysias due to arrive in a day or two, and with the city walls destroyed, the only compact area which offered any defensive opportunities was the Temple Mount, which Judah had fortified the previous year. It is probable that Judah left a Maccabee unit there to hold out as long as it could and then proceeded to Gophna with the rest of his forces. Seeing little chance of victory over Lysias at this stage, he was anxious to preserve at least a minimal capacity for continuing his resistance. The Temple unit would thus fight a delaying action and enable Judah with the remaining Maccabees to establish themselves anew in the Judean hills as a simple guerilla force. Lysias, after capturing Jerusalem, would assuredly leave behind an occupation army to subdue rural Judea, and the Maccabees would then revert to their former partisan role.

The Maccabee holding force continued to give battle from the fortified Temple Mount and surprised Lysias by the ferocity of its defence. After his decisive success at Beth Zechariah, Lysias expected no opposition when he entered Jerusalem and joined up with his Acra garrison; but he now found the Temple area barred to him. He sent in assault units, but they were hurled back, and he was compelled to resort to siege. This, however, was a lengthy process, whereas he had planned on a quick campaign, and as day followed day, with the Jews refusing to surrender, he became concerned lest Philip take advantage of his lengthy absence from Antioch. Lysias therefore 'set up emplacements and siege-engines' round the Temple Mount, 'with flame-throwers, catapults for discharging stones and barbed missiles, and slings'. But the Maccabees, too, 'constructed engines to counter his engines, and put up a prolonged resistance' (I Macc. 6: 51, 52).

However, the fact – unknown to Lysias – was that the situation of the Jewish defenders was getting more desperate from hour to hour, and they would soon be physically unable to hold out. They had run out of food. Like their comrades at Beth Zur, they had suffered a shortage of provisions because of the sabbatical year, and despite rationing their supply stores were now bare. They could not sustain their resistance on empty stomachs and were already preparing plans for stealthy flight or surrender.

They were saved at the last moment. News reached Lysias that Philip was on his way back to Antioch 'with the late king's expeditionary force, and that he was seeking to take over the government'. Lysias could tarry no longer. With the regency at stake, Judea was of lesser import, and he promptly decided to abandon the Jerusalem siege and rush back to the capital, taking the young king and the army with him.

It was a bitter decision. Victory was within his grasp, and now it would be claimed by his enemies, the Jews. But there was no alternative. However, as he reflected on the vexatious problem of Judea, he conceived a design of compromise which would diminish both his own failure and the Maccabee success, allow him to make a graceful departure and smooth his future relationship with the rebellious province. Trouble with Judea, he recalled, had erupted only with the hellenistic decrees of Antiochus IV, who had hoped to achieve unity and loyalty through an enforced cultural and religious homogeneity. Instead, he had reaped incessant conflict, repetitive military defeat and grave damage to the empire. It was now clear to Lysias that, in the cold hard terms of imperial interests, the policy of the former emperor had been an act of extravagent folly, and if he, Lysias, prolonged it, he would face the same Judean nightmare. There was now no need to do so, for Antiochus IV was dead, and power, for the moment, was in his hands.

Lysias accordingly despatched a herald to the besieged Judeans with a compromise offer of peace. Its principal item was the annulment of the anti-Jewish decrees imposed by Antiochus IV. The ancient records dwell only on this grant of freedom of worship. As Josephus observes, Lysias promised 'to allow them the liberty of conscience, and to protect them in the exercise of their laws and religion'. It is almost certain, however, that religious toleration was to be granted in return for Judean political loyalty to Antioch and the continued presence of a Seleucid garrison in Judea. Amnesty to the rebels was granted in return for an end to the rebellion.

A clue to the thinking which inspired this offer is contained in the First Book of Maccabees 6:58–61, which records the proposal made by Lysias to the young king and his commanders:

'So let us offer these men terms and make peace with them and their whole nation. Let us guarantee their right to follow their laws and customs as they used to do, for it was our abolition of these very customs and laws that aroused their resentment, and produced all these consequences.' The proposal met with the approval of the king and the commanders, and an offer of peace was sent and accepted. The king and his commanders bound themselves by oath, and on the agreed terms the besieged emerged from their stronghold.

The Second Book of Maccabees 11:23–6 presents the remission

order in the form of a letter addressed by the boy-king to Lysias (presumably dictated by Lysias), solemnly renouncing the policy of the former emperor:

Now that our royal father has gone to join the gods, we desire that our subjects be undisturbed in the conduct of their own affairs. We have learnt that the Jews do not consent to adopt Greek ways, as our father wished, but prefer their own mode of life and request that they be allowed to observe their own laws. We choose, therefore, that this nation like the rest should be left undisturbed, and decree that their Temple be restored to them and that they shall regulate their lives in accordance with their ancestral customs . . .

Following the presentation and acceptance of the agreement, the Temple Mount was thrown open and Lysias went in to inspect it. When he 'saw how strongly the place was fortified, he went back on the oath he had sworn, and gave orders for the surrounding wall to be demolished' (1 Macc. 6:62). There was nothing the Maccabee holding unit could do to prevent it, and they could take slight comfort only in the thought that Judah was away in the hills and was thus spared the painful sight.

Perhaps to appease the Maccabees for dismantling the Temple fortifications, and to reassure them that his oath on religious freedom would be respected, Lysias took action against Menelaus, the High Priest appointed by Antiochus IV who symbolized all that was abhorrent to the traditionalist Jew. It was also a shrewd political act, and in keeping with the renunciation of the hellenist decrees, for, as Josephus observes, Lysias 'represented that it would be impossible to keep the Jews in peace and subjection while [Menelaus] was living; for he had instigated [Antiochus IV] . . . to compel the Jews to practice a religion that was contrary to their sentiments.' And the Second Book of Maccabees 13:4 says that Lysias regarded Menelaus as the 'criminal [who] was responsible for all Antiochus' troubles', suggesting that had this man not persuaded the emperor that hellenism could take root in Judea, the decrees might never have been imposed. Menelaus was therefore removed to Beroea (today's Aleppo, in northern Syria), tried and executed.

Lysias' final act before leaving Jerusalem was to appoint a new military governor for the area, headquartered in the Acra citadel. He then sped back to Antioch, to find Philip, with the forces who had returned with him from the east, ready to enforce his claim to the regency. In the ensuing conflict, Lysias emerged the victor. He was now the *de facto* ruler of the Seleucid empire.

The Jews of Judea could well congratulate themselves on having secured their war aim. Five years earlier, they had resisted, at first passively and then by battle, the governmental order compelling them to abandon their Judaism and adopt hellenistic paganism. After their initial sufferings of martyrdom, they had fought a grim fight against the might of an empire for the right to follow their traditional religious laws and customs. And now, miraculously, at the most critical moment in their fortunes, when they were within a hair's breadth of being wiped out, the battle had been broken off and they had been granted the very right for which they had struggled. It was natural for many to feel that having gained their objective, there was no longer a need for a Maccabee army, no further need for a militia, and they could all revert to their former pattern of living. Among them were the Hasidim, the devoutly orthodox who in the early months of Antiochus' persecution had given their lives rather than defend themselves on the Sabbath but who had been among the first volunteers to join the guerillas at Gophna. They had soon accepted Mattathias' formula of defensive action, but not the initiation of an attack, on the Sabbath, and they had been among the most valiant fighters in all the subsequent battles. Now that religious toleration had been regained, that they could worship at the Temple, that the renegade High Priest Menelaus had been removed and they could pursue their traditional lives unmolested, they took their leave of Judah and their other comrades-in-arms.

Judah did not share their views. He understood their reasoning, but considered it short-sighted. True, they had secured their initial aim of religious freedom, and at the beginning it had been their sole aim. But now, in the light of their subsequent military and political experience, this was not enough. What they needed was political freedom. Only with independence could the Jews of Judea enjoy true freedom of worship, for only then would they be free of the fear of renewed persecution. If they remained a subject province, they and their religion would always be vulnerable, exposed to the whim of whoever was emperor at Antioch. Until the arrival of Antiochus Epiphanes, it would never have occurred even to Jews like Judah that anyone would seek to uproot the Jewish religion and murder Jews because of their faith. But Epiphanes and his anti-Jewish decrees had been a traumatic fact, and what had happened once could happen again. Antiochus was now dead, and Lysias had rescinded those decrees. He had done so for reasons of current expediency, not for love of Jews. If at any time in the future he deemed it useful to renew the persecution, he would not hesitate to do so; and if not he, one of his successors. Independence alone would make the Judeans free of future threat to their traditional ways. Until they gained it, it was essential to keep their defence organization intact. For even the expedient Lysias must harbour vengeful thoughts after his bitter defeats at the hands of the Maccabees, and their disbandment might tempt him to punitive action against Judea. That, alone, was reason enough to maintain a deterrent force. But it was more important for that force to continue its resistance with a new war aim – independence.

To many Judeans this may have seemed an impossible target. But not to Judah and his colleagues. Not now. It was no less possible of attainment than religious freedom, yet that had seemed beyond their reach when they had first taken up arms. They had decided then to go down fighting rather than submit passively to the tyrant's decrees or his executioners. None had expected to live. But after surviving their initial skirmishes, they had suddenly realized that resistance was possible and through it they might secure a change of policy. They had now achieved this, having convinced Antioch that her religious coercion simply did not pay. It was costly in men, resources and imperial prestige – and it was ineffective. By the same methods they could 'persuade' Antioch that political subjection would be equally burdensome to the Seleucids. There was no reason why they should not reconcile themselves to Judean political independence – with appropriate friendship treaties as safeguards – in the same way as they had now accommodated themselves to Jewish religious independence.

Judah had another reason for thinking that independence was an attainable goal. Despite his preoccupation with combat, he had kept abreast of political developments within the empire and in the eastern Mediterranean region. He knew that the Seleucid throne was shaky, even after the despatch of Philip by Lysias. Factionalism was bound to remain, for Philip had had his adherents both in the army and the political councils, and such dissident elements could produce a new rival to challenge the incumbent regent. They could also be exploited by one of the relatives of the emperor – and there were several such princes scattered about who were eager to depose the young Antiochus, possibly with the backing of an outside power. Antioch was rife with intrigue. So were the courts of every kingdom in the region. As for powerful Rome, while she was not yet prepared to take military action, it was known that she was doing all she could through diplomatic emissaries in the surrounding states to undermine the Seleucid empire. The minimal product of such an atmosphere of internal and international intrigue was political uncertainty – and in such uncertainty lay opportunity. Anything might happen.

Judah was determined to continue the Maccabee struggle.

# 11 The Escape

Developments moved faster than Judah had imagined, and dramatic events in Antioch and Rome were to have a vital impact – at first tragic, but ultimately triumphant – on the course he had planned. The year 162 BC saw the inauguration of a bitter and bloody dynastic struggle for Seleucid power, complete with royal plot and counter-plot, the murder of kings (and even of a queen and princess), emperor pitted against pretender, the victor vanquished by a new rival and he in turn routed by a new claimant, all flavoured with the classic ingredients of duplicity, guile, treachery and retribution. These dynastic conflicts were eventually to tear the Seleucid empire apart. In the process, as Judah had judged, they were to offer political opportunities which the Maccabees were able to exploit to advantage.

The opening move in the scramble for power was taken in the sedate and subdued atmosphere of the Roman Senate by a bright, ambitious and dashing young man of twenty-three who had the legitimate right and the keenest craving to assume the Seleucid monarchy. He was Demetrius, cousin to the nine-year-old emperor Antiochus V Eupator. His legal claim was unexceptionable, for he was the son of the emperor Seleucus IV and should have succeeded him. But when Seleucus was murdered, Demetrius, then a boy of eleven, was in Rome, having been sent there as a hostage during his father's reign (under the treaty of Apamea), and it was his uncle, younger brother to Seleucus, who seized the throne, reigning as Antiochus IV Epiphanes. During Epiphanes' rule, Demetrius grew to manhood in Rome, under surveillance but with few restrictions beyond the ban on leaving the country. He was thus able to pursue the gay life of a high-spirited young prince, hunting the wild boar with nets and dogs and keeping his cup-bearer busy at nightly dinner parties, but also managing to acquire the arts of politics and

A 2nd-century BC statue of the dashing and ambitious young Prince Demetrius, a hostage in Rome, who escaped and became Seleucid emperor

A boar hunt played a part in Demetrius' escape plan. Detail of a hunt, from a 6th-century BC pottery vase

diplomacy through friends in high places. (One of his mentors was the distinguished and well-connected Greek statesman and historian Polybius.) Demetrius was thus in Rome when the news came through that his uncle Epiphanes had died in Persia, and he promptly appeared as a suppliant before the Roman Senate for permission to return to Antioch and assume his rightful position as head of state. The Senate turned down his request.

Polybius records the very convincing arguments advanced by Demetrius and says that while the Senators were personally moved,

their public decision was to keep Demetrius in Rome and help to establish on the throne the surviving child of Antiochus IV. The Senate acted thus, in my opinion, because they were suspicious of a king in the prime of life like Demetrius and thought that the youth and incapacity of the boy who had succeeded to the throne would serve their purpose better (*Histories* XXXI.2).

Lysias was apprised of this episode by his intelligence agents in

Rome, and though he was relieved that the Senate had neutralized Demetrius – for the time being, at least – he was disquieted by the intentions of the royal relative. Out of this he developed a neurotic mistrust of all members of the family, fearing that they might seek to oust his young ward as the son of a usurper. There were two such persons who happened to be living in Antioch at that very time. One was the daughter of the redoubtable Antiochus III, and thus the sister of Seleucus IV and Antiochus IV and aunt both of Antiochus V and of Demetrius. Her name was Antiochis, and she went to the Seleucid capital, with her daughter, after the death of her husband, King Ariarathes IV of Cappadocia. (Cappadocia in Asia Minor, adjoining Seleucid Syria, is the ancient name of the eastern region of modern Turkey. After a spell as nominal vassal of the Seleucid empire, the nation proclaimed its independence in the middle of the third century BC, though its ruler, Ariarathes III, married a daughter of the reigning Seleucid. So did his successor, Ariarathes IV, taking to wife Antiochis. After the Seleucid defeat at the battle of Magnesia, Cappadocia became a client state of Rome.)

Though Lysias must have foreseen its effect on Cappadocia and Rome, he now instigated the assassination of these two women and thought he had thereby made his position more secure. He would soon rue this action.

In Rome, after Demetrius' appearance before them, the Senate took another decision which confirmed Polybius' surmise as to why they had held back the royal claimant, favouring a more fragile monarch.

*above* Polybius, the remarkable historian of the period and friend of Demetrius, as depicted on a stele found in Arcadia

*below* Patricians portrayed in stone, looking like a group of Roman Senators

A terracotta figurine, uncovered at Myrina (in Asia Minor), of an Indian war elephant attacking a Galatian soldier

They resolved to send a commission to Antioch to settle such matters as the breach of the treaty of Apamea by Lysias' use of war elephants in the campaign against Judea. Three legates, headed by Gnaeus Octavius, were accordingly sent to Syria with instructions, says Polybius, 'to burn the decked warships' – such ships had been banned under the treaty – 'to hamstring the elephants, and by every means to cripple the royal power'. No one was likely to oppose the Senate's orders 'since the king was a child' and the reigning clique, led by Lysias, 'were only too glad that the government had not been put in the hands of Demetrius'.

The Roman legates were also given additional missions in several of the neighbouring kingdoms, including Cappadocia, and it is possible that the murder of the queen mother and her daughter in Antioch may have occurred while they were *en route*, for king Ariarathes v, son and brother of the victims, urged upon Octavius that action be taken against the Seleucid rulers for their deed. Octavius took note of this counsel, and though he declined the offer of assistance for a joint punitive venture, he proceeded to Antioch and set about his task with greater fervour.

Vigorous action was taken to eliminate the fleet and the elephant squadrons – 'a pitiful sight', says Appian, 'the killing of these gentle and rare beasts'. But before it was completed, Octavius was assassinated by a fanatical Syrian Greek named Leptines. The records say that this occurred at Laodicea, the coastal city some 50 miles south of Antioch in the north-east corner of the Mediterranean, and it was probably there that the ships were being burned, a sight likely to inflame local passions.

The murder of a Roman legate, even one less distinguished than Octavius, could have disastrous consequences, understandably serving as a pretext for war if Rome so wished. Lysias appears to have been horrified and alarmed, fearing that he would be suspected of complicity, particularly after the assassination of Antiochis and her daughter. He therefore accorded Octavius a handsome funeral, with full honours, and hurriedly sent envoys to Rome who, says Polybius, 'were profuse in their assurances' to the Senate 'that the friends of the king had had no part in the deed'. The Senate decided to take no immediate action but to keep Lysias dangling in a state of uncertainty. They received the envoys coldly and gave no indication as to whether or not they accepted their master's plea of innocence.

The one man who was delighted with the news of Octavius' murder, and whose exploitation thereof was to have a profound effect on Judea and the rest of the empire, was Demetrius. In a fever of excitement, he at once sent for his sagacious friend Polybius, and

A flaming, torch-like *hanukkiah* kindled at a gathering on top of the dramatic rock of Masada, overlooking the Dead Sea, to celebrate the Hanukkah Festival

it is through him (*Histories* XXXI.11–15) that we have a first-hand account of the dramatic happenings that followed.

Demetrius wondered whether it would not be a good idea to appear again before the Senate, for they might now welcome his replacement of the young king and Lysias. 'Polybius' – he writes of himself in the third person – 'begged him not to stumble on the same stone', but rather 'to trust in himself and take some bold course worthy of a throne; for, he said, there were many opportunities for action suggested by the present situation'. Nevertheless, on the advice of another friend, young and inexperienced, Demetrius did petition the Senate and was again turned down. This was only to be expected, says Polybius, 'for on the former occasion it was not because Demetrius was not right in what he said that they had decided [as they did], but because it suited their own interest'.

Demetrius regretted his step, but was still ready to take a 'bold course' even though it was now more dangerous. He was encouraged in this by the latest intelligence he now received on the state of affairs in Antioch from an old and trusted friend who had just returned from a visit to Syria. This was Diodorus, who had been his foster-father and who was a shrewd political observer. Diodorus told Demetrius that there was 'great disturbance' in Antioch following the death of Octavius; that there was mutual distrust between 'Lysias and the populace'; and that 'the time was very favourable for his appearing suddenly on the scene. For the Syrians would at once transfer the crown to him, even if he appeared accompanied only by a single slave, while the Senate would not go so far as to help and support Lysias after his conduct.'

Thus, says Polybius, 'all that remained then was to escape from Rome secretly without anyone's having any notion of his plan', and Polybius himself was asked by Demetrius to help in contriving his adventurous departure. It has been suggested by modern scholars that though this would be an act contrary to the decision of the Senate, Polybius had reason to know that it would not displease men of influence among his Roman friends, though he was discreet enough not to mention the fact in the subsequent account he wrote.

Now come the cloak-and-dagger details of the escape. The principal snags were that Demetrius could not openly charter a boat, for this would quickly become known; he could not absent himself from Rome without arousing the curiosity of his friends – and the suspicions of the Senate; and, on the designated night, he could not dine at home, as he was wont to do with all the members of his large suite, for only a few trusted intimates were to be let into the secret.

Fortunately, an old confidant of Polybius, a certain Menyllus,

Demetrius attended a party on the night of his escape as a diversionary tactic. A party scene depicted on a Greek cup (*ca.* 500 BC)

happened to be in Rome at the time as an envoy of Ptolemy VI Philometor of Egypt. (Known as the elder Ptolemy, he was feuding with his brother, the younger Ptolemy, with whom he was sharing the throne at this period, with their sister Cleopatra as queen and wife of the elder Ptolemy.) Menyllus readily fell in with the escape plan and openly chartered a Carthaginian ship for the ostensible purpose of 'conveying himself home', back to Egypt. He could thus 'without any suspicion send on board a month's stock of provisions and could speak openly to the ship's officers and make arrangements with them'. The ship was anchored at Ostia, at the mouth of the Tiber.

As to Demetrius' absence from Rome, he would let it be known that he was off to hunt the wild boar for a few days. To give his story verisimilitude, he would send his slaves ahead to the hunting centre, keeping back only one who would accompany him on the voyage.

The dining problem on the appointed night was solved by arranging for a party at the house of an acquaintance which Demetrius would attend. Those of his trusted group who would be travelling with him would dine at home and make their way individually to the ship, 'each attended by one slave', after sending the other slaves to the hunting rendezvous 'saying they would follow them on the following day'.

The ship was ready. The time of departure was set for shortly before dawn so that the passengers would embark and be under way during the hours of darkness. They could leave Rome shortly after midnight and reach the vessel in good time. Demetrius went happily off to his party, having arranged for his travelling clothes to be taken earlier to a nearby hut.

The planning was meticulous. Every detail had been thought of. Polybius, who would be remaining in Rome, had fallen sick and was confined to bed. Now, as he lay there on that crucial evening pondering the bizarre enterprise in which he had become so intimately involved, he was suddenly struck by a shattering doubt. There was one tiny chink in an otherwise foolproof scheme, and it could put the entire venture at risk: Demetrius might get drunk at the party and pass out. The central character in this high drama, with control of an empire at stake, might miss the boat!

At this alarming thought, the old man jerked himself into a sitting position and dashed off a short but careful note calculated to sober the recipient. He summoned his slave and sent him off to the house where Demetrius was partying with orders to tell no one who he was but to ask for Demetrius' cup-bearer. To him he was to entrust the note with the urgent demand that his master read it at once.

The words of his mentor which Demetrius now read were interspersed with the wisdom of Epicharmus and Euripides, favourites of Polybius who knew their poetry and plays by heart:

> The doer is away with all the tarrier's gear.
> Night favours all alike but most the brave.
> Be brave and risk it, act to lose or win,
> Anything but to give thyself away.
> Be sober and remember to distrust;
> These are the sinews of the mind.
>
> (*Histories* XXXI.13, trans. W. R. Paton)

The note had the intended effect. Demetrius promptly excused himself to his hosts on the plea of sickness. After changing at the hut, he hurried off to Ostia and there found Menyllus waiting for him. Menyllus had just performed his final act in the stratagem by informing the captain that he had received a message from his king commanding him to stay in Rome for the present but 'to send on to him in advance the most trustworthy of his young soldiers'. These young men now appeared, eight of them in all, together with eight slaves, and climbed on board. 'The pilot heaved anchor just as it was getting light and set sail, having no idea at all of the truth, but fancying he was conveying some soldiers from Menyllus to Ptolemy.'

It was five days before the suspicions of the Senate were confirmed; but they took no precipitate action. Instead, they sent observers to Asia Minor to await the outcome of Demetrius' move and to gauge the reactions of the neighbouring kingdoms. Demetrius reached the Syrian shore at Tripolis (in today's Lebanon), 110 miles south of Antioch, where an advance group of his supporters had prepared the ground for his homecoming. The local population rallied to his cause and the army defected. Lysias and Antiochus V Eupator were seized by their troops and brought to Demetrius. The young royal cousins had never met. 'Don't let me see them', Demetrius told the guards, and they were immediately put to death. He was acclaimed by the people as the legitimate king and took the throne as Demetrius I. (A year and a half later, after a successful campaign in the east, he took the title Soter – Saviour – to mark his victory.)

Rome withheld recognition of the new monarch for the time being – and Judah was soon to take diplomatic advantage of the fact. Of more immediate concern to Demetrius was that Timarchus, the satrap of the Seleucids for Media and Babylonia, had proclaimed himself king, and Rome had promptly recognized his independence. This, too, was noted by Judah for future reference – and action. The Senate's diplomatic moves were designed to sharpen the conflict between the rebellious Timarchus and Demetrius and to leave both uncertain as to what Rome would do if they went to war. (In the event, when Demetrius finally took action against his eastern provinces, Rome failed to render military assistance to Timarchus and allowed him to go under. Indeed, with Demetrius' victory, the Senate granted him recognition. It all seems very confusing – and very contemporary – but, as Soloman Zeitlin points out, Rome's policy was 'to harass and confuse the governments of Asia Minor, in order ultimately to absorb them'. Judah was to learn something of the sophisticated intricacies of Roman diplomacy and seek to put it to useful effect – though there would be a Timarchus lesson for him too.)

Shortly after his accession, Demetrius appointed a new High Priest in Judea. This oak figure of a High Priest is an early 18th-century Dutch conception

It appears that shortly after Demetrius' arrival he appointed a new High Priest in Judea to replace the deceased Menelaus. The man he chose was Eliakim (or Jakim, better known by his hellenized name of Alcimus). The new king was in no mind to suffer the Judean experiences of his predecessors, and he thought Eliakim would be acceptable both to the traditionalist Jews – because he belonged to a priestly family of proper Aaronic descent – and to the hellenistic group in Jerusalem, to whom he had been close, although not an extremist. He was, in fact, welcomed by the hellenists and also accepted by many orthodox Jews, including the Hasidim; but he was anathema to the Maccabees because he was a Seleucid choice and was installed in Jerusalem with the support of foreign troops.

Demetrius had sent him back from Antioch accompanied by a military force under the command of a powerful general named Bacchides, who left some of his soldiers behind to bolster the new High Priest's authority.

(Exactly when Eliakim was appointed is the subject of controversy, for in the Books of Maccabees he first appears in the reign of Demetrius, whereas Josephus says the appointment was made several months earlier by Lysias. Some scholars hold to the Josephus view, considering that Lysias would not have left a hiatus after the elimination of Menelaus. It is clear, however, that Eliakim became active only after the accession of Demetrius.)

One of Eliakim's first acts in Jerusalem was to order the execution of sixty Hasidim, a deed which has baffled historians, since the Hasidim had been prepared to recognize him. It may be that the victims had caused trouble upon discovering that Eliakim (as mentioned in the Second Book of Maccabees 14:3) had participated in pagan practices during the bitter days of persecution. Or Eliakim may have had grounds for thinking that they were still in league with the Maccabees, and he wished to demonstrate his loyalty to Demetrius. It is probable that many Hasidim, cruelly surprised by Eliakim's action, returned to join Judah in the hills.

At about the same time, Bacchides, on his way back to Antioch after installing Eliakim, 'encamped in Bethzaith', a village not far from Gophna, and killed many of the Jews there, presumably suspecting them of Maccabean sympathies.

This behaviour by the new High Priest and the Seleucid general stirred up popular indignation and roused Judah to renewed action. He, his brothers and his veteran commanders again made their stealthy rounds at night to the Judean villages, gathering support for a continued struggle, reactivating the militia, harassing and killing the hellenizers and preventing Eliakim from officiating in the Temple or conducting the administrative affairs that went with his office. Eliakim appealed to Antioch for help, as his predecessors had done, and Demetrius sent a force to deal with the Maccabee rebels. It was headed by Nicanor, probably the same general who had been routed by Judah at Emmaus three years earlier.

Nicanor led his force straight to Jerusalem – probably via the south, for he encountered no opposition – and then moved north into the hills to flush out the Jewish rebels. But Judah, a guerilla once again and operating on home ground, set up elaborate ambush positions at Capharsalma (Kfar Shalem), roughly midway between Jerusalem and Beth Horon, and routed him. An infuriated Nicanor returned with his survivors to Jerusalem.

Nicanor now seems to have decided that the only way to put an

*overleaf* Judean hillsides, from which the Seleucid general Nicanor tried to flush the Jewish rebels

end to the Jewish rebels was to secure reinforcements from Antioch and, operating from his solid Jerusalem base and with an expanded army, proceed systematically to comb the hills. It was at the beginning of 161 BC that he was informed that troops from Syria were on their way to join him. The accounts in the ancient records of what happened next are somewhat obscure, the only positive details being that Nicanor met his reinforcements at Beth Horon and that the subsequent confrontation with Judah took place at Adasa, some 7 miles south-east of Beth Horon. It is probable that to save time, Nicanor ordered his Syrian reinforcements to take the quicker route through the Beth Horon pass rather than go all the way round and reach Jerusalem from the south. To ensure their safety in the hill-country, he would proceed with his force from Jerusalem and meet them at the pass. Together they would march to their Jerusalem base, familiarize the newcomers with the terrain and concert plans for their mopping up task.

On the appointed day, the reinforcements moved warily up the Beth Horon pass, after their long trek down the coast from the north, and Nicanor marched out with his men from Jerusalem in full battle array, with larger gaps than usual between his detachments, keenly on the alert for a surprise assault by the Maccabees. But the Maccabees seem to have melted into the countryside, for Nicanor reached the pass and joined up with his coastal force without mishap. He judged that Judah, who would have received intelligence on the reinforcements, must have been reluctant to expose himself to so large an army. Full of confidence, he led his combined force back to Jerusalem. They were less vigilant on the return journey, though Nicanor, as an experienced commander, would have warned them to be on the lookout for a possible attack from the north, where the rebels were concentrated, and had no doubt sent reconnaissance patrols ahead to investigate the territory north of his route.

Through his observers Judah knew the movements of both enemy forces and of their meeting at the pass. Even if he had not guessed their next step, his scouts would have seen the combined units heading back towards Jerusalem. He and his men had no doubt been only a short distance north of the midway point along the Jerusalem–Beth Horon route when Nicanor had passed by earlier and had probably seen him. Judah now took his followers quickly over the few hills and wadis that separated him from the main track, crossed it and set up assault positions along its southern edge, just south of Adasa. There they waited.

A short while later the enemy approached, expecting little trouble from their right flank, and the Maccabees took them by surprise. Nicanor himself was among the first casualties, and his troops panicked. Cut off from Jerusalem, they sought safety in escape and made for the coastal plain. The Maccabees gave chase, sounding trumpet signals in their pursuit which brought out the villagers along the way to join in the hunt. The enemy was driven as far west as the Seleucid fortress of Gazara (Gezer). The First Book of Maccabees 7:43 records that this battle occurred 'on the thirteenth day of the month of Adar' (about March). Thenceforth, this day would be observed by the Judeans as an annual holiday, known as the 'Day of Nicanor'.

Judea was peaceful. No immediate action was taken by Antioch to avenge the defeat of Nicanor. The emperor's prime concern at this moment was with the recovery of Media and Babylonia and the overthrow of his insubordinate tributary, Timarchus. Judah and his Maccabees were thus once again in virtual control of their land – still with the exception of the Acra citadel. It is not clear from the records whether Eliakim remained in Jerusalem or fled to Antioch; but even if he stayed, he would have lived within the protection of the Acra, unable to officiate at the Temple or exercise power as he had, briefly, after his installation by Bacchides. He and his hellenists were neutralized.

Judah now turned his mind to the prospects of advancing his cause by political means. This strange man, brought up on farming and the study of the religious books, who had taken naturally to guerilla fighting and risen to the leadership of his people by his military, organizational and administrative talents, showed ingenuity in his political thinking as he had in his operational planning. Lacking any formal training in politics or diplomacy, remote from imperial seats of power and the centres of decision making, he yet possessed a genius for thinking things out from first principles. Now, as he studied his political intelligence reports, his attention was caught by four facts. They made a pattern, and in its central motif he saw opportunity.

None of these facts was a secret. All were common knowledge throughout the region and had been included in his observers' accounts as routine items. These told of the Senate's displeasure at Demetrius' escape from Rome; its refusal to recognize his monarchy; the assertion of independence by Timarchus; and his recognition by Rome. Judah thought this pattern indicated a Roman willingness to help the enemies of Demetrius, and it was worth trying to secure the kind of treaty which had been granted to Timarchus.

Judah was not so naïve as to imagine that such a treaty was an automatic passport to independence, or that Rome's policy was guided by anything other than self-interest. She would not do battle on behalf of Judea for motives of benevolence; but she might claim to be doing so if she were seeking an additional pretext to make war on Antioch. Conversely, Demetrius would not throw up his arms and allow Judea to secede – unless he had reason to fear or mollify Rome. This seemed unlikely at the moment, for Judah had heard that Demetrius was well advanced in his plans to campaign against Timarchus despite the latter's alliance with Rome. Nevertheless, Demetrius would not wish to go on flouting Rome,

Judah the Maccabee sent ambassadors to the Senate to conclude a 'treaty of alliance with Rome'.
A 19th-century reconstruction of Rome's Forum

and the Senate's political friendship with Judea might conceivably serve as a deterrent. At any rate, it could create uncertainty in Demetrius' mind, and Judah did not feel there was anything to lose. He might be rebuffed by Rome, or he might secure a treaty which Demetrius would ignore. Either way, he would be in no worse position than he was now, enjoying temporary relief from danger but threatened at any time by another Seleucid attack.

He seems to have been unworried by his lack of any official authority. It was true that, in formal terms, he was no more than a simple Jew from the subject province of Judea, holding no appointment by the Seleucids and none by his own people. He might be their leader, but there had been no legally constituted assembly with a formal resolution elevating him to supreme office. However, Judah judged that Rome was familiar with his deeds and was well aware that he was for all practical purposes the ruler of Judea. Lack of title would prove no hindrance if Rome were willing; and a title was no crutch if she were reluctant.

He accordingly summoned two trusted colleagues and sent them to Rome. The men he chose were 'Eupolemus, son of John, son of Hakkoz, and Jason, son of Eleazar' (1 Macc. 8:17). (Hakkoz was the centuries-old name of a priestly family mentioned in Ezra 2:61 and is probably the same as Coz which appears in 1 Chronicles 4:8). Their Grecized first names suggest that they came either from hellenized homes which they had left to join the Maccabees or from upper-class families who had been influenced by hellenistic culture but had remained faithful to the Jewish religion. They were no doubt more worldly and articulate than the other officers in Judah's forces and well suited to argue the Maccabean case.

The two Judean ambassadors made the long journey to Rome and soon after their arrival were told that the Senate would receive them. This was indication enough that their mission was viewed with favour, and they wasted little time in coming to the point when they addressed the august Roman body: 'Judah, known as the Maccabee, his brothers, and the Jewish people have sent us to you', they said, 'to conclude a treaty of friendly alliance with you, so that we may be enrolled as your allies and friends'. The Romans found the proposal acceptable and inscribed the protocol on tablets of bronze, depositing one copy in the Capitol and sending the other to Judea. The text is recorded in the First Book of Maccabees 8:23-30:

The Rome-Maccabee treaty was inscribed by the Romans on 'tablets of bronze', and they retained one copy and sent the other to Judea. This 5th-century BC bronze tablet records a treaty between two Greek cities

Success to the Romans and the Jewish nation by sea and land for ever! May sword and foe be far from them! But if war breaks out first against

Rome or any of her allies throughout her dominion, then the Jewish nation shall support them whole-heartedly as occasion may require. To the enemies of Rome or of her allies the Jews shall neither give nor supply provisions, arms, money or ships; so Rome has decided; and they shall observe their commitments, without compensation.

Similarly, if war breaks out first against the Jewish nation, then the Romans shall give them hearty support as occasion may require. To their enemies there shall be given neither provisions, arms, money, nor ships; so Rome has decided. These commitments shall be kept without breach of faith.

These are the terms of the agreement which the Romans have made with the Jewish people. But if, hereafter, both parties shall agree to add or to rescind anything, then they shall do as they decide; any such addition or rescindment shall be valid.

To this the Romans added: 'As for the misdeeds which king Demetrius is perpetrating against the Jews, we have written to him as follows: "Why have you oppressed our friends and allies the Jews so harshly? If they make any further complaint against you, then we will see that justice is done them, and will make war upon you by sea and by land."'

Doubts have been expressed about the genuineness of this document on the grounds that recognition of Jewish independence would have been a *casus belli* between Rome and Demetrius and that, in fact, Rome did not intervene when Demetrius subsequently attacked Judea. But, as Edwyn Bevan writes: 'These objections have no force in view of the fact that Rome behaved in just the same way in regard to the rebel Timarchus. It recognized him as king, but allowed him to fall before Demetrius unassisted. The Senate had indeed no intention of intervening by armed force in Syria: it desired only to embarrass Demetrius, and that it did by giving countenance to his enemies.' Solomon Zeitlin says the same, and most other modern scholars are agreed on the authenticity of Rome's expression of friendship.

(Ninety-eight years later, Rome would conquer Judea and put her under subjection; and 133 years after that, a Roman general would destroy Jerusalem and drive the Jews from their land.)

Callous, cynical, calculating, the members of the Roman Senate were assuredly the shrewdest policy-makers at this period. They were in no hurry to make war on Seleucia, but they seized upon any occasion to hasten her internal collapse. Their friendly response to Judah's emissaries is a good example of how they operated. The treaty might dissuade Antioch from proceeding against Judea, in which case it would lose that province; or it might provoke both Demetrius and Judah into a more violent clash, which would further drain Antioch's resources. Either way the Seleucid empire would be weakened, and Rome would have enfeebled her foe with the simple inscription of a few astute words. (Even Justin, observing that 'on revolting from Demetrius, and soliciting the favour of the Romans, they [the Jews] were the first of all the eastern people that regained their liberty', finds himself moved to comment: 'the Romans readily affecting to bestow what it was not in their power to give'.)

We cannot know whether or not Judah harboured any illusion that Rome might come to his aid. But he was certainly aware of one consequence of the treaty to which the Senate had given no thought: its effect upon the Jews of Judea. This may have been a contributory purpose in his trying to secure it. Judah and his nucleus of Maccabee regulars were as popular as ever among their people, the traditionalists; but, as we have seen earlier, not all were enthusiastic about the fight for political independence now that religious freedom had been won. Yet their zealous support was essential for the success of Judah's new cause. It was crucial to the morale of his fighting men – and to his militia system. Earlier, before the anti-Jewish decrees had been annulled, families had willingly sent off their menfolk to fight the good fight and had cheerfully denied themselves to supply provisions for their troops. Now, unconvinced of the urgency or feasibility of the struggle, many were less eager to suffer these hardships, preferring to resume the untroubled pattern of their former lives. The Maccabee forces were thereby much reduced, and the fighting spirit even of Judah's stalwart supporters could well be impaired when next they went into action, knowing that they lacked whole-hearted popular backing.

In sending his emissaries, Judah may have thought that a treaty with powerful Rome might fire anew the waverers and the doubters, showing them that his goal of independence was no pipe dream but a practicable, realizable aim. For the very fact of an alliance, whatever the contractual obligations and whether they were kept or not, would mean that this mighty régime was treating Judea as an independent Jewish state – a status she had not enjoyed for more than four hundred years.

Subsequent events would show that Judah was overoptimistic. The compact with Rome did raise general morale, but this was not immediately reflected in the level of volunteering. However, the small though solid core of Maccabee fighters were more convinced than ever that the struggle for independence was worth pressing at all costs, and through them Jewish freedom would ultimately be regained.

But Judah would not live to see it.

# 12 The Death of Judah

The emperor Demetrius would have heard from his friends in Rome the somewhat startling news that rebel emissaries from one of his own provinces had arrived in the city. Knowing Rome so well, he would have been less startled by the follow-up report that the Senate had received them and approved their treaty request. It was just the kind of suave, sophisticated gesture he thought the Senate would make to remind him of its displeasure and to indicate its readiness to use the poison-tipped arrows in its diplomatic quiver to make his monarchic life difficult. It would incite his dependencies, intrigue with his neighbouring kingdoms, encourage his potential rivals. His every move would be watched, and he would need to tread warily. But he had no reason to panic. He judged that the Senate's act concealed no military threat, for he knew of its political conviction that it could afford to wait; and anyway if the Senate wanted war, it would have acted sooner, upon learning of his escape. He would therefore proceed undeterred with the policy he had apparently formulated upon reaching the throne: rehabilitate his kingdom, restore authority in all his tributaries and make manifest his firm control over the empire. He would then be able to deal with Rome – and with the other realms in the region – on terms of equality and from a position of strength.

Since his courier service was faster than Judah's, Demetrius probably learned of the treaty before anyone in Judea, and he decided on immediate action against the Maccabees. He would show Rome that he was not prepared to accept her dictates on his internal imperial affairs; and he would show Judea, and any other rebellious province, that seeking outside aid was a worthless exercise. Indeed, if he failed to act, he would be demonstrating to all that he could be frightened out of independent governance by a shake of the Senate's head.

Roman Senators, a detail from a 1st-century BC relief on the Altar of Peace in Rome

Moreover, one element in the Judean problem became urgently obtrusive at this time: the proximity of this province to Egypt. Ptolemaic designs to recover the territory between Egypt and Syria – wrested from them by Demetrius' grandfather – had never been abandoned, and every change of government in Antioch raised fresh hopes in Alexandria. There had been stirrings in the Egyptian capital upon the death of Epiphanes; and now, with the accession of Demetrius, there was renewed expectancy. The loss of Judea would thus greatly magnify the danger from Egypt; for Judean independence, coupled with a Rome-Judea mutual-aid pact, could well lead to an alliance between Alexandria and Jerusalem, and the Ptolemies would be almost at his doorstep. If for no other reason than to stifle this threat, Judea had to be subdued.

Demetrius did not think the task would be difficult if he put his resources behind the effort and chose a good general. Nicanor's reverses were put down to incompetence, for Seleucid intelligence sources showed that the Judeans were less discontented and resistance was not as strong or as widespread as it had been. The problem was simply one of eliminating the Maccabee rebels, and they were now fewer in number. Thereafter, religious toleration would be maintained, to give the population no pressing cause for revolt, and the province would be fortified and properly garrisoned to keep it quiet. He would send in Bacchides and put a large force at his disposal to conduct a swift and effective operation.

Bacchides left Syria at the head of twenty thousand infantry and two thousand cavalry and marched south through eastern Galilee, taking time off to slaughter the Jews of Arbela, just west of the Sea of Galilee, which lay along his route. He then made straight for Jerusalem. Judah could do little to stop him, for he now had comparatively few men under his command. All he could muster were 'three thousand picked men' (1 Macc. 9:5), and his only hope lay in the possibility that Bacchides might split his army when he came to scour the hills.

The Seleucid general completed his preparations and moved north from Jerusalem, establishing his base at 'Berea' (1 Macc. 9:4), which some scholars identify with the modern El-Bireh, close to Ramallah, 8 miles north of Jerusalem; some put it nearer to Gophna; while others hold it was closer to the capital. According to Josephus (*Antiquities* XII.422), Judah and his men were encamped near the village of Berzetho, just south of Gophna. When Bacchides proceeded further north, Judah wheeled slightly south-west, possibly with the intention of cutting him off from his operational base, and the two armies clashed at a place called Elasa, some 6 miles east of Beth Horon.

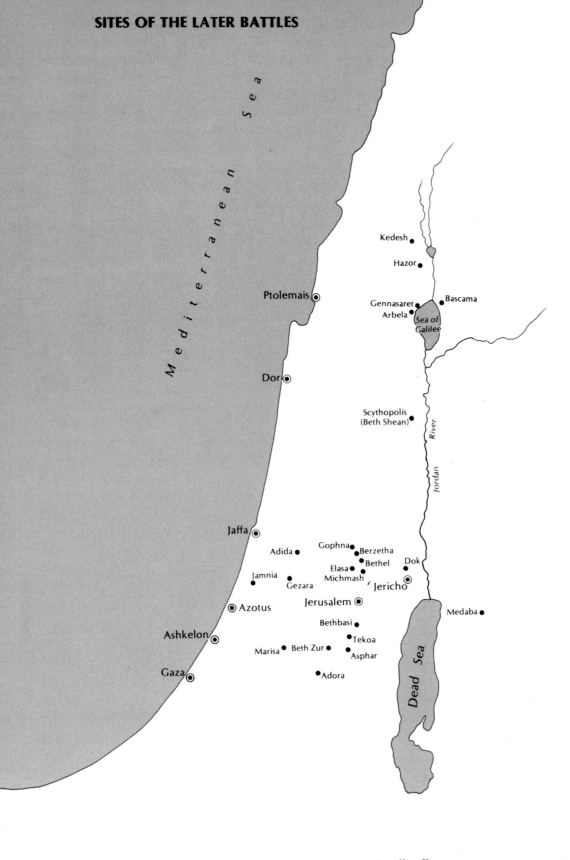

# SITES OF THE LATER BATTLES

Mediterranean Sea

Kedesh

Hazor

Ptolemais

Gennasaret
Arbela
Bascama
Sea of Galilee

Dor

Scythopolis
(Beth Shean)

Jordan River

Jaffa

Adida
Gophna
Berzetha
Bethel
Elasa
Dok
Jamnia
Michmash
Gezara
Jericho

Azotus
Jerusalem

Bethbasi
Medaba

Ashkelon
Tekoa
Marisa
Beth Zur
Asphar

Dead Sea

Gaza
Adora

0    10    20
km

The numerical odds were so overwhelmingly against him that Judah's attack was suicidal. He had started out with only three thousand combatants, few enough to face the host of well-armed enemy troops. But even those few became fewer still when they saw what they were up against. When their eyes beheld 'the size of the enemy forces, their courage failed, and many deserted, leaving a mere eight hundred men in the field' (1 Macc. 9:6). It was the saddest moment of Judah's life.

He tried to rally those who were left: 'Let us move to the attack and see if we can defeat them.' The very phrasing of his appeal showed desperation. His comrades sought to dissuade him, citing the course he himself would have followed during the early days at Gophna. 'Impossible,' they said. 'No; let us save our lives now and come back later with our comrades to fight them. Now we are too few.' But Judah replied: 'Heaven forbid that I should do such a thing as run away! If our time is come, let us die bravely for our fellow-countrymen, and leave no stain on our honour' (1 Macc. 9:8–10).

His men, brave as he, followed him, though they clearly felt, for the first time, that he was making a gross tactical error. He was abandoning one of the key principles he had taught them of guerilla warfare – to 'melt' when faced by a superior foe who was in a position to exploit his advantages. Judah, for his part, did not feel he was spurning that guerilla axiom. True, he had frequently avoided a confrontation with the enemy when he considered the conditions unfavourable. But his decision in those cases to 'melt into the countryside' and let the enemy chase phantom targets had always been taken *in advance*. He had never 'run away' once he had decided on battle, and his persistence had proved itself. When he had planned his response to the threat of Bacchides, he thought he might succeed with a force of three thousand. Now that it had dwindled, he knew the chances were slender; but he judged that flight, added to the earlier desertions, would demoralize the people of Judea and crush the very heart of the resistance movement, whereas fighting to the death could keep it alive. He and his eight hundred went into action.

There are enough details in the ancient records to reveal the pattern of the battle.

The [enemy] cavalry was divided into two detachments; the slingers and the archers went ahead of the main force, and the picked troops were in the front line. Bacchides was on the right. The phalanx came on in two divisions . . . When Judah saw that Bacchides and the main strength of his army was on the right flank, all his stout-hearted men rallied to

Bacchides' army, from an illuminated manuscript made by the Crusaders in Acre

him, and they broke the [enemy's] right; then he pursued them . . . When the [enemy] on the left wing saw that their right had been broken, they turned about and followed on the heels of Judah and his men, attacking them in the rear . . . (I Macc. 9:11–16).

Judah concentrated his attack on the enemy's right flank because Bacchides was there, and if he could eliminate the commander he might break the spirit of the other ranks. He accordingly summoned for this task his best fighters, leaving a weaker unit to face the enemy's left flank. In the event, he won through with his daring and tenacious assault against such heavy odds, and the Seleucid right flank crumbled, turned and fled, with Judah and his unit in hot pursuit. But Bacchides was not a casualty; and he had also been fortunate in his choice of a subordinate, the divisional commander on his left flank. Seeing what happened, this officer, who had almost overwhelmed the weaker Maccabee unit opposing him, left them to help his fleeing right flank and he started chasing the Jewish pursuers. Judah's unit thus found themselves sandwiched between the two enemy divisions, with Bacchides ahead in flight and his subordinate in the rear in pursuit. At some point during this grim dawn to dusk battle, Bacchides must have gathered what his other division was up to, and he turned to face Judah, holding him until the arrival of his subordinate. The two enemy divisions thus formed two arms of a nutcracker, with Judah in the middle. 'The fighting became very heavy, and many fell on both sides.' Among the killed was Judah.

The death of Judah, as conceived by the illustrator of the 12th-century Latin Bible in Winchester Cathedral

Demetrius and Bacchides could rejoice at having succeeded where their predecessors had failed, and for the first time in six years there was a feeling of confidence in Antioch that troublesome Judea held no further dangers. To them, the death of Judah clearly spelled the death of the Maccabee movement, Jewish resistance and the prospects of renewed Jewish independence. The Judeans were indeed dispirited as they mourned the passing of their hero: 'How is our champion fallen, the saviour of Israel!' (1 Macc. 9:21). But Judah, the ingenious fighter, magnetic leader and imaginative statesman, had also been a great educator, and his influence was greater than he knew. He had educated by fervent inculcation and above all by example, and had re-sown an historic seed which would grow into an ineradicable plant, a flowering plant that would long outlive him. The struggle would be continued by his faithful comrades, and some of them would live to see the realization of his aim, though they would traverse the long dark valley before they gained it.

Bacchides returned to Jerusalem after his decisive victory and promptly put into effect a systematic plan to preserve imperial authority in Judea. He built a series of fortresses and strengthened existing ones, which effectively ringed the province, and in them he 'placed forces and stores of provisions'. He refortified the Acra citadel, the fortress of Beth Zur to the south of Jerusalem and Gazara to the north-west. The new bases were established at Emmaus and Beth Horon to the north-west; at Bethel, due north; at Jericho, north-east of the capital; and at 'Timnath, Parathon and Tephon', whose exact location is not known but which filled the gaps in the ring. These forts constituted a strong military presence in the most populous sector of Judea – the hills north of Jerusalem – and commanded the passes and gateways into the province, thus making guerilla operations intensely difficult in the very region which had given birth and growth to the Maccabees. As an added measure to keep the Judeans subdued, Bacchides rounded up the sons of the leading traditionalist and nationalist families 'as hostages and put them under guard in the citadel at Jerusalem'.

Eliakim could now function as High Priest without disturbance, and he and his hellenistic Jewish group conducted the day-to-day administration of the land under the overall direction of Bacchides and with the support of his troops. Though freedom of Jewish worship was respected, Eliakim and his colleagues, loyal to Antioch, 'set inquiries on foot, and tracked down the friends of Judah and brought them before Bacchides, who took vengeance on them . . . It was a time of great affliction for Israel' (1 Macc. 9:26,27). To root out the spirit of Jewish revolt, Bacchides was determined to destroy the surviving rebels, and though Judah was already dead, the Seleucid general had heard with disquiet that his three remaining brothers, Johanan, Simon and Jonathan, were still at large. They had in fact participated in the battle of Elasa and had somehow managed to retrieve the body of Judah from the battlefield and bury him in the family tomb at Modi'in.

Hiding out in their familiar haunts in the hills during the days and weeks following their disaster at Elasa, the Maccabee veterans learned from their trusted friends in the villages of the steps being taken by Bacchides and Eliakim to reduce Judea to rigorous subjection. Bacchides, they heard, unlike the earlier generals, was remaining to supervise the 'pacification' of the province, together with the bulk of his considerable force, and their all-pervasive presence, plus their new fortresses, would make positive action virtually impossible. They had no intention of abandoning their struggle, but there was no immediate future for them in this region north of Jerusalem. They would be fugitives constantly on the run, a danger to the friendly villagers who gave them shelter and powerless even to dent the formidable military machine the enemy now disposed. They could of course disperse, and their small scattered detachments could engage in minor harassment. But this would be no more than pin-pricking, doing no major damage yet bringing violent reprisals upon the population. Moreover, the odds were now such that rebel detachments would soon be caught. They were not repelled by this thought for they had long proved their readiness to die in the struggle; but they felt it was better to give their lives to more effective purpose, and the wisest course was clearly to lie low for a time, rebuild their strength and renew their operations when circumstances were more propitious and they could strike a more telling blow.

The first act of the assembled survivors of Elasa was to choose a replacement for Judah, and they turned to Jonathan, although he was the youngest of Mattathias' sons. 'Since your brother Judah died, there has not been a man like him to take the lead against our enemies, Bacchides and those of our own nation who are hostile to us. Today, therefore, we choose you to succeed him as our ruler and leader and to fight our battles' (1 Macc. 9:29,30). Jonathan commanded them with the close support of his older brothers Johanan and Simon.

Jonathan was equally of the opinion that if they were to live to fight another day they needed a period of recovery, and it would be prudent for them to remove themselves from populated Judea –

The wilderness between Jerusalem and the Dead Sea, where Jonathan took refuge and built up his strength. After defeating Bacchides, he was able to return to northern Judea

and from the heavy hand of Bacchides. They accordingly set off at night and made their way southwards, taking 'refuge in the desert of Tekoa' and 'encamping by the pool of Asphar'. The wilderness of Tekoa is part of the Judean Desert, lying south-east of Jerusalem between the capital and the Dead Sea, and this rugged region, pocked with caves, had long been a favoured hide-out for rebels and a refuge for the persecuted despite its comparative proximity to the fringe settlements of Judea. (David had come here eight centuries earlier when fleeing from the wrath of Saul.) The village of Tekoa, birth-place of the prophet Amos, lies some 5 miles south-east of Bethlehem, and the pool or well of Asphar is about 3 miles further south.

Bacchides made an initial foray against the fugitive Maccabees, but they slipped from his grasp. He would have wished to eliminate the last of the rebel leaders, but he found that hunting them down in the bleak and rocky Dead Sea terrain would take too much time and too many men, and they were not worth this expense, for they were few in number and isolated from the main body of their people. He therefore returned to Jerusalem and continued with his fortification programme, to isolate them further and strengthen his hold on Judea. Jonathan, for his part, established his group in the wilderness, where they lived off the flocks and herds they had brought with them from the north, and resolved to await a favourable opportunity for the renewal of active rebellion. It was evidently his belief that before long, with Judea quiescent, the occupation forces would be reduced and those who remained, bored with inactivity, would be less vigilant. That would be the appropriate moment for the Maccabees to infiltrate, expand their volunteer force, start harassing the ruling hellenists and the enemy troops and revive popular support for the resistance. Jonathan would also watch out for changes in the political constellation in Antioch which could be to his advantage – and he, of all the Hasmonean brothers, was particularly responsive to political opportunity.

In the meantime, he would maintain the military organization of his veteran group, hold to a regular training programme and restore contact with the villagers by frequent nightly couriers. This service would also provide him with intelligence on developments in Judea. It is probable, too, that the three brothers paid occasional secret visits to their old village friends – just as they had when they first reached Gophna – to encourage volunteering even during this waiting phase. It was their aim, while in the wilderness, to build a capacity to swing into action, in strength, when the time was ripe.

In their new life, the Maccabees were in frequent contact – at times friendly, at times hostile – with tribal groups on both sides of the Jordan and the Dead Sea. There was, for example, a warm association with the Nabateans in Transjordan, the people who had been so helpful to Judah a few years earlier when he had sped to the relief of the beleaguered Jews in Gilead. As for hostility, the records speak of an early conflict with the 'sons of Jambri' who 'appeared from Medaba', a few miles east of the Dead Sea, and attacked a party being led by Johanan. The Maccabees had just arrived in the area and were presumed by this tribe to be easy prey. Johanan was killed and the flocks in his charge were stolen. Jonathan and Simon quickly retaliated. Setting up a skilful ambush after careful reconnaissance, they avenged their brother's death and recovered their animals. Thereafter, most of the local tribes gave them no trouble.

More than a year passed, with Bacchides still in Jerusalem, exerting his authority over an outwardly placid Judea, and the High Priest Eliakim and his hellenistic colleagues conducting their administrative functions under his patronage. Since the general wanted calm in the province, his minions were careful to give the traditionalist Jews no cause for popular disturbances, and they were allowed to follow their religious rites and worship at their sanctuary in Jerusalem in the time-honoured fashion. However, in the

The courts of the Temple, from the reconstruction at the Holyland Hotel, Jerusalem

spring of 159 BC, Eliakim gave 'orders for the wall of the inner court to be demolished', which would have had the effect of allowing idolaters to approach the sanctuary. Adjacent to the Temple buildings were three courts in which the Jews alone were allowed to set foot: the Court of the Priests, the Court of the Israelites and the Court of the Women. Surrounding these inner courts was a wall or screen which separated them from the outer court, where Gentiles were permitted. Eliakim's order would thus have given pagans free access to an area reserved for members of the faith, and it greatly angered the devout Jews. Fortuitously, at the very moment when the demolition work was about to begin, Eliakim 'had a [paralytic] stroke, which put a stop to his activities'. He died soon after.

Bacchides was in no whit put out by Eliakim's death. He had gained no profit from this man. If anything, Eliakim had been an embarrassment. He was unpopular with most traditionalist Jews and barely tolerated by the others; he was given to impulsive follies which aroused needless passions and added to Bacchides' burdens; he had converted none of the reluctant populace into Seleucid enthusiasts; and he could hold office only with the backing of the occupation troops. With such military backing Bacchides reckoned that any hellenistic Jew could administer the sullen Judeans, and if he did so without an official appointment to the high priesthood, he would probably be more acceptable to the public. It was assuredly at Bacchides' recommendation that Demetrius named no successor to Eliakim, and for the next seven years the Jews were to be without a High Priest. Indeed, so confident was Bacchides of a relaxation of tensions in Judea by the introduction of this policy that he returned to Antioch shortly after the death of Eliakim. And 'for two years Judea had peace' (I Macc. 9:57).

Jonathan put those two years to good use, taking advantage, after Bacchides' departure, of the growing military laxity which crept into the occupation garrisons, and of the faltering administration of Eliakim's untitled hellenistic heirs. He and his men were still outlawed, but they could now make more frequent visits to the villages, albeit still stealthily, and rebuild a national organization of revolt. It was by such visits that Jonathan, Simon and their veteran commanders were able to fire the people with a renewed spirit of resistance, establish underground cells among the trusted villagers, reconstitute the intelligence and communications system and encourage volunteering. After a time, having gained more adherents, they were able to start small-scale guerilla operations along the lines they had conducted seven years earlier from Gophna. They harassed

enemy patrols and made life dangerous for the hellenistic collaborators. Gradually, as their forays grew in scope and intensity, the
garrison forces in the province stayed close to their fortresses, and
the hellenistic Jews and headquarters troops were largely confined
to Jerusalem. Judea was again being lost to the rebels.

The cry went out from the Acra to Antioch that Bacchides again
be sent south to re-establish imperial authority. It was suggested
to him by the hellenistic Jews that while their rivals, the Maccabee
nationalists, had become stronger, they could be crushed if their
leading commanders were caught, and this might not prove difficult.
They themselves had contrived a plan to kidnap Jonathan and his
fellow officers. In response to their appeal, Bacchides began the
march to Jerusalem. Meanwhile the hellenists put their kidnap plan
into effect, but Jonathan had received advance intelligence, and the
trappers were themselves trapped. The Maccabees caught fifty of
them and put them to death.

Jonathan then occupied 'Bethbasi in the desert, built up its ruined
fortifications, and strengthened it'. (The geographer Felix Marie
Abel identifies Bethbasi with Khirbet Beit-bassa, south-east of
Bethlehem.) Jonathan apparently now felt confident enough to
establish a base in this old abandoned fortress quite close to a settled
sector of Judea. He refortified it so that it might withstand a long
siege, though he had no intention of shutting up all his men behind
its walls. When Bacchides arrived in Jerusalem and learned where
the rebels were, he soon moved south to engage them.

Jonathan had expected it. He split his forces in two, left one under
Simon's command inside Bethbasi and took the other out into the
desert, after arranging a stratagem with his brother. Bacchides
reached the Maccabee base and tried to take it by assault to snatch
a quick victory; but he was repulsed and forced to take the longer
course and put it under siege. Simon was well able to hold out
during the time the enemy was building its field works and erecting
its siege-engines. Meanwhile, Jonathan had made contact with two
desert tribes, Odomera and Phasiron, and, according to Josephus,
persuaded them to join in an attack on Bacchides. (There is a textual
contradiction on this point. The standard Greek translation of the
original Hebrew First Book of Maccabees records that, in fact, the
two tribes were hostile and Jonathan 'attacked Odomera and his
people and the tribe of Phasiron in their encampment' [1 Macc.
9:66]; but some early Greek manuscripts suggest that the tribesmen
were Jonathan's friends, and Josephus presumably based himself on
one such translation.) At all events, either with or without reinforcements from these two tribes, Jonathan eventually made his way
back to Bethbasi and launched a surprise assault on the rear of

Bacchides' besieging forces. Simon had been waiting for this, and, by pre-arrangement, he now sallied forth from his fortress, set fire to the siege-engines and engaged the enemy in close combat. Bacchides' men, worn down by frustration and boredom during the lengthy vigil outside the walls, were now caught between the two contingents of the Maccabees who were pressing them from front and rear in unexpected strength. Bacchides quickly saw that the rebels had the upper hand and he broke off as soon as he was able, retiring with the remnant of his army to Jerusalem.

He was filled with fury – less towards the fighting Jews he had just met on the battlefield than towards the hellenized Jews of Jerusalem who had misled him. They had promised him an easy victory, and the strength and stubbornness of the Maccabees had thus taken him by surprise. He was so angry with 'the renegades at whose instance he had invaded the land' that 'many of them were put to death' (1 Macc. 9:69).

It was a dismal act for an experienced general, who should have relied on his own combat intelligence; and his vengeance on the hellenists, to show that they were to blame, was a poor face-saver for his bitter defeat. But Jonathan, who soon heard the news, was quick to exploit it with a timely approach to the Seleucid general. He judged that Bacchides, exasperated with the hellenists, irritated by their impotence in administering the province and tired of having to be called in time and again to restore authority, might be receptive to a proposal for a *modus vivendi* with the Maccabees. He accordingly despatched envoys to Bacchides, and when the general announced his readiness to receive them, it was clear that, as Jonathan had guessed, he was in a mood to negotiate.

The records give no details of the negotiations, saying only that Jonathan's representatives went 'to arrange terms of peace with him [Bacchides] and a return of Jewish prisoners' and that 'Bacchides agreed and did as Jonathan proposed, swearing to do him no harm for the rest of his life' (1 Macc. 9:70, 71). It is evident from subsequent events that Jonathan did not press for outright independence, for the general was neither disposed nor empowered to grant it. Instead, he limited his demands to those which might commend themselves to Bacchides as reasonable and innocent, yet which would in fact advance the cause of autonomy. The concessions by Bacchides were an amnesty for the rebels; permission for them to return to and reside in Judea; the return of Jewish prisoners of war, though not of the hostages who were in the Acra; and the reaffirmation of Jewish religious freedom. Jonathan, in return no doubt, promised to keep the peace and accept the continued status of Judea as a Seleucid dependency. It would be administered by the Jewish hellenists with the aid of the main Seleucid force garrisoned in the Acra Fortress. It is not clear from the records whether it was now or later that, by government permission, 'Jonathan took up residence in Michmash' (the site of a dramatic battle between Saul and the Philistines eight centuries earlier). Following this agreement, Bacchides left the land of the Jews and 'never again did he enter their territory. So the war came to an end in Israel' (1 Macc. 9:72, 73). The date was 156 or 155 BC.

The Maccabees were no longer outlaws, no longer on the run. For the first time, they could plan their moves in the drive towards independence calmly, unhurriedly and in comparative security. Michmash had been well chosen as their base. It was in the heart of their own familiar country, the Judean hills north of Jerusalem, and surrounded by villages they had known in their youth. It lay roughly midway between Jerusalem and Gophna, about 9 miles from each, and about 17 miles east of Modi'in.

It would have been easy for Jonathan to have launched a guerilla campaign on the morrow of Bacchides' departure. But to what purpose? It would only invite another invasion, perhaps another flight, possibly another return, and then what? Their goal would be as distant as ever, and they would lose what they had already gained. Jonathan considered that the urgent need now was not to go back to their Gophna beginnings but forward from the point to which their military exploits had brought them, using their considerable accomplishments as a spring-board for a further leap towards independence. That leap should now be political, albeit backed by a military potential, and Jonathan thought the circumstances favourable for political manoeuvering. The Bacchides agreement represented the second occasion, after the compromise peace offer by Lysias, that a Seleucid general had treated with the rebels; but it was the first time that the rebels, and the rebel leader, were officially recognized. This, to Jonathan, provided an important political base from which to advance.

Such thinking brought about a change in Maccabee tactics and a change in emphasis on certain immediate targets. So far, while there had been a good deal of fighting against the Jewish hellenists, the Maccabee shafts had been directed primarily at the Seleucid army. Jonathan now thought that they should avoid clashes with enemy troops for a time and seek instead to crush the hellenist party. He knew that Antioch must be sorely disappointed in these Jewish collaborators who had consistently failed to 'deliver' a peaceful Judea. Yet the imperial authorities continued to treat them as the official representatives of the province and to administer the territory through them. However, both Lysias in his day and now Bacchides had, at critical moments and over their protest, put them in their place and dealt directly with the rebels. They had done so for the pragmatic reason that the rebels were the only ones with the power to give them – for a price – what they wanted on those occasions: a trouble-free province. If Jonathan could now so weaken the hellenists as to demonstrate to Antioch their utter uselessness as a Seleucid political instrument, Antioch might eventually turn to the Maccabees as the only effective and representative party, however much she hated them and however reluctant she would be to pay their political price.

To put his plan into operation, Jonathan needed an initial period of quiet. If he gave the authorities no trouble, he would induce in them a sense of security. The troops, with little to do, no revolt to crush and no guerillas to chase – or fear – would fall into a routine of indolence. They would become complacent, indifferent to Judea's domestic affairs and less inclined to appear as instruments of the Jewish hellenistic administrators. The hellenists might wish them to take vengeful action against the Maccabees, but after the Bacchides agreement, they were unlikely to do so unless the Maccabees harassed them. Jonathan, Simon and their commanders would use this peaceful period to move around the province, quietly expanding their popular base and preparing both old supporters and new enthusiasts for the day when they could move forward to political freedom.

Thus it came about, as observed in the records, that 'war came to an end' and Judea knew peace. This was duly reported to Antioch in the regular despatches from the commander of the Acra, and apparently the occupation forces were gradually reduced and only token garrisons retained to man the fortresses in the province. Meanwhile, Jonathan and his colleagues were enjoying considerable success in their psychological preparation of the public. They were popular heroes, but they were also respected for their proven judgement. After all, it had been their resistance policy and deeds which had saved Judaism and won them the restoration of religious liberty in Judah's time; and now Judah's young brother had secured an agreement, and recognition, from General Bacchides. If Jonathan now assured them that independence was within their reach, his words were worth heeding. He was certainly not an impulsive man. He was a thoughtful soldier who knew how and when to fight, and also when to sheathe his sword, and he won the trust of his people as a wise and mature leader.

There came a day when Jonathan judged he was ready for action. The records say only that he began 'rooting the godless out of

Israel' (1 Macc. 9:73), but it is not difficult to reconstruct the pattern. He probably started by moving out with his men to one or two villages known to be harbouring some prominent Jewish hellenistic collaborators and killing them, to demonstrate that such conduct would henceforth not be tolerated in Judea. After a few days of this grim activity, the appeals for help by the families of the victims – and the projected victims – would reach the administrators in Jerusalem, and these would call upon the troops to act. The garrison commanders would have been reluctant to do so, since there had been no attacks on their troops and it was no longer their business, as it had been under Antiochus, to impose hellenism upon the public. Nor would they have been eager to intervene in what they would have considered a private squabble between the Jews which was being fought out in the rural areas. It would have been different if the lives of the administrators in Jerusalem were in danger, for they were the representatives of Seleucia and it was the army's job to protect them. But they had not been threatened, and the Maccabees had made no attempt to extend their activities to Jerusalem, the Seleucid administrative and military centre in Judea. An appeal by the hellenists to Antioch would have been similarly ignored, for the same reasons: so long as there was no general rising, no armed attack on the imperial garrisons and no threat to Jerusalem, Seleucid prestige was not involved and no action was called for. Certainly no one in Antioch now would have felt disposed to sending an expedition to prevent the killing of a few Jews, whether hellenist or traditionalist. But there were more pressing reasons for Antioch's failure to intervene. The emperor Demetrius had run into grave difficulties with several of his neighbouring kingdoms, and they were in the process of forming an alliance to dethrone him. He could spare little thought and few men for Judea; and what thought he did give to that province, based on reports of the dwindling power of his hellenistic nominees, only confirmed his melancholy conviction that they were, and had always been, a broken reed. It was best to write them off.

Without Seleucid help, the hellenist administrators were powerless, unable to assert their authority over a hostile public. The population rallied to their nationalist leader who held out the hope of independence, and Jonathan was able to proceed from sector to sector rooting out the would-be collaborators until the whole of rural Judea was under his control. And Jonathan 'began to govern the people' (1 Macc. 9:73).

He still lacked official status; but formal recognition would soon be forthcoming. And Jerusalem was still outside the area of his effective rule; but that, too, would not be for long.

# 13   The Royal Bidders

Major rewards for their tenacious resistance – and political sagacity –
began to flow to Jonathan and the Maccabees in the year 152 BC.
The dramatic upswing in their fortunes was occasioned not by
any fresh military action by them but by the diplomatic intrigues
of others, and by events not in Judea but in Antioch and Rome,
Cappadocia, Pergamum and Egypt. By following these events and
being alert to the changes of alignment they wrought, Jonathan
was able to bring Judea to the very threshold of independence.

The ambitious Demetrius had vigorously striven to restore the
greatness and grandeur of the Seleucid empire, the aim he had set
himself upon his escape from Rome. In the decade since then, he
had worsted his enemies in the eastern provinces, secured a form of
stability in Judea and begun to make his influence felt in the Asia
Minor kingdoms to his north-west (which had once belonged to
the House of Seleucus). In the process, he had inevitably deepened
the disapproval of Rome and the anxieties of the neighbouring
kingdoms, all of whom would have preferred a weakling in his
place. Anxiety turned to downright hostility when Demetrius took
a hand in the power struggle between his cousins in Cappadocia.
The king, Ariarathes v (whose mother and sister had been murdered
by Lysias), was backed by King Attalus II of Pergamum (near the
western coast of modern Turkey); Ariarathes' rebellious brother
(Ophernes) was supported by Demetrius. Ariarathes won, and
he and Attalus never forgave Demetrius. These two kings were soon
joined in their hostility to the Seleucid monarch by a more important third. He was Ptolemy vi Philometor of Egypt. (It was his
ambassador, Menyllus, who had chartered the ship at Ostia on which
Demetrius had fled from Rome.) Philometor had been friendly
with the young king, but he was incensed when Demetrius tried
(by bribing the local governor) to take one of his prized possessions,

Ptolemy vi Philometor of
Egypt, who supported the
royal claims of Alexander
Balas and helped overthrow
Demetrius

Bronze statuette of Alexander Balas, who defeated Demetrius and succeeded to the Seleucid throne

Coins struck by Seleucid rulers, from left to right: *top row* Antiochus IV Epiphanes; Antiochus V Eupator *second row* Demetrius I Soter; Alexander Balas *third row* Demetrius II Nicator; Antiochus VI Dionysos; Tryphon *fourth row* Antiochus VII Sidetes; Cleopatra Thea with her son Antiochus VIII Grypus

the island of Cyprus. (The attempt failed. The plot was discovered and the governor hanged himself.)

The three monarchs made a compact to oust Demetrius from his throne, and it was Attalus who fathered an ingenious scheme to gain this end. He found a young man in Smyrna who bore a strong resemblance to a former Seleucid emperor – Demetrius' uncle, Antiochus IV Epiphanes! The youth was a certain Balas – he was given the added name of Alexander for obvious promotional purposes – and King Attalus asserted that he was Epiphanes' son and thus a serious claimant to the Seleucid monarchy. [Edwyn Bevan is right to point out (in his *House of Seleucus*) that Alexander Balas is referred to in all the early Greek sources as an imposter, and this came to be accepted as the standard view by later historians. But the main source was Polybius, and he, as we have seen, had been very close to Alexander's rival, Demetrius. Bevan adds this charitable conclusion: 'On the whole, it seems to me probable that Alexander was an imposter; but unless we have reason to believe that later on someone concerned in the deception (e.g., Attalus or Ptolemy Philometor) made an avowal, I do not see that we can speak positively.']

Attalus arranged for a trusted envoy, sophisticated in the ways of the Senate (and with good personal reason, as the brother of the dead satrap Timarchus, to hate Demetrius), to take Alexander to Rome and present him as the authentic son of the late Emperor Antiochus. Polybius says (in *Histories* XXXIII. 15) that the envoy 'made a long stay there, trying by means of jugglery and base intrigue to work upon the Senate'. He succeeded, for it appears that Rome, as anxious as the three kings to see Demetrius replaced, granted recognition to Alexander at the beginning of 152 BC. What happened next, in the summer of that year, caused consternation in the court at Antioch as Demetrius saw his imperial world about to tumble: Alexander Balas, with the support of the allied monarchs, principally Philometor, landed on the coast of Palestine and secured a footing in Ptolemais (Acre). He was greeted by the local populace and proclaimed himself king.

Demetrius was in a serious predicament, with nowhere to turn. He was without allies and unpopular with his own subjects, for whom he had shown open contempt. (Polybius says he took solace in drink, 'and was tipsy for the greater part of the day'.) He was sadly aware of the backing enjoyed by Alexander, and if he took immediate action against this pretender, he might find himself at war with Egypt, Cappadocia, Pergamum – and possibly Rome. If this happened, some of his provinces might seize the occasion to rise against him. On the other hand, he could hardly remain passive,

for this would be a display of craven weakness which his enemies and his champing tributaries would be quick to exploit. He saw as his immediate danger an attempt by Alexander, with Philometor's help, to swing the buffer province of Judea over to his side. This would give him a solid hinterland running south from Ptolemais all the way to Egypt to brace a determined northern thrust at Antioch, the heart of the empire. The logical first step for Demetrius was thus to secure the active support of Judea, which would cut Alexander's land contact with Egypt and pose a threat to him from the south. Demetrius could then move from Antioch with his local forces and attack the pretender from the north. Caught between the two, Alexander could be crushed before his allies might think of rushing to his help.

There now began a desperate flurry of royal overtures to Judea, with bounteous offers pouring into Jonathan's lap as king and claimant sought to outbid each other for his friendship and military help, or at least for his neutrality. The first move was made by Demetrius, who 'sent Jonathan a letter in friendly and flattering terms; for he said to himself, "Let us forestall Alexander by making peace with the Jews before Jonathan comes to terms with him against us, for he will remember all the harm we have done him by our treatment of his brothers and of his nation"' (1 Macc. 10:3–5). He accordingly ordered that all the Jewish hostages interned in the Acra citadel be returned to Jonathan; conferred on Jonathan the 'title of ally'; and gave him authority to raise and equip an army, including the forging of weapons.

Jonathan took quick and full advantage of these unconditional concessions. He promptly assembled his men and marched to Jerusalem, where he read the emperor's letter 'aloud before all the people' and then presented it to the commander of the Acra. The men of the garrison 'were filled with apprehension when they heard that the king had given Jonathan authority to raise an army', but the commander was forced to respect the royal will, and he 'surrendered the hostages' to Jonathan, who 'restored them to their parents'. (1 Macc. 10:7–9). The Acra remained in the hands of the imperial troops, for the king's order had not included its evacuation: a military presence in the capital was important to Seleucid prestige and showed that Judea was still a dependent province. Jonathan, however, decided to establish himself in Jerusalem, and no attempt was made to stop him. His first instruction was to refortify the Temple Mount. His right to levy an armed force offset the earlier Seleucid need for the fortresses round Judea which Bacchides had erected, and they were abandoned. Beth Zur alone was retained as a place of refuge for the Jewish hellenists. Thus, with the exception

Brussels tapestry showing Jonathan as High Priest wearing the purple robe he received from Alexander Balas

of this fort and Jerusalem's Acra, the entire province of Judea came under the operational control of Jonathan. He enjoyed the privileges of a royal commander, but he held no official title; and Judea was now virtually free, but it was still without formal independence.

Jonathan felt under no obligation to his erstwhile enemy. He had made no commitment, for none had been demanded, though Demetrius had certainly hoped his 'generosity' would soften Jonathan's hostility. His concessions had been offered under constraint, and Demetrius might well retract if and when he ever recovered. Above all, Jonathan considered that Demetrius had done little more than accept Judean realities. He had given him the right to levy troops – which merely legalized what Jonathan had already done. He had withdrawn most of his garrison forces, for they were needed less in Judea than they were nearer home. And he was now pinning his hopes on a rebel leader because his own hellenist nominees had proved impotent. Demetrius was simply recognizing what had been obvious for years – that the Maccabees, relying on their own Jewish resources and strength of spirit to fight their battles, were the most powerful and popular party in Judea, whereas their Jewish opponents, the hellenizing party, were isolated. They could never act without Seleucid support; and when their foreign prop was weakened, their fragility was apparent to all. Jonathan might find private satisfaction in the implicit acknowledgement of this fact by a Seleucid emperor, but it called for no thanks from him. Indeed, the only real concession by Demetrius had been the release of the hostages, but this was hardly a momentous sacrifice on his part for what he hoped to get in return.

Jonathan therefore calmly accepted the rights he had been given and proceeded to organize the administration of Judea, expand his Maccabee force, and arrange for his intelligence service to extract all possible information from the camps of the royal contenders. It thus came as no surprise to him to receive a letter from Alexander Balas, though the offer it contained was unexpected:

King Alexander to his brother Jonathan, greeting. We have heard about you, what a valiant man you are and how fit to be our friend. Now therefore we do appoint you this day to be High Priest of your nation with the title King's Friend, to support our cause and keep friendship with us (1 Macc. 10:18–20).

Accompanying the letter was a package containing a purple robe and a gold crown, the vestments of the High Priest.

Alexander had made a shrewd bid. After analysing the concessions granted by his rival, he quickly perceived how he could improve upon them in a manner likely to commend itself to Jonathan. He

Dyeing installation of the hellenistic period discovered in archaeological excavations at Tel Mor, the ancient port of Ashdod. The deep hole (left) contained a pile of murexes (right), the shell-fish which yielded purple dye

would offer him formal recognition and appointment to an office which had been in abeyance since the death of Eliakim seven years earlier. The High Priest was not only the religious but also the secular leader of the people, and Alexander thought the Judeans would welcome the designation of Jonathan to this post, for he was their true leader, and he would be the first traditionalist Jew to hold this office since the days of Antiochus Epiphanes.

In the event, Alexander's offer was well received, but more for its political than for its religious implications. As to its religious aspect, the traditionalist Jews, the Maccabees included, had never conceded the right of an outsider to initiate such an appointment. This was a matter for the Jews alone, though the imperial rulers had always reserved a veto right on the Jewish choice, and the Jews were not yet ready to see a man of the sword in the highest ecclesiastical office. However, they interpreted Alexander's gesture as formalizing Jonathan's administrative and military leadership, and there is a hint of this in the records which refer to his spiritual and martial activities in the same breath: 'Jonathan assumed the vestments of the High Priest . . . at the Feast of Tabernacles, and he gathered an army together and prepared a large supply of arms' (1 Macc. 10:21). It is not unreasonable to suppose that Jonathan had worn the priestly garments sent by Alexander, at what may well have been the most joyous celebration of a Pilgrim Festival since Judah's reconsecration of the Temple, as a political signal to whoever might be interested. Its implications would not have been lost on the imperial troops in the Acra who saw, but no longer sniped at, the crowds of worshippers. The citadel commander would have reported the event to Demetrius, and though the emperor may already have heard of Alexander's bid, it was probably only upon learning of Jonathan's appearance in his sacerdotal robes before an enthusiastic populace that he was moved to cap his rival's offer.

He now outdid himself in outbidding Alexander, and his next message to Judea offered the people a profusion of bounties which were beyond belief – in more than one sense: the Judeans questioned his sincerity ('the people . . . did not believe or accept them' [1 Macc. 10:46]); and later historians questioned the authenticity of his letter as it appears in the ancient records listing his concessions. These included exemption from a wide range of imposts and levies, such as the tax on salt, one-third of the grain-harvest and the half of the fruit-harvest; the restoration to Judea of 'three administrative districts' with Jewish populations, 'Apherema, Lydda and Ramathaim', which had been detached and given to Samaria by Antiochus Epiphanes; Jerusalem and its environs 'to be sacred and tax free'; the Acra citadel to be evacuated by his troops; 'Ptolemais and the lands belonging to it' – which were now occupied by Alexander Balas – to be made over to the Temple 'to meet the expenses proper to it', together with an annual grant of 'fifteen thousand silver shekels' from the royal treasury; the cost of repair of the Temple, the walls of Jerusalem and all Judean fortresses also

Recently excavated Hasmonean remains in Jerusalem's Citadel

to be borne by the royal exchequer; and the enlistment of Jews 'in the forces of the king to the number of thirty thousand men; they shall receive the usual army pay. Some of them shall be stationed in the great royal fortresses, others put in positions of trust in the kingdom. Their commanders and officers shall be of their own race, and they shall follow their own customs, just as the king had ordered for Judea' (1 Macc. 10:29–45; 11:34).

Whether or not Demetrius promised all the rights, privileges, territories, tax relief and financial grants attributed to him in the First Book of Maccabees, there is little doubt that the concessions he offered were indeed formidable and far-reaching. The largesse he displayed was to weigh considerably with Jonathan – though in an unexpected way – when he came to decide which rival to support.

Jonathan was in no hurry to make known his choice. The armies of Demetrius and Alexander were engaged for months in indecisive combat, and the crucial clash was still a long way off. Each sought in the meantime to augment his forces, improve his political position and win over Jonathan to his side. Both knew, as did Jonathan, that at some point in their struggle, he might hold the key to its outcome. During this period Jonathan expanded his fighting ranks, strengthened his administration – and remained an enigma to the two royal supplicants.

He had almost certainly made up his mind at the outset to support Alexander. Demetrius had been his bitter foe; Alexander was new to the scene, with no history of enmity towards Judea. If Demetrius won, as he might with Jonathan's help, he would be more powerful and more tyrannical than ever, giving scarcely a thought to the promises he had made and keeping Judea firmly in its tributary place. Alexander might do the same, but he was as yet an unknown quantity. He was unlikely to be worse than Demetrius, and he might be very much better than any emperor since the Ptolemies, for he would be starting his relationship with the Jews as friend and ally. Demetrius was isolated in the region; Alexander had the active support of three kingdoms and the tacit approval of Rome. As time went on, Jonathan learned that Demetrius was encountering grave domestic difficulties, and was not at all certain of the loyalty of his generals. He had even sent two of his young sons, Demetrius and Antiochus, out of the country for safety (though the eldest, Antigonus, remained in Syria – and was murdered shortly after his father's death). Alexander, on the other hand, was enjoying more than political encouragement from his allies. There was talk that Cappadocia and Pergamum might strike at Demetrius from the north in a co-ordinated strategy with Alexander, while Ptolemy Philometor in the south might despatch a force from Egypt.

Demetrius was defeated in his fateful battle with Alexander Balas. Combat scene from a hellenistic sarcophagus found in Sidon

Incidentally, Philometor's commitment to Alexander held another acutely relevant implication for Jonathan: if he, Jonathan, threw in his lot with Demetrius, Philometor's first act to aid his ally could well be the invasion of nearby Judea.

An added reason for joining Alexander was the very generosity, sincere or spurious, of Demetrius' last bid. It was so extravagant, so outrageously at odds with every intention, attitude and sentiment which Demetrius was known to have harboured towards Judea, that it could only have been born of desperation or dishonesty or both. Whichever it was, it bespoke a deeply troubled Demetrius, his position so precarious that only Jonathan's help could save him. The man and his followers who had started out as simple guerillas with an ideal in their hearts and only sickles for swords, dismissed by the mighty men of Antioch as unruly bandits, now had it in their hands to tip the scales between emperors. Jonathan tipped them in favour of Alexander.

There are few details in the ancient records of the fateful battle between the two rivals for the Seleucid throne which took place in 150 BC. It appears, however, that early in the fighting Demetrius had the upper hand, his left wing gaining on the adversary's right flank and even putting it to flight. But Demetrius himself was with his other wing and was hard pressed. Josephus describes the final scene on the battlefield: 'Demetrius acted wonders, killing and pursuing his enemies, and defending himself; till at length his horse plunged into a bog, and being oppressed by multitudes, he was obliged to yield; which, however, he disdained for some time to do,

fighting on foot till his body was covered with darts and arrows' (*Antiquities* XIII. 60, 61). With Demetrius' death, his forces crumpled. Alexander Balas was now the new emperor of Seleucia, titular head of the territories of Syria in the west and south and Babylonia in the east.

Ptolemy Philometor could derive deep satisfaction from the presence on the Seleucid throne of a man who was beholden to Egypt and who possessed none of the masterful qualities of his predecessor, Demetrius I Soter. It is not clear from the records as to who initiated the proposal, but shortly after his accession, Alexander was given the daughter of Philometor to wife. She was Cleopatra Thea. Philometor stipulated, however, that the wedding ceremony would take place not in Antioch but in Ptolemais, on the northern coast of Palestine, and that is where the two kings met. (Edwyn Bevan says that it was 'a sign of the subordination to Egypt which marked the new state of things in Syria that Alexander seems to have resided more in Ptolemais than in Antioch'.) One of the distinguished guests invited to the wedding celebrations was Jonathan. His relations with Alexander had become very cordial, and now, in Ptolemais, the king advanced him to a higher degree in the order of 'King's Friends', and appointed him commander (*strategos*) and governor (*meridarches*) of Judea in the service of the king.

Jonathan returned to Jerusalem 'well pleased'. Though he had earlier received offers of considerable power by a Demetrius in grim straits and by an Alexander who was a pretender to the throne, this was the first time since his family had raised the standard of revolt in Modi'in that the Jews of Judea were officially given genuine home rule by a reigning emperor who had the will, authority and power to grant it. This was not yet independence. Jonathan was still subject to the king, whose troops continued to retain the Acra citadel. But this apart, Jonathan was able to govern the people of Judea as though he and they were completely free. There was no interference from Alexander. Early protests to him by the Jewish hellenists were brushed aside. The Maccabee nationalist party was the dominant power in what was the Jewish state in almost all but name.

Life in Judea was peaceful for the next three years, and the people were able to pursue their productive and traditional lives with no trouble from within and no meddling from without. Jonathan maintained his close friendship with the king, and Alexander, for his part, allowed Jonathan full license to govern his province in his own way. Neither gave the other any cause for complaint.

Alexander, however, apparently gave others cause for disappointment, though the reasons are obscure. (The ancient histories shed little light on this brief period, and some of the accounts are contradictory.) One of the disenchanted seems to have been his father-in-law, Ptolemy Philometor, possibly because he had not succeeded in deepening Egypt's influence in the Seleucid territories. This may have been because, as we have seen, Alexander spent most of his time in Ptolemais and left the imperial administration in the powerful hands of his chief minister in Antioch. His absence from Antioch also gave other leaders in the capital opportunies for conspiratorial activity. It is possible, too, in the light of her subsequent behaviour, that Cleopatra, Alexander's wife and mother of his infant son, Antiochus, also took a hand in events which were to lead to the emperor's downfall. (This formidable lady, daughter and wife of emperors, was to marry her husband's rival, then the rival's brother, both of whom became emperors; to have sons with all three, all of whom were to reach the throne; and finally to murder her second husband and then the son she bore him.)

In 147 BC, to Alexander's alarm, the son of Demetrius I, also named Demetrius, landed in Cilicia, adjoining Syria, with the backing of a large force of Cretan mercenaries. (The Cretan commander, Lasthenes, was no doubt in charge of this action, for Demetrius was but a youth.) This was the Demetrius who, with his young brother, had been sent for safety out of the country before his father's final confrontation with Alexander, and he had now been brought back to claim his throne. Alexander rushed north

from Ptolemais to Antioch and on towards the border to engage the forces of Demetrius. To his anguish, he found that he was deserted by his former supporters – all except Jonathan.

Jonathan's friendship was soon put to the test. While the king was in the north, Demetrius sent a trusted general, Apollonius, to establish himself as governor of Coele-Syria, and he brought an army which occupied the coastal plain south of Ptolemais. Apollonius' next task was to discipline Judea and eliminate the man who championed the cause of Alexander. He set up his main base at Jamnia and, according to the First Book of Maccabees, sent a taunting demand to Jonathan to surrender, citing the isolation of Alexander, the powerful allies of Demetrius and the hopelessness of Judea's position. He also enlarged upon the power of his cavalry, which would quickly overwhelm the Jews, and he added the mocking challenge that if Jonathan had confidence in his troops, he should leave the safety of his Judean hills and come down to do battle in the coastal plain.

To his surprise, this is precisely what Jonathan now did. Heading an army of ten thousand well-trained men, he marched out of Jerusalem, across the hills and down the pass, joined by auxiliary

A 19th-century lithograph by David Roberts of Acre (called Ptolemais in the Hasmonean period), where Alexander Balas proclaimed himself king

contingents under his brother Simon. They made straight 'for Joppa' (Jaffa), where they routed Apollonius' garrison and took the port city. Jonathan then wheeled south to confront the main enemy force. As they neared Jamnia, Apollonius resorted to the stratagem of appearing to retreat southwards towards Azotus with 'three thousand cavalry and a large force of infantry'. But he 'had left a thousand cavalry in hiding in their rear, and Jonathan discovered that there was an ambush behind him'. He and his men were heavily pressed from front and rear by enemy archers and cavalry assaults 'from dawn till dusk. But they stood fast . . . and the enemy cavalry grew weary.' At this point Simon appeared with his force 'and joined battle with the enemy phalanx, now that the cavalry was exhausted. They were routed by him and took to flight' (1 Macc. 10:74–82). The Judeans pursued them to Azotus, which they captured, went on to Ashkelon, whose citizens greeted them with honours, and then returned to Jerusalem. This victory added to the already high military prestige of Judea in the region, and it gave Alexander one of the few moments of relief he was to enjoy in his campaign against Demetrius. He was so delighted with Jonathan's act of friendship – and with its success – that he advanced him to the highest degree in the royal order, that of 'King's Kinsmen', and presented him with Ekron, in the coastal plain, together with 'all its districts'.

It was now that Ptolemy Philometor decided to intervene in the Alexander-Demetrius conflict, but no one, apart from Philometor, seems to have known on whose side. He set out from Egypt at the head of a large army and pushed northwards up the coastal plain towards Syria. Alexander assumed that he was coming to help him, and instructed the coastal cities to treat him with all respect, which they did. Jonathan left Jerusalem and met the Egyptian emperor in state at Jaffa, where they exchanged salutations and spent the night, and Jonathan then accompanied him for some distance on his journey northwards before returning to Jerusalem. Philometor proceeded from city to city, leaving a detachment of garrison troops in each, so that by the time he reached the Syrian border he was master of the principal coastal towns between Egypt and Seleucia.

Josephus, probably drawing on Polybius and Diodorus for his sources, says that Philometor's original intention had indeed been to support his son-in-law, but he changed his plan when told that Alexander had plotted to kill him. Edwyn Bevan suggests as one possibility that he marched north with an open mind and may 'have left it to future events to determine his line. He will almost certainly have intended in any case to recover Coele-Syria for his house.' The First Book of Maccabees states quite baldly that his clear purpose

Bronze panther of the hellenistic period discovered at Ashdod (ancient Azotus), where the Maccabees defeated the forces of a later General Apollonius

A female figure crowned with battlements, the emblem of the city of Antioch, resting her foot on a youthful figure representing the Orontes River

when he set out from Egypt was 'to make himself master of Alexander's kingdom by treachery and add it to his own. He set out for Syria with professions of peace . . . [but] he was harbouring malicious designs against Alexander' (11:1, 2,8).

If little is known of Philometor's original aim, there is nothing obscure about his actions upon reaching Syrian soil. He dropped Alexander and opted for the youth Demetrius – even offering him the hand of his daughter Cleopatra Thea, Alexander's wife. Alexander promptly escaped to Cilicia, and Philometor entered Antioch amid public acclamation. There, according to the First Book of Maccabees, 'he assumed the crown of Asia; thus he wore two crowns, that of Egypt and that of Asia'. If indeed he did so, it was only temporary, as a gesture to the local populace, for he would have known that Rome would consider it a provocative act.

Josephus' account seems the more feasible. He says that Philometor, being a wise man, 'determined to avoid the envy of the Romans; so he called the people of Antioch together to an assembly, and persuaded them to receive Demetrius'. It is evident that he felt he could achieve the same extension of Egyptian influence in the Seleucid empire through a young puppet without exciting the anxieties of the other powers in the region. Demetrius became king.

When Alexander eventually gathered fresh forces in Cilicia and re-entered northern Syria, he was met by the combined armies of Philometor and Demetrius and was defeated. Ptolemy Philometor, though victorious, received battle wounds from which he would shortly die. Alexander, though vanquished, managed to escape and sought protection from an Arab tribe; but 'Zabdiel the Arab chieftain cut off Alexander's head and sent it to Ptolemy', who was shown the grisly sight two days before he died. With his death, the occupation by his garrisons of the coastal cities in Coele-Syria ended. The year was 145 BC.

Jonathan had taken no part in the northern fighting. Even if he had wished to help Alexander, it would have been difficult to do so once Philometor had brought his army north from Egypt and occupied the territory between Judea and Antioch. He had now to deal with a new emperor, still in his early teens, who reigned as Demetrius II Nicator. Though the young king might be personally acceptable to his people, the Cretan troops who had brought him to power were not, and his consequent domestic troubles, added to his youth and ineffectualness, provided Jonathan with an opportunity to edge Judea a little closer to independence. He set siege to the imperial troops in the Acra Fortress in Jerusalem, so as to remove the last vestige of a Seleucid presence in the land. His act provoked an outcry by the small, though vocal, Jewish hellenizing party in Jerusalem, and they joined the Acra commander in sending a protest report on Jonathan's conduct to Demetrius. The king and his advisers were furious. The Judean leader was instructed to raise the siege immediately and was summoned to a meeting with Demetrius in Ptolemais.

Jonathan took his time, gave orders for the siege to be continued, and then, 'selecting elders of Israel and priests to accompany him, he set out on his dangerous mission'. The conference called by the emperor to discipline a rebellious underling ended as a triumph for Jonathan. By skilful diplomatic argument, he won the confidence of Demetrius, no doubt playing on the king's insecurity, his need for a trouble-free province, the lessons his predecessors had been forced to learn and the advantages of granting Judea greater autonomy – and more territory. As a result, Demetrius confirmed Jonathan as High Priest; 'appointed him head of the first class of the King's Friends'; and transferred three districts (toparchies) from Samaria to Judea, 'Apherema, Lydda and Ramathaim . . . together with all lands adjacent thereto' (1 Macc. 11:34). (It will be recalled that his father, Demetrius I, had also offered to add these three Samarian districts to Judea; but whereas then the offer had been somewhat nebulous and made in circumstances which rendered its royal implementation difficult, the present concession was part of a firm agreement, and conditions were such that it could be put into immediate effect.) Jonathan also asked that Judea be freed of tribute, with no further tithes, tolls, crown-money or taxes on salt and crops, and all he offered for the huge concessions he had been granted were three hundred talents. Demetrius agreed, and the full details were inscribed in a royal document signed by the emperor.

Though no mention of the Acra appears in the document, it is probable that Jonathan decided to lift the siege. It was a small price to pay for what he had managed to secure, and he no doubt thought there would be an opportunity later to free the citadel of foreign troops. Jonathan returned to Jerusalem to resume his governance of a larger, freer and richer Judea – unbowed by heavy tribute – and to enter the final stretch along the hard road towards national independence.

By contrast, the emperor was plagued with local troubles, occasioned largely by the disaffection of veteran troops who stirred up the citizens of Antioch. Discontent in the capital eventually became so acute that Demetrius urgently appealed to Jonathan for help. Jonathan agreed to send aid but set as one of his conditions the evacuation of the Acra. The emperor was forced to comply when he was faced with a popular rising, apparently led by a certain Diodotus who had served Alexander and had then deserted him for Demetrius. Jonathan despatched a contingent of three thousand men who arrived in the nick of time: the crowds were storming the palace in which the emperor had taken refuge. After bitter street fighting, order was restored. The king's life was saved, Diodotus escaped, Antioch was calm and the Judean troops returned home. Demetrius then repudiated his promise, a breach of faith that was to cost him dearly when a rival to the Seleucid throne appeared – or rather was thrust – upon the scene.

This occurred in the year 144 or 143 BC (the exact date is not clear from the records), and the rival was his infant step-son, Antiochus, son of his wife Cleopatra by her first husband, Alexander Balas. The child had been entrusted to an Arab chieftain for safe-keeping when his father was in danger from Demetrius, and he had remained

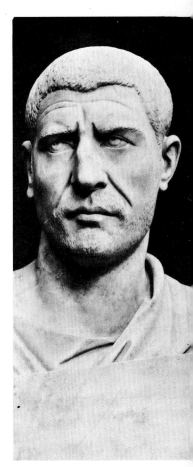

Alexander Balas was in turn overthrown by the son of the emperor whom he had ousted, and he sought refuge with an Arab tribe; but 'Zabdiel the Arab chieftain cut off Alexander's head'. An ancient portrait of an Arab chieftain

in the Arab's charge after Alexander was killed. An ambitious general now retrieved him from the chieftain and put him forth as the rightful emperor, with the style Antiochus VI Dionysos, and himself as all-powerful regent.

The general was none other than Diodotus, whose earlier rebellion had failed, and now, as prospective regent, he assumed the name of Tryphon. Several fellow commanders and their troops, equally dis-satisfied with Demetrius and ready to exploit the discontent of the people, defected to him and moved against the reigning emperor in the name of Antiochus VI. Many rallied to their cause, and Tryphon and his royal ward entered Antioch in triumph. Demetrius fled to the coastal town of Seleucia, some 17 miles south-west of Antioch, and for a time the Seleucid empire was divided between two emperors: Demetrius II Nicator, headquartered in Seleucia, controlled much of the Mediterranean seaboard and the eastern provinces, while Antiochus VI Dionysos, installed in Antioch and with Tryphon behind him, occupied the Orontes Valley, which runs south of the capital.

Once again, Jonathan was courted by two royal rivals, though this time only hesitantly by one. Demetrius knew that he could expect little support from the man with whom he had dealt so dishonourably. Tryphon, on the other hand, anxious to consolidate his adventurous move, was eager to secure all the allies he could, and Jonathan was now one of the most formidable military commanders in the region and his Maccabean army the strongest military force in the territory lying between Syria and Egypt. Tryphon therefore quickly sent a despatch to Jonathan, in the name of Antiochus, confirming him in the high priesthood and endorsing his 'authority over the four districts' (1 Macc. 11:57). Josephus says they were the 'four districts which had been added to the territory of the Jews'. Three of them were those which, as we have seen, had been detached earlier from Samaria. Professor Avi-Yonah suggests that the fourth was a province in Transjordan, for 'Jonathan had meantime added the Perea – Jewish "Transjordan" – a legacy from the Tobiads, to his dominions'.

Jonathan accepted Tryphon's offer and promised his support. Tryphon then appointed Simon, Jonathan's brother, 'as officer commanding the area from the Ladder of Tyre [today's Rosh Hanikra on Israel's northern frontier] to the borders of Egypt' (1 Macc. 11:59). This made Simon the military commander of Coele-Syria with the exception of Phoenicia (today's Lebanon). The Maccabees were getting closer to their goal, and the territory they now controlled was approaching the size of the original Land of Israel.

The two brothers now made the most of their new powers, moving throughout Coele-Syria to add substance to their formal authority, 'showing the flag' in regions which were friendly or neutral and reducing the opposition where there was hostility. In the coastal plain, for example, which Jonathan visited first, he was greeted warmly in Ashkelon but not in Gaza, and he imposed his will on that city by force of arms. He then marched north through the entire country and reached as far as Damascus before turning back towards the Sea of Galilee. Simon, meanwhile, operating south of Jerusalem, captured the fortress of Beth Zur and replaced the Seleucid garrison with his own men.

Jonathan and Simon were taking advantage of the conflict between Demetrius and Tryphon to strengthen Judea and enhance its political and military status; but Demetrius had every reason to believe that they were acting on behalf of Tryphon, and he decided to strike at Jonathan and secure control of Judea and the rest of Coele-Syria. This would give him a strong base from which to make a decisive thrust against his principal rival. He accordingly despatched an army through southern Syria towards Galilee and

The Ladder of Tyre (today's Rosh Hanikra). Under the emperor Tryphon, the Maccabee leader Simon became military commander of 'the area from the Ladder of Tyre [in the north] to the borders of Egypt [in the south]'

they encamped at Kedesh. Jonathan and his men were 18 miles to the south, at Gennesaret, on the north-western shore of the Sea of Galilee, when they learned of the enemy's intentions, and Jonathan marched north to engage them. The two armies met in the plain of Hazor, some 3 miles south of Kedesh, and at first the battle went hard for the Maccabees. The enemy generals had flung their main force against Jonathan but had also posted units in the hills, ambushing his detachments in the rear and setting them in flight. However, Jonathan, aided by two forceful officers, Mattathias, son of Absalom, and Judah, son of Chalphi, put up a determined stand and routed the enemy. The Maccabee units that had fled now rejoined the main force, and they pursued Demetrius' troops and overran the enemy camp at Kedesh.

The monarchic rivals Demetrius and Tryphon, each controlling a portion of the empire, appeared to have reached a stalemate, and Jonathan, after his considerable military successes and now the *de facto* ruler of a substantially stronger and larger Judea, considered the moment opportune for a diplomatic initiative. He accordingly sent envoys to the Roman Senate to renew the friendly ties which had been contracted under Judah. He was under no illusions about the cynicism of Rome, and he well remembered her failure to come to his brother's aid despite their mutual assistance pact; but he thought that even the formal friendship of Rome would raise the political standing and prestige of Judea in the eyes of the emperors and peoples of Seleucia.

His emissaries were well received by the Senate, which 'gave them letters requiring the authorities in each place to give them safe conduct [back] to Judea'. Josephus says that on their homeward journey they visited Sparta, and the First Book of Maccabees gives 'a transcript of the letter which Jonathan wrote to the Spartans . . . about the renewal of our pact of brotherhood'. In it, Jonathan refers to a letter sent some one hundred and fifty years earlier 'to Onias the High Priest from Arius your king . . . in which the terms of the alliance and friendship were set forth. We do not regard ourselves as needing such alliances, since our support is the holy books in our possession. Nevertheless, we now venture to send and renew our pact of brotherhood and friendship with you, so that we may not become estranged, for it is many years since you wrote to us . . .' (1 Macc. 12:7–11). While most scholars agree as to the authenticity of the Jewish embassy to Rome, they are sceptical about the document to the Spartans. As Solomon Zeitlin points out, 'The apparent disorder of its introductory verses has aroused suspicions of its genuineness.' However, Zeitlin shows that there is in fact 'no real

The Hills of Gilead as seen across the Jordan Valley, through which Jonathan marched to meet Tryphon

disorder', and he concludes that there is 'no reason to doubt the authenticity of the letter to the Spartans'.

The records are silent about the activities of Tryphon at this time; but there is a report of Demetrius' attempt to wipe out his defeat by Jonathan at Kedesh. He now assembled an army to invade Judea; but they had barely left their headquarters area on their southern journey when Jonathan learned of their aim and marched north. He was resolved to do battle on enemy soil, 'giving them no chance to set foot in his territory' (1 Macc. 12:25). He moved through Lebanon, penetrated the country ruled by Demetrius and encamped close to Hamath, some 50 miles north-east of today's Beirut, where the enemy forces were gathered. His spies managed to infiltrate Demetrius' encampment and they returned with the report that a night attack was being prepared. Jonathan responded by ordering his troops to 'stand to arms all night, ready for battle', and he established 'outposts all round the camp'. Bereft of the element of surprise, the enemy stood little chance against the Maccabee army, and they retired stealthily at night, covering their withdrawal by 'first lighting watch-fires in their camp' to deceive the Jews into thinking they were still there. By morning, when Jonathan discovered their ruse, he set off in pursuit, but he was too late to catch them, for they had already 'crossed the river Eleutherus' (1 Macc. 12:26–8,30).

Jonathan struck camp and marched south-east to Damascus, subduing a pro-Demetrius settlement on the way. From there he freely traversed the breadth of Coele-Syria and encountered no opposition. His brother Simon had again been active in the coastal plain, recapturing Jaffa, after learning that its people intended to hand it over to Demetrius, and fortifying Adida, a strategic site roughly midway between Jaffa and Jerusalem.

When the two brothers returned to Jerusalem after these military operations, Jonathan 'called together the elders of the people' and together they decided 'to build fortresses in Judea, to heighten the walls of Jerusalem, and to erect a high barrier to separate the citadel from the city' (1 Macc. 12:35,36) and thus isolate the Acra garrison. It is evident that he expected trouble and made haste to strengthen his defences.

Trouble was not long in coming, and this time the source was not Demetrius but the regent Tryphon. The First Book of Maccabees says that Tryphon 'now aspired to be king of Asia; he meant to rebel against King Antiochus and assume the crown himself. But he was afraid that Jonathan would fight to prevent this, so he cast about for some means of capturing and killing him' (12:39,40). It is true that Tryphon was determined to be emperor – he was soon to dethrone

A Macedonian war helmet on the obverse of a coin of Tryphon

the infant Antiochus VI and put him to death four years later, in 138 BC. But there is probably an additional reason why Tryphon now turned against Jonathan. While taking satisfaction from the defeats of his rival Demetrius at the hands of Jonathan, he was disquieted by the rising power of the Judean leader, who was in touch with Rome and possibly other kingdoms and who had left his military and administrative mark on territory stretching from Damascus almost down to the Egyptian border. Moreover, Tryphon aspired to be monarch over an intact empire, and here was Judea slipping from his grasp. Though formally his tributary, it was virtually independent; and though Jonathan was his appointee, he behaved like a free ruler, expanding and strengthening his domain at will. If Jonathan were to be curbed and Judea to remain an imperial province, the time to act was now.

Tryphon accordingly took his army on a southward march to Judea, selecting the Jordan Valley route. Jonathan's intelligence service gave him early news of this move but not of Tryphon's intentions. These remained unclear; but the action seemed odd for a friendly regent, and so the prudent Jonathan set out northwards, also along the Jordan Valley, at the head of a very strong force.

Beth Shean, scene of the dramatic confrontation between Tryphon and Jonathan. In the *foreground*, the archaeological site where the Philistines displayed the body of King Saul; *middle right*, the recently restored Roman theatre; *top*, the modern town developed since 1948

The two armies met at Beth Shean and encamped close to each other, neither making a hostile move. Jonathan presumably waited to see what Tryphon would do. Tryphon, sizing up the military strength behind Jonathan, saw little hope of victory in combat. He promptly changed his plans – and his manner, donning the mask of sweet diplomacy; and he succeeded in duping the usually cautious Jonathan.

He sent for the Judean leader, received him with honours, commended him to all the distinguished members of his entourage and ordered his troops 'to obey Jonathan as they would himself'. He then asked Jonathan why he had brought his army? 'Why have you put all these men to so much trouble, when we are not at war? Send them home now and choose a few to accompany you, and come with me to Ptolemais. I will hand it over to you with all the other fortresses, the rest of the troops, and all the officials, and then I will leave the country. This is the only purpose of my coming' (1 Macc. 12:43–45). Jonathan took him at his word. He sent his army back to Judea, leaving only three thousand men to accompany him as he set out for the Mediterranean coast with Tryphon. Before reaching Ptolemais, he left two thousand in Galilee. Thus it was that

The Gates of Acre, where
Jonathan was trapped by
Tryphon

he had only one thousand troops with him when he entered the
open gates of the coastal city – walking right into Tryphon's trap.

Historians have found it hard to explain why so experienced and
vigilant and circumspect a commander as Jonathan, particularly
with his guerilla training, should have proved so unwary. It is

evident, however, that he had been badly let down by his intelligence service, which had failed to discover Tryphon's true motives. He had therefore planned for the worst and taken the appropriate precaution of setting out from Jerusalem with a large army. By so doing he had tipped his hand; for the moment he reached Beth Shean, the very presence of his forces showed Tryphon that Jonathan had been suspicious. Yet Tryphon had not attacked him; nor, when they met, had he expressed anger at Jonathan's military demonstration of his unfriendly doubts. His reproval had been mild and gentle. Indeed, he had treated Jonathan as an honoured comrade. As for his southern march, far from harbouring warlike designs, he had come for the specific purpose of showering Jonathan with further gifts, including the lavish prize of the city of Ptolemais. Such gracious and generous behaviour was thoroughly disarming, and though Jonathan had met duplicity countless times and was by no means naive, he may well have thought in this case that his apprehensions had been groundless. After all, it was feasible for Tryphon to sue for his favours, since he could have felt that Jonathan had proved an effective instrument to beat Demetrius, and the gifts could be regarded as a reward for service rendered and an inducement to continue such service. Thus, Jonathan must have considered that he had gravely misjudged the regent and was anxious to make amends. He had therefore readily fallen in with Tryphon's suggestion. It was to be his last free act.

As soon as he and his escort entered Ptolemais, the gates were closed behind them. Jonathan was seized and made captive, and his men were put to death.

Tryphon, thinking of Judea in his own terms and knowing what happened to his mercenaries when their general was killed, believed that the loss of Jonathan would mean the collapse of the Maccabee army. He therefore quickly sent a force of infantry and cavalry into Galilee to wipe out the two thousand Jewish troops who had been deployed there by Jonathan. It is possible that Tryphon's commander used psychological warfare as a softening-up weapon by getting the news through to the Maccabees that Jonathan and his escort were dead. To his surprise, the Jews, instead of laying down their arms upon hearing of this calamity, promptly formed up for battle. When the enemy commander saw that there would be determined opposition, he broke off and retreated. The Maccabee contingent then left Galilee and marched safely back to Judea, where they relayed their sad report. They apparently did not know that Jonathan was a prisoner. They assumed that he had been killed together with his men; and 'all Israel was plunged into grief'.

Simon took immediate control, with the spontaneous backing of the public. He now mustered all the fighting men and hastily completed the fortifications of Jerusalem, realizing that a full-scale attack by Tryphon was imminent. He was not worried by the enemy garrison in Jerusalem, for the Acra was sealed off by the wall Jonathan had erected and its inmates must by now have been close to starvation. Anxious to deny Jaffa to the enemy and secure it as a foot-hold in the coastal plain, he despatched a crack unit under the command of a certain Jonathan, son of Absalom, to turn the hostile port city into a Jewish outpost.

Information soon came through that Tryphon had left Ptolemais and was heading south with a large force to invade Judea. Simon set out with his army and established himself at Adida, the site he had fortified shortly before, which commanded the road from Jaffa to the hills of Judea. Tryphon seems to have thought he would encounter little opposition, and he was surprised to learn that a powerful Maccabee army awaited him at Adida under the leadership of Jonathan's brother. Anxious to avoid a direct confrontation at that site, where he would find himself at the edge of the coastal plain and the Judean foothills – and with a Judean force at Jaffa in his rear – Tryphon sought to reassure Simon by sending him envoys with a special message. In it he revealed that Jonathan was alive and was actually with him in his camp. He had been 'detained' because of 'certain monies which he owed to the royal treasury . . . To ensure that he will not again revolt if we release him, send one hundred talents of silver and two of his sons as hostages, and we will let him go' (1 Macc. 13:15,16).

Simon was in a quandary. He 'realized that this was a trick, but he had the money and the children brought to him, fearing that otherwise he might arouse deep animosity among the people, who would say, "It was because you did not send the money and the children that Jonathan lost his life." So he sent the children and the hundred talents, but Tryphon broke his word and did not release Jonathan' (1 Macc. 13:17–19).

It was presumably while these negotiations were proceeding that Tryphon pushed his army further south along the coastal plain, bypassing Adida and avoiding the Judean hill country. He now continued southwards into Idumea and turned east through Marisa, 'taking a roundabout way through Adora', a few miles south of Beth Zur, with the intention of wheeling north so as to reach the settled districts of Judea from the south. But 'Simon and his army marched parallel with him everywhere he went' (1 Macc. 13:20), using his interior lines of communications as in earlier days. While Tryphon was on the march, he kept receiving urgent appeals from

the beleaguered Acra garrison 'to come to them by way of the [Judean] desert, and to send them provisions'. Tryphon sent his cavalry to relieve them; but as luck would have it, the region was struck by an unusual and severe snowstorm 'which prevented their arrival'. The weather, together with the considerably stronger Maccabee force than he had expected, were enough to persuade Tryphon to abandon his invasion plan. He set his army on a direct course for the warm, below-sea-level Jordan Valley and marched north to Gilead. 'When he reached Bascama', just beyond the north-eastern shore of the Sea of Galilee, 'he had Jonathan put to death, and there he was buried. Tryphon then turned and went back to his own country' (1 Macc. 13:23,24).

Simon had the body of his brother brought to the village of Modi'in and there it was laid to rest in the Hasmonean family tomb. The year was 142 BC.

Simon was now the last surviving son of the priestly Mattathias, whose act in the village square of Modi'in had launched the Jews on their road to liberty. Judah had led them most of the way and over the toughest stretch. Jonathan had brought them almost within reach of their mark. It would be up to Simon to break through the final barrier and regain freedom for his people.

Snow in Jerusalem. A sudden snowstorm forced Tryphon's cavalry to abandon its attack on the Judean capital

# 14 Independence

Simon, like Jonathan before him, saw opportunity for the advancement of Judean independence in the continued division of the Seleucid empire. The royal rift deepened when Tryphon returned to Antioch after his unsuccessful essay at invading Judea and his execution of Jonathan. He deposed the infant monarch Antiochus VI Dionysos and usurped the throne. He was thus the first sovereign (at least over part of the empire) who did not belong to the House of Seleucus, a fact which made his action even more galling to his competitor of royal birth, Demetrius II Nicator, who still held the other part of the imperial possessions. (Tryphon added a sting by striking new coins to mark the start of what he hoped would be a new era.) The rivalry between the two emperors was bitter indeed, and though the clashes between them had not yet been decisive, each sought to prepare for the inevitable critical confrontation by gathering military and political support wherever he could.

This was the moment chosen by Simon to address himself to Demetrius – and a chagrined Tryphon realized the folly of his treachery towards Simon's brother. Demetrius welcomed the representatives of the Maccabee leader, commander of so potent a military force, and granted all Simon's demands. His crucial concession was the one freeing Judea from taxation and renouncing all claims to arrears of tribute. The letter from 'King Demetrius to Simon, the High Priest and Friend of Kings, and to the elders and to the nation of the Jews', affirmed that 'All our agreements with you stand, and the strongholds which you built shall remain yours . . . We remit the crown-money which you owed us, and if there is any other tax collected in Jerusalem, let it be collected no longer . . . Let there be peace between us' (1 Macc. 13:36–40).

Freedom from taxation was tantamount to the recognition of Judea's independence, and since Demetrius wrote that it was 'to

The seven-branched candelabrum (*menorah*) used for the first time as a state symbol on a coin minted by the last Hasmonean king, Mattathias Antigonus, who reigned from 40 to 37 BC

take effect from the date of this letter' (142 BC), that was the year hailed by the Jews as marking the lifting of 'the yoke of the heathen . . . from Israel. The people began to write on their contracts and agreements "In the first year of Simon, the great High Priest, general and leader of the Jews" ' (1 Macc. 13:41,42). This, then marked the beginning of the Hasmonean era, and Simon is formally considered to have been the first of the Hasmonean dynasty. [In the Mishna and the Talmud, as well as in Josephus, Mattathias and his descendants are referred to not as the Maccabees but as members of the House of Hashmon, or Hasmoneans. Even in the Books of Maccabees, it is Judah alone who is called 'the Maccabee'. The term, however, subsequently became associated somewhat loosely with his brothers, too, and I have used it even more loosely in this book to cover also the Jews who fought with all the sons of Mattathias.]

The evacuation of the imperial troops from the beleaguered Acra was all that remained to render Jewish independence complete. This was effected in the early summer of the following year, when the starving garrison (and presumably the remnant of the hellenistic Jews) 'clamoured to Simon to accept their surrender, and he agreed'.

He expelled them from the citadel and cleansed it from its pollutions. It was on the twenty-third day of the second [Hebrew] month in the year 171 [of the Seleucid era, corresponding to 141 BC] that he made his entry, with a chorus of praise and the waving of palm branches, with lutes, cymbals and zithers, with hymns and songs, to celebrate Israel's final riddance of a formidable enemy (1 Macc. 13:50–52).

The singular exhilaration engendered by this event is well explained by Solomon Zeitlin: 'The Jews looked upon the Acra as a symbol of their humiliation and suffering at the time of Antiochus Epiphanes, and its capture by Simon was considered a double victory – the triumph of Judaism over Hellenism, and the removal of the last vestige of dependence on Syria.' Simon then tore down those sections of the Acra which dominated the Temple Mount – Josephus says that he razed the entire structure – and eventually the palace of the Hasmoneans was erected upon its ruins.

The whole of Jerusalem was at last under Maccabean control and Judea was again an independent Jewish state. But its boundaries were now wider than they had been when it was a tributary province of Seleucia, for they now included part of the coastal plain in the west and fringes of territory beyond the southern border with Idumea, the northern border with Samaria and the eastern border in Transjordan. Simon, as we have seen, had already secured Jaffa, 'which he took for a harbour, and made it a place of entrance to the isles of the sea' (1 Macc. 14:5). After assuming the leadership of

his people, and expecting a further invasion by Tryphon, he 'invested Gazara [Gezer]'. This well-fortified city commanding the Jerusalem-Jaffa road was captured with the aid of 'a siege-engine', and Simon turned it into a strong military base, appointing his son Johanan (better known as John Hyrcanus) as its commander. He considered that Gezer, together with the previously fortified Adida to its north, would prove an effective deterrent to an enemy seeking to reach the Judean hills from the coastal plain. (In Gezer, Simon also 'built a residence . . . for himself'. In his 1902–5 archaeological excavations of the site of ancient Gezer, Stewart Macalister found a building stone in the debris with an imprecation scratched on its surface containing the phrase 'the palace of Simon'.)

Tryphon failed to launch his expected attack, reflecting, no doubt, that he would fare no better than he had on his earlier attempt. Demetrius, too, took no action against what he could well have interpreted as Simon's expansionist, rather than defensive, operations. The reason for his passivity was to be found not in Judea but in Babylonia, and it probably explains why he had given way on the

'Boundary of Gezer', a Hebrew inscription on the boundary marker (with the name of the city ruler in Greek) from the Hasmonean period. Simon turned Gezer into a fortified base commanded by his son Johanan Hyrcanus

very point on which every emperor before him had held fast – the retention of the Acra. The fact is that the main source of what strength he commanded lay in the eastern territories of the empire, which had now shrunk to Babylonia alone, and in his conflict with Tryphon, this province had remained loyal to his royal house. In 141 BC, however, the year in which Simon had taken the Acra, Babylonia had been overrun by the Parthians, the strong eastern kingdom whose threat had given such concern to Antiochus Epiphanes two and a half decades earlier. Demetrius was now busily making preparations for a campaign to recover this territory, for without it he thought he stood little chance against Tryphon. In these circumstances it would have been suicidal for him to try to compel a determined Simon to vacate the Acra and give up Jaffa and Gezer. He therefore followed the prudent course of reconciling himself to the new Judean situation; and whatever his inner feelings, he behaved towards Simon in the spirit of his concessionary letter: 'Let there be peace between us.'

It was in this atmosphere of tranquillity that an event took place which was of considerable importance to the character of Judea's religious and political leadership. In the year 140 BC, a great assembly was held in Jerusalem of 'priests and people and leaders of the nation and elders of the country', and they agreed that

Simon should be their leader and High Priest for ever, until a true prophet should arise. He was to be their general, and to have full charge of the Temple; and in addition to this the supervision of their labour, of the country, and of the arms and the fortifications was to be entrusted to him. He was to be obeyed by all; all contracts in the country were to be drawn up in his name. He was to wear the purple robe and the gold clasp . . . It is the unanimous decision of the people that Simon shall officiate in the ways here laid down. Simon has agreed and consented to serve as High Priest, general and governor of the Jews and of the priests, and to preside over all (1 Macc. 14:28–47).

The political implication of this formal decision was its demonstrative expression of independence: the source of power of Judean leadership stemmed from the will of the Judean people. Heretofore, the legal basis for the power of the governors of Judea had been their appointment by the Seleucid emperor. Even Simon himself, for the previous three years, and Jonathan before him, had been royal appointees. Now his rule rested upon the decision of the people, and the political title of Simon was Prince of the People of Israel.

The religious implications of his popular appointment as High Priest were revolutionary – and were to hold the seeds of future internal friction. Until the reign of Antiochus Epiphanes, the high

Simon being installed as High Priest, from the Book of Maccabees in an illustrated 17th-century pocket Bible

priesthood was a hereditary office in the House of Onias, which traced its line back eight centuries to Zadok. (Zadok was one of the two High Priests appointed by David and father of the first High Priest to officiate in Solomon's Temple.) After the deposition of Onias III, as we have seen, the successive High Priests had all been imperial appointments, and the traditionalist Jews had been outraged not only because they were hellenists, and not only that some had not belonged to the high priestly, or any priestly family, but also because they had been appointed by a Gentile ruler. Jonathan had been the first traditionalist Jew to hold this office since Onias, but he had been given this position by the emperor Alexander Balas. As we have indicated earlier, the people accepted it largely for its political import, but there were some who had reservations.

When Simon assumed the leadership after his brother's death, he too was confirmed in the office of High Priest by Gentile emperors. Clearly the position had to be regularized; but the Jews of Judea were in a quandary. There was no surviving representative of the House of Onias in Judea; and there was no 'true prophet' in Israel to interpret the will of the Lord and name a successor to the last legitimate incumbent of the highest priestly office. They therefore did the next best thing: they, the Jews, conferred the appointment, thus re-assuming this authority from the hands of the Gentiles; they made the appointment provisional 'until a true prophet should arise'; and they granted it as a hereditary office ('for ever') to the House of Hashmon, for it was Mattathias and his sons who had 'risked their lives in resisting the enemies of their people, in order that the Temple and the Law might be preserved, and they brought great glory to their nation'. Moreover, though Simon and his brothers were not of high priestly stock, their father was 'a priest of the Joarib family', and the Joarib branch was one of the most aristocratic of the priest-hood. One difficulty was that Simon was also a man of the sword; but now, after years of fighting – and particularly since only by fighting had Judaism been saved – it was no longer deemed incongruous for the High Priest also to be a military commander. Ten years earlier, the people were not yet ready to accept such a notion, and it was no doubt on this account that Judah, the most outstanding of the Maccabees, had not been considered for this office. But now it was acceptable to the majority of the public, and Simon became the religious, political and military leader of the nation. The ultra-orthodox Jews, however, clung to their reservations. They may have been silent at the time because of the warm personality of Simon, who had endeared himself to the people; but the undercurrent of feeling against the Hasmonean high priesthood would find expression in later decades.

Silver tetradrachm bearing a portrait of the Parthian king Mithridates I, who defeated, captured and eventually released Demetrius II

Simon, like his brothers Judah and Jonathan, was active diplomatically, and early in his rule he sent envoys to Rome and Sparta to renew the treaties of friendship and alliance. There has been a good deal of scholarly controversy over the details in the First Book of Maccabees (14:16–24 and 15:15–24) of Simon's embassy to the Senate, which some suggest belong to the later mission sent by Hyrcanus. However, even those inclined to agree with this theory consider it likely that Simon, too, renewed contact with Rome. Not that any of the successive Judean leaders expected military help; but the moral authority of Rome was accounted worth securing (her diplomatic intervention was to prove helpful on one occasion to Hyrcanus) and it was an added and demonstrative gesture of independence.

As Seleucid authority in the divided empire grew weaker, Simon continued to advance the strength, size and welfare of Judea. This peaceful and fruitful situation lasted until 138 BC, when it was threatened by a tough new emperor. We have already seen that the eastern territory of Babylonia, which had been loyal to Demetrius, had been wrested from him in 141 by the Parthians, led by king Mithridates I. Demetrius set off to campaign against him in 140, leaving his wife, Queen Cleopatra Thea, to safeguard his cause. He registered initial military successes but was captured in the following year, and though well treated by Mithridates (he would be released and return to the throne ten years later), for the

A 1st-century BC relief of a Roman warship, similar to the earlier ships of war mentioned by Antiochus VII in his written appeal to Simon for help

time being he was out of action. Tryphon was thus the sole ruler of the Seleucid empire. But not for long.

Demetrius' younger brother, Antiochus, was in 'the islands of the sea' – Rhodes, according to Appian – when he heard that Demetrius had been taken prisoner, and he soon appeared in Syria determined to restore a united empire to the House of Seleucus. He married his brother's wife, becoming Cleopatra's third husband, and proclaimed himself the legitimate emperor in 138 BC, reigning as Antiochus VII Euergetes (but better known by his nickname Sidetes). He made overtures to the supporters of Tryphon and soon brought them over to his side. He also sought help from Tryphon's enemies, among them Simon, to whom he had written before setting out from Rhodes that he had 'raised a large body of mercenaries and fitted out ships of war.'

I intend to land in my country and to attack those who have ravaged my kingdom. Now therefore I confirm all the tax remissions which my royal predecessors granted you, and all their other remissions of tribute. I permit you to mint your own coinage as currency for your country. Jerusalem and the Temple shall be free. All the arms you have prepared, and the fortifications which you have built and now hold, shall remain yours ... When we have re-established our kingdom, we shall confer the highest honours upon you, your nation and Temple, to make your country's greatness apparent to the whole world (1 Macc. 15:3–9).

No endorsement of Judean independence could have been more explicit.

Within weeks of Antiochus Sidetes' arrival and marriage,

Tryphon was on the run. He put to death the boy Antiochus VI, whom he had deposed four years earlier, and fled to Dor (some 9 miles north of today's Caesarea on Israel's Mediterranean coast), which Sidetes quickly blockaded. Simon despatched a force of two thousand to assist him, but the new emperor, with victory in his grasp, refused the offer, repudiated his previous commitments to the Judean leader and broke off relations with him. When Tryphon escaped by ship (he was eventually caught and forced to commit suicide), Simon knew what to expect and made suitable preparations.

He soon received a visit from Athenobius, a trusted counsellor of Antiochus Sidetes, who came to Jerusalem bearing the royal demand that Simon give up Jaffa and Gezer and the Acra citadel, which 'you are occupying' and which 'belong to my kingdom.'

I demand the return of the cities you have captured and the surrender of the tribute extracted from places beyond the frontiers of Judea over which you have assumed control. Otherwise, you must pay five hundred talents of silver on their account, and another five hundred as compensation for the destruction you have caused and for the loss of tribute from the cities. Failing this, we shall go to war with you (I Macc. 15:28–31).

Simon rejected the monarch's ultimatum. 'We have not occupied other people's land', he told Athenobius, 'or taken other people's property, but only the inheritance of our ancestors, unjustly seized for a time by our enemies. We have grasped our opportunity and

Archaeology-minded soldiers of the Israel Defence Forces recently discovered the conduits which brought water to Dok, the Maccabean fort near Jericho where Simon was murdered

have claimed our patrimony.' As for Jaffa and Gezer, 'these towns were doing a great deal of damage among our people and in our land'. Nevertheless 'for these we offer one hundred talents' (1 Macc. 15:33-5).

Athenobius left in a rage, and Antiochus was equally furious when he received his report. He immediately instructed Cendebeus, his commander in the coastal plain, to march on Judea. By this time Simon had raised a small cavalry force, and he sent this unit together with twenty thousand picked men under the command of his sons Johanan and Judah to engage the invaders. The critical battle took place in the southern coastal plain near Kedron (today's Gedera), some 12 miles south-west of Gezer, and the Seleucid forces were routed. Johanan chased them to Azotus (his brother Judah had been wounded), destroyed its fortifications and inflicted heavy casualties on the enemy. Thereafter, for as long as Simon lived, no further attempt was made by Antiochus to invade Judea, and for the next three and a half years the last surviving Maccabee brother and the first head of the restored independent Jewish state was able to consolidate its strength.

Early in the year 134 BC, while Simon was on an inspection tour of the cities and strongholds in the Jericho plain, he called on his son-in-law, Ptolemy, son of Abubus, who was military commander of the region. Ptolemy received him 'at the small fort called Dok', some 4 miles north-west of Jericho, and entertained him to a festive meal. At a given moment, when Simon and his entourage were relaxed and drowsy with wine, Ptolemy gave a signal and his accomplices rushed into the banquet chamber and killed the distinguished guests. 'It was an act of base treachery in which evil was returned for good.' Unsuspected by Simon, the ambitious Ptolemy had been in secret league with Antiochus and had hoped to become a vassal governor under the Seleucid emperor as a reward for returning Judea to its tributary status. Killing his father-in-law, he thought, was the quickest way to achieve this. He had also killed two of his brothers-in-law, who had accompanied their father Simon on his tour. But Simon's third son, Johanan (Hyrcanus) was still at large (he was in Gezer). Ptolemy promptly despatched his men to seize him and sent another unit to take Jerusalem. But one of the survivors of Simon's party managed to escape and rushed straight to Johanan with the news. Johanan set off post-haste to intercept the men who had come to kill him, wiped them out and continued on to Jerusalem, which he reached before Ptolemy. He was quickly recognized as Simon's heir and installed as the new High Priest, commander and leader of the nation.

Coins minted by the Hasmonean kings:
*top* Alexander Jannai (103–76 BC)
*centre* Hyrcanus II (63–43 BC)
*bottom* Aristobulus II (67–63 BC)

For most of the years of Simon's rule, Judea knew the blessings of peace, and there is an idyllic description of this period in the First Book of Maccabees 14:8–15:

The people farmed their land in peace, and the land produced its crops, and the trees in the plains their fruit. Old men sat in the streets, talking of their blessings; and the young men dressed themselves in splendid military style. Simon supplied the towns with food in plenty and equipped them with weapons for defence. His renown reached the ends of the earth. He restored peace to the land, and there were great rejoicings throughout Israel. Each man sat under his own vine and fig-tree, and they had no one to fear. Those were the days when every enemy vanished from the land and every hostile king was crushed. Simon gave his protection to the poor among the people; he paid close attention to the law and rid the country of lawless and wicked men. He gave new splendour to the Temple and furnished it with a wealth of sacred vessels.

Johanan Hyrcanus would have a hard time preserving his father's gains in the initial years of his rule, for he was under heavy pressure from Antiochus VII Sidetes. This monarch was to prove the last strong emperor of the House of Seleucus, and he could now exert the full force of his imperial might against the Jews. Hyrcanus was not disposed to lose all that the Jews had gained on a single military throw, and for a short period he held office as a feudal prince. However, through the exertion of diplomatic pressure on Antiochus by Rome, he was allowed to retain the cities beyond the former frontiers of Judea which the Maccabees had captured, though he had to pay tribute for them. Politically, therefore, the Judeans were again a subject people, and it may have seemed to some that they had been given but a brief hour of glory and that their regained freedom within an independent Jewish state had been no more than an ephemeral achievement. But Hyrcanus and his core of Maccabee colleagues were biding their time, and within five years of his accession, in 129 BC, Antiochus was killed in battle by the Parthians while campaigning to retrieve his eastern possessions. With his death, the Seleucid empire began to crumble, shattered by civil war, as rival branches of the House of Seleucus battled each other for power. The opportunity this offered was quickly seized by Hyrcanus, who promptly restored the independence of Judea. (To mark this status, he struck bronze coins which bear the Hebrew words 'Johanan the High Priest and the Commonwealth of the Jews'.)

This was the start of an age of Jewish freedom which was to last two-thirds of a century. During the long reign (134–104 BC) of

Hyrcanus and under his sons Judah Aristobulus I and Alexander Jannai, the Jewish state would prosper and its frontiers would be extended until it was roughly the size of the Land of Israel over which David had ruled. The national and religious resurgence would touch not only those living within the State; it would also add a dimension to the lives of Jews who had been scattered to sundry lands of the Diaspora, but to whom Jerusalem was the vibrant spiritual centre.

This era of independence would not be one of unalloyed triumph. There would be internal religious dissension and a growing rift between the ruling house and some of its subjects, particularly during the despotic reign of Alexander Jannai, who would deviate from the traditionalist path. Independence would also come to an end in 63 BC when Rome's Pompey, the conquering general of the now undisputed great power in the region, would subdue Jerusalem after a bitter siege. (There would be two brief flickers of sovereignty thereafter, each lasting three years: under Hasmonean King Mattathias Antigonus, 40–37 BC, and under Bar-Kokhba, AD 132–135). But short though it was, the Hasmonean period would exercise an undying impact on the lives of the Jews and on the course of their history ever after. The Hasmonean family of the old priest Mattathias and his remarkable sons created something greater than they knew.

In regaining freedom for the Jews of their own times, these glorious Maccabees fashioned a mould for the preservation of the Jewish identity for all time. Their strength of spirit in appalling adversity and their prodigious deeds against incredible odds became part of the heritage and collective memory of the nation. The Jews in the years to come would suffer the most horrendous cruelties, be victims of the most hideous holocausts, but never would they go under. The record of this most extraordinary Maccabee struggle to safeguard their faith and their liberty would sustain the hopes and nourish the will of the Jewish people throughout the long, dark centuries of their exile – and would lead to the rebirth of the State of Israel in our own day.

# Chronological Table

| | |
|---|---|
| 13th century BC | Moses – Exodus of the Children of Israel from Egypt. |
| | Joshua – Conquest and settlement of Palestine. |
| 12th–11th centuries | The Judges |
| 10th century | King David establishes Jerusalem as capital of United Kingdom of Israel. King Solomon builds the Temple in Jerusalem |
| 922 | Division of Kingdom into Israel and Judah (Judea). |
| 587 | Destruction of Jerusalem and of the Temple by Nebuchadnezzar, and exile of Jews to Babylon. |
| 537–332 | The Persian Period |
| 537 | Under Persian rule, Jews allowed to return from Babylon to Judea. |
| 515 | Restoration of the Temple (henceforth called the Second Temple). |
| c. 440 | Nehemiah arrives from Babylon and rebuilds the walls of Jerusalem. |
| c. 435 | Ezra the Scribe comes from Babylon and joins Nehemiah in rebuilding the city of Jerusalem and the community in Judea. |
| 332–134 | The Hellenistic Period |
| 332 | Alexander the Great conquers the Persians and gains their territories, including Palestine. |
| 301–200 | Palestine under the Ptolemies of Egypt. |
| 200 | Seleucid Emperor Antiochus III of Syria wrests Palestine from the Ptolemies. |
| 190 | Antiochus III loses decisive battle of Magnesia to Romans. |
| 188 | Under treaty of Apamea, Antiochus' son (the future Antiochus IV) is sent to Rome as hostage. |
| 187 | Accession of Seleucus IV, son of Antiochus III. |
| 175 | Accession of Antiochus IV Epiphanes, brother of Seleucus IV. |
| | Onias III (Honya), traditionalist Jewish High Priest in Jerusalem, is ousted by the emperor; pro-hellenist Jason installed in his stead. This marks the start of Seleucid attempts to hellenize Judea. |
| 172 | Jason dismissed, flees to Transjordan, and extreme hellenist Menelaus appointed High Priest in his place. |
| 170 | Antiochus IV launches first campaign in Egypt. |
| 168 | Rome conquers Macedonia. |
| | Antiochus IV, on his second campaign in Egypt, is about to complete his conquest of the country when Rome orders him to retreat. |
| | Uprising in Jerusalem. |
| | Antiochus sends punitive expedition to Jerusalem. Many Jews massacred; the Temple looted; and formidable Acra Fortress built as a Seleucid military base. |
| 167 | Antiochus IV issues anti-Jewish decrees. |
| December 167 | Desecration of the Temple. |
| 166 | Incident at Modi'in. Mattathias and his sons raise banner of revolt. |
| | Judah creates guerilla force. |
| | The Book of Daniel given forth. |
| 166/165 | Death of Mattathias. Judah succeeds him as leader of the Maccabees. |

|  | Apollonius defeated near Gophna in first Maccabee battle against Seleucid forces. |
|  | Seron defeated at battle of Beth Horon. |
| 165 | Antiochus IV departs on his eastern campaign. |
|  | Nicanor and Gorgias defeated at battle of Emmaus. |
| 164 | Lysias repulsed at battle of Beth Zur. |
| December 164 | Maccabees rededicate the Temple. Inauguration of Festival of Hanukkah. |
| 163 | Judah's expedition to rescue the Jews of Gilead. |
|  | Simon's relief expedition to western Galilee. |
|  | Judah campaigns in coastal plain and Idumea. |
|  | Death of Antiochus IV Epiphanes. Succeeded by his young son Antiochus V Eupator, with Lysias as regent. |
| 162 | Judah's brother Eleazar killed in battle of Beth Zechariah. |
|  | Lysias reaches Jerusalem. |
|  | In the name of Antiochus V, Lysias annuls anti-Jewish decrees. High Priest Menelaus removed and executed. |
|  | Demetrius escapes from Rome, becomes new Seleucid emperor (Demetrius I Soter). |
|  | Antiochus V and Lysias put to death. |
|  | Eliakim (Alcimus) appointed High Priest. |
|  | Nicanor repulsed at battle of Capharsalma. |
| 161 | Nicanor killed at battle of Adasa. |
|  | Judah's treaty of friendship with Rome. |
| 160 | Maccabees defeated by Bacchides at battle of Elasa. Judah killed. |
|  | Jonathan succeeds Judah as Maccabee leader. |
|  | The eldest Maccabee brother, Johanan, murdered by Transjordanian tribe. |
| 159 | Death of High Priest Eliakim. No successor appointed. |
| 156 or 155 | Bacchides repulsed at battle of Bethbasi; negotiates armistice treaty with Jonathan. |
|  | Jonathan establishes himself in Michmash; secures control of rural Judea. |
| 152 | Alexander Balas, pretender to Seleucid throne, lands at Ptolemais; vies with Demetrius I for Jonathan's support; appoints Jonathan High Priest. |
| 150 | Alexander defeats and kills Demetrius in battle and becomes emperor. |
|  | Alexander marries Cleopatra Thea, daughter of Egyptian emperor Ptolemy VI Philometor; appoints Jonathan commander and governor of Judea. |
| 147 | Demetrius, son of Demetrius I, lands in northern Syria and campaigns against Alexander. |
|  | Jonathan repels attack by Demetrius' forces under Apollonius. |
|  | Ptolemy Philometor arrives in Antioch; switches allegiance from Alexander to Demetrius. |
|  | Alexander flees to Cilicia. |
|  | Cleopatra Thea, Alexander's wife, marries Demetrius. |
| 145 | Alexander returns to battle Demetrius and is defeated; he is murdered shortly afterwards. |
|  | Demetrius reigns as Demetrius II Nicator; confirms Jonathan as High Priest; grants Judea greater autonomy; adds three Samarian districts to its territory. |
| 144–143 | Tryphon engineers rising against Demetrius; puts forth Antiochus VI Dionysos, infant son of Alexander Balas and Cleopatra Thea, as rival to throne, with himself as regent. |

Seleucid empire divided for a time between Demetrius, reigning from Selucia, and Antiochus, reigning from Antioch.

Tryphon, in name of Antiochus VI, confirms Jonathan as religious and political leader of Judea and appoints his brother Simon military commander of territory from Ladder of Tyre to Egyptian border.

Jonathan defeats Demetrius' forces in plain of Hazor and at Hamath; renews pact with Rome.

|     |     |
|-----|-----|
| 142 | Jonathan killed by Tryphon. |
|     | Simon succeeds Jonathan; repels Tryphon's attack on Judea. |
|     | Tryphon dethrones Antiochus VI and establishes himself as sovereign. |
|     | Simon secures from Tryphon's rival emperor, Demetrius Nicator, freedom from tribute, tantamount to the recognition of Judah's independence. |
| 141 | Simon expels Seleucid garrison from their last stronghold, the Acra Fortress. The whole of Jerusalem at last under Maccabee control and Judea again an independent Jewish state. |
| 140 | Great assembly in Jerusalem proclaims Simon High Priest, commander and ruler of the Jews. Simon renews treaty of friendship with Rome. |
|     | Demetrius II Nicator captured by Parthians and kept prisoner (he regains throne in 129). |
| 138 | Tryphon executes Antiochus VI, whom he had dethroned four years earlier. |
|     | Demetrius Nicator's brother, Antiochus, lands in Syria, marries his brother's wife, defeats Tryphon, and proclaims himself king, reigning as Antiochus VIII Sidetes, sole Seleucid emperor. |
|     | Simon's son Johanan (Hyrcanus) defeats Antiochus' forces under Cendebeus at Kedron (Gedera) in southern coastal plain. |
| 134 | Simon murdered. Succeeded by Johanan Hyrcanus. |
| 134–133 | Antiochus VII puts Judea under tribute but confirms its autonomy. |
| 129 | Antiochus killed campaigning against the Parthians. |
|     | His brother, Demetrius II, returns from captivity and resumes throne. |
|     | Johanan Hyrcanus restores the independence of Judea. During his reign, Judean realm extended to include Idumea, Samaria and portions of Transjordan. |
| 104 | Death of Hyrcanus, who is succeeded by his son Judah Aristobulus, the first Hasmonean to adopt the title of king. |
|     | Aristobulus incorporates Galilee into kingdom. |
| 103 | Aristobulus succeeded by his brother, Alexander Jannai. |
|     | Under Jannai, the Jewish State is enlarged until it is roughly co-extensive with the kingdom ruled by King David, including the coastal plain from Sinai to Mount Carmel (except for Ashkelon), the country west of the Jordan from Dan to just south of Beersheba, and considerable territory across the Jordan. |
| 76 | Jannai succeeded by his wife, Salome Alexandra. |
| 67 | Accession of their son, Aristobulus II. |
| 63 | Succeeded by his brother, Hyrcanus II. |
|     | Roman conquest, under Pompey. |
| 40–37 | Last flicker of independence under a Hasmonean sovereign, Mattathias Antigonus, son of Aristobulus II. |

# The Seleucids in the Second Century BC

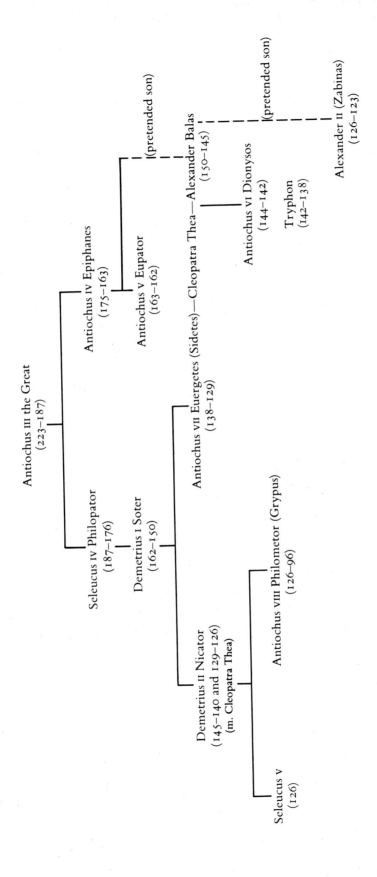

# The House of Hashmon

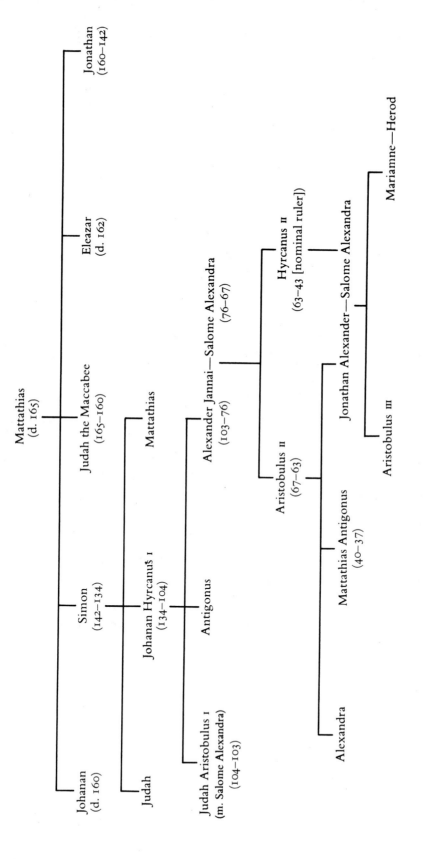

Mattathias
(d. 165)

Johanan
(d. 160)

Simon
(142–134)

Eleazar
(d. 162)

Jonathan
(160–142)

Judah the Maccabee
(165–160)

Judah

Johanan Hyrcanus I
(134–104)

Mattathias

Judah Aristobulus I
(m. Salome Alexandra)
(104–103)

Antigonus

Alexander Jannai—Salome Alexandra
(103–76)

Alexandra

Mattathias Antigonus
(40–37)

Aristobulus II
(67–63)

Jonathan Alexander—Salome Alexandra

Hyrcanus II
(63–43 [nominal ruler])

Aristobulus III

Mariamne—Herod

# Selected Sources and Bibliography

The First Book of Maccabees. (Originally written in Hebrew, it is preserved only in its Greek translation. It is the most important historical source for our knowledge of the Maccabee revolt, with its detailed account of the forty-one year period following the accession of the Seleucid emperor Antiochus IV Epiphanes in 175 BC. It was composed, probably in the second half of the second century BC, by a Palestinian Jew who may have lived through the stirring events in Judea or heard about them later from eyewitnesses. Both the First and Second Books of Maccabees are part of the Standard Apocrypha.)

The Second Book of Maccabees. (It was originally written in Greek and it is an abridgement of a five-book work, not preserved, by a certain Jason of Cyrene. Though the interests of the writer, a traditionalist Jew, are more religious than historical, it is a vital supplement to the First Book of Maccabees and covers a fifteen-year period from 176 BC to shortly before the death of Judah. There has long been scholarly controversy over its date, but Victor Tcherikover presents persuasive arguments to show that it was written between the years 124 and 110 BC; that Jason's work, on which it is based, was composed between 160 and 152 BC; and that Jason was a contemporary of Judah and probably an eyewitness to the events he described.)

The Fourth Book of Maccabees. (Written in Greek, its presumed date is the end of the first century BC or the first half of the first century AD. It differs from the first two Books of Maccabees in that it is largely philosophical in character, but it makes dramatic use of the historical events during the Maccabee period to pursue its purpose of religious edification. Most of it is an embellishment of two chapters in the Second Book of Maccabees. It is the work of a loyal Jew addressed to other Jews, stressing, through stories of Jewish martyrdom, the sovereignty of pious reason over the passions. Though not part of the Standard Apocrypha, it is included in two great manuscripts of the Septuagint, the fourth-century Codex Sinaiticus and the fifth-century Codex Alexandrinus.)

The Book of Daniel.

Josephus (first century AD), *The Antiquities of the Jews*, Books XII, XIII.
——, *The Wars of the Jews*, Book I.
——, *Against Apion*, Book II.
Appian (second century AD), *Roman History*, Book XI.
Diodorus Siculus (first century BC), *Bibliotheca Historica*, Fragments from Books XXIX–XXXIV.
Justin (third century AD), *An epitome of Historiae Philippicae* . . . (a 44-book work by the first-century BC Roman historian Pompeius Trogus), Books XXXII–XXXIX.
Livy (first century BC), *The History of Rome*, Books XXII–XXXIX.
Polybius (second century BC), *The Histories*, Books XXII–XXXIX.
Strabo (first century BC), *Geography*, XIV, XVI.

Abel, Felix Marie, *Géographie de la Palestine*, Vol. II, Paris, 1933.
——, *Les Livres des Maccabées*, Paris, 1949.
——, *Histoire de la Palestine*, Paris, 1952.
Abrahams, Israel, *Campaigns in Palestine from Alexander the Great* (Schweich Lectures – British Academy), Oxford, 1927.
Albright, William Foxwell, *From the Stone Age to Christianity*, New York, 1957.
Avissar, Eitan, *The Wars of Judah the Maccabee* (Hebrew), Tel Aviv, 1965.
Avi-Yonah, Michael, *Historical Geography of the Land of Israel* (Hebrew), Jerusalem, 1950.
——, 'The Second Temple' in *A History of the Holy Land*, ed. by M. Avi-Yonah, Jerusalem, 1969.
—— and Y. Aharoni, *The Macmillan Bible Atlas*, Jerusalem and New York, 1968.
Bevan, Edwyn Robert, *The House of Seleucus*, London, 1902.
——, *A History of Egypt under the Ptolemaic Dynasty*, London, 1927.
——, 'Syria and the Jews' in *The Cambridge Ancient History*, VIII, 495–533.
Bickermann, Elias, *Der Gott der Makkabäer*, Paris, 1937.
——, *Les Institutions des Séleucides*, Paris, 1938.
——, *From Ezra to the Last of the Maccabees*, New York, 1962.
Box, George Herbert, *Judaism in the Greek Period*, Oxford, 1932.
Cary, Max, *A History of the Greek World from 323 to 146 BC*, London 1932.

Finklestein, Louis, ed., *The Jews: Their History, Culture, Religion*, New York, 1949.

Galili El'azar, 'The Battlefield Enemies of the Hasmoneans' (Hebrew), *Ma'arachot*, June 1968, Tel Aviv.

———, 'The Foes the Maccabees Fought' (Hebrew), *Molad*, No. 218 (8), Jerusalem, 1968.

Ginzberg, Louis, *Studies in Daniel*, New York, 1948.

Griffith, G.T., *The Mercenaries of the Hellenistic World*, Cambridge, 1935.

Hadas, Moses, Introduction, translation, commentary and critical notes to *The Third and Fourth Books of Maccabees*, New York, 1953; and to *Aristeas to Philocrates*, New York, 1951.

Klausner, Joseph, *History of the Period of the Second Temple* (Hebrew), Jerusalem, 1949.

Kolbe, Walther, *Beiträge zur syrischen und Jüdischen Geschichte*, Stuttgart, 1926.

Launey, Marcel, *Recherches sur les Armées Hellenistiques*, Paris, 1950.

Lieberman, Saul, *Greek in Jewish Palestine*, New York, 1942.

———, *Hellenism in Jewish Palestine*, New York, 1950.

Niese, Benediktus, *Kritik der beiden Makkabäerbucher*, Berlin, 1900.

Oesterly, William O.E., *A History of Israel*, Oxford, 1932.

Olmstead, Albert T.E., *History of Palestine and Syria to the Macedonian Conquest*, New York, 1931.

Reifenberg, Adolf, *Ancient Jewish Coins*, Jerusalem, 1947.

Renan, Ernest, *Histoire du Peuple d'Israel*, IV and V, Paris, 1926, 1927.

Rostovtzeff, Mikhail Ivanovich, *The Social and Economic History of the Hellenistic World*, Oxford, 1941.

Roth, Cecil, *A Short History of the Jewish People*, London, 1948.

Saulcy, Felicien de, *Histoire des Machabées*, Paris, 1880.

Smith, George Adam, *The Historical Geography of the Holy Land*, London, 1903.

———, *Jerusalem, From the Earliest Times to AD 70*, London, 1907.

Stern, Menahem, *Documents of the Hasmonean Revolt* (Hebrew), Tel Aviv, 1965.

Tarn, William Woodthorp, *Hellenistic Military and Naval Developments*, Cambridge, 1930.

———, *Hellenistic Civilization*, London, 1947.

Tcherikover, Victor, *Hellenistic Civilization and the Jews*, tr. Shimon Applebaum, New York, 1970.

Yadin, Yigael, *The Art of Warfare in Biblical Lands*, Jerusalem and New York, 1963.

Zeitlin, Solomon, *The History of the Second Commonwealth*, Philadelphia, 1933.

———, *Introduction and Commentary to the First and Second Books of Maccabees*, Dropsie College Jewish Apocryphal Literature Series, New York, 1950, 1954.

# Index